ENDORSEMENTS

I've come to know Ryan Bridgeo over the last decade, and I am totally impressed by what the Lord has done in and through him. I've seen his fruit by my visits to his church in Plumtree, NC, and in the lives of members of his church who came to our Charis Bible College. Everywhere I look I see the Lord using Ryan to make disciples, not just converts. Ryan has put into writing what I see working in his life. From this tiny place in the hills of North Carolina, the Lord is touching people all over the world through Ryan's ministry. Only the Lord could do that, and in this book, you will find out why.

Ryan understands the grace of God that empowers him to do things beyond his ability. These truths have set Ryan and those who come in contact with his ministry free from the bondages of religion. I believe you will be challenged and set free to become the disciple the Lord intends you to be through the truths Ryan shares in this book, *Discipling Nations*. Get ready for a radical change. The best is yet to come.

Andrew Wommack
Founder and President
Andrew Wommack Ministries and Charis Bible College

✳ ✳ ✳

As I was in a small group meeting with a pastor of what has come to be known as a Mega-Church, the question was asked; "What is your biggest challenge in leading a congregation of over 20,000 people?" I have to admit that I didn't get the answer I expected when he answered, "Making disciples." Now, with so many people and that large of a property, you would think that surely there was at least one thing that was bigger than making disciples. But there wasn't! It seems that the age-old problem stems from the command found in Matthew 28:19: "Go therefore and make disciples of all nations." Thankfully, there are men of faith who have taken this seriously and have made it easier for those who will follow in the coming days. Such a man is Pastor Ryan Bridgeo. His book, *Discipling Nations*, comes at a critical time in history. Upon reading this book, I was impressed with three words: Simple, Direct, and Relevant.

Simple in the fact that it's done in such a way that whether you are a new believer or have been walking with Christ for years, it's just simple to understand. It's so easy to get caught up in trying to impress with big words and deep meanings that we forget that the gospel is not for a select few but for all mankind. Thank you, Pastor, for making it simple enough that even someone like me can understand it.

Direct in the fact that there are no gray areas that are easily misinterpreted. This book cuts to the chase and answers questions that are often asked by those who are seeking to know more about being a believer. In an era when many shy away from answering in a way that some might find offensive, it's refreshing to find someone willing to speak the truth in such a direct manner. Thank you, Pastor, for holding true to His Word.

Relevant in the fact that we find our world, including the Church, in search of true purpose. This book is designed not only for those who are born again, but for those outside of the Church who are seeking meaning for their lives. Thank you, Pastor, for hearing the voice of the Spirit as you captured the message that is so needed in this hour.

I encourage leaders to make good use of this book as you lead your assigned people into the full purpose that God intends for their lives.

Chuck Waldrup
Director of Eden-Land Outreach and Encounter Ministries

❋ ❋ ❋

I can certainly tell that Ryan Bridgeo has a pastor's heart with his book, **Discipling Nations**. He has taken the mandate of making disciples seriously and has put together an impressive foundational group of teachings that every believer needs to understand. These short, yet comprehensive, teachings cover a large portion of truths that are essential for believers to walk with the Lord and fulfill God's commission for their life. It is especially helpful for new Christians, as it not only answers common questions that those new to the faith are asking, but it also addresses areas that are not on their radar but really do need to be understood to have a strong biblical foundation. Even seasoned Christians will benefit to fill in the gaps in their walk with the Lord. I highly recommend this book and ask pastors to consider using this as a resource to build a solid foundation for their members to expand the Kingdom of God.

Dr. Rodney Hogue
Rodney Hogue Ministries

※ ※ ※

Discipling Nations is more than just a publication; it is an expression of God's framework of reproducing Himself to the world He created and has so loved. Each of the 52 chapters of this book have been birthed by God to us through the ministry of Pastor Ryan Bridgeo. The chapters offer a unique structure whereby individuals and groups can asynchronously or synchronously engage in sound biblical doctrinal discourse. This is important in the time in which we live, "That we henceforth be no more little children, tossed to and fro, and carried about with every wind of doctrine …" (Eph. 4:14). Since my introduction to Pastor Ryan over five years ago, I have found him to have a bottomless passion for the maturing of the Bride, and a commitment to love and cherish her even as Christ gave His life for the Bride.

I have known Pastor Ryan Bridgeo for several years, as a friend and as a brother. His friendship has become dear to myself and my family. We had the opportunity to be hosted by his wonderful church, nestled superbly in the beautiful mountains of Western North Carolina. The Spirit and Presence of God were matched by their hospitality and graciousness toward us. Pastor Ryan's peaceful disposition always reassures us of the peace of God that passes all understanding.

The ministry of Christ through Pastor Ryan Bridgeo can be trusted. The content provided in the book is user friendly and easy to follow. It can be used for study groups or conversation starters. As an educator, I loved the assessment questions and fill-in-the-blank items at the end of various sections. This adds an element of accountability to readers.

One of the takeaways that was so exciting for me was when Ryan stated that "(Christians) have spent a lot of time asking God for more faith. We do not need to pray and ask God for more faith. We already have enough. We have been given the measure of faith." I had been meditating on this very concept for months, and when I read this, I leapt within. God has truly given us everything we need! It is a matter of accessing ALL that He has given.

In summary, this book is a curriculum in and of itself. It is a journey across the landscape of topics that we all want to know more about. Ryan, thank you so much for this gift to us.

I intend to utilize this material in ministry and teaching sessions. I have successfully trained and equipped many for the working of the ministry. I prophesied to Pastor Ryan years ago, and it is a delight to see the manifestation of so much that God is doing. I see and value the importance of sound Bible-based teaching and *Discipling Nations* is just that.

Pastor James Woods
The Spirit Without Measure Church
Flint, Michigan

※ ※ ※

It's my pleasure to recommend Pastor Ryan's new book, *Discipling Nations*. Ryan has taken a plethora of important biblical doctrines and concisely packaged them for a study guide to teach "new and not so new believers" a Kingdom-minded presentation of the Gospel. These scripturally-founded teachings will clearly assist in training disciples for the assignment of fulfilling the great commission.

Doug Johnson
Pastor of Merit Harvest Church

DISCIPLING NATIONS

DISCIPLING NATIONS

MATTHEW 28:19

By Ryan Bridgeo

LAURUS BOOKS

Unless otherwise noted, Scripture quotations are taken from the New King James Version © 1982 by Thomas Nelson. Used by permission. All rights reserved.

Scripture quotations taken from the Amplified® Bible (AMPC), Copyright © 1954, 1958, 1962, 1964, 1965, 1987 by The Lockman Foundation. Used by permission. www.Lockman.org

Scripture quotations taken from the New American Standard Bible® (NASB), Copyright © 1960, 1962, 1963, 1968, 1971, 1972, 1973, 1975, 1977, 1995 by The Lockman Foundation. Used by permission. www.Lockman.org

Scripture quotations marked (NIV) are taken from the Holy Bible, New International Version®, NIV®. Copyright © 1973, 1978, 1984, 2011 by Biblica, Inc.™ Used by permission of Zondervan. All rights reserved worldwide. www.zondervan.com. The "NIV" and "New International Version" are trademarks registered in the United States Patent and Trademark Office by Biblica, Inc.™

The Holy Bible, English Standard Version. ESV® Text Edition: 2016. Copyright © 2001 by Crossway Bibles, a publishing ministry of Good News Publishers.

Scripture quotations marked KJV are from the King James Version, available in the Public Domain.
Scripture quotations marked WEY are from the Weymouth New Testament, Public Domain.
Scripture quotations marked YLT are from Young's Literal Translation, Public Domain.
All italics in Scripture quotations were added by the author for emphasis.

Discipling Nations

By Ryan Bridgeo

Copyright © 2022 by Ryan Bridgeo

All rights reserved. This book is protected under the copyright laws of the United States of America. This book may not be copied or reprinted for commercial gain or profit. The use of short quotations or occasional page copying for personal or group study is permitted and encouraged. Permission will be granted on request.

Paperback: ISBN: 978-1-943523-89-4

Mobi (Kindle): ISBN: 978-1-943523-99-3

Published by LAURUS BOOKS

LAURUS BOOKS
www.TheLaurusCompany.com

This book may be purchased in paperback from:
www.TheLaurusCompany.com, Amazon.com, and other retailers around the world.
May also be available in formats for electronic readers from their respective stores.
Available to booksellers at Spring Arbor.

Dedication

I would like to dedicate this book to all my family and friends who believe in me and are invested in my life. I would not be the man I am today without them. I am very thankful for my rich Christian heritage from my dad and grandfather, who have gone home to be with the Lord. They taught me so much. I am thankful for my mom, who has believed in me from the beginning, even when I did not believe in myself. I am thankful for my brother, who has been a true friend throughout my life. I am thankful for my wife's parents, who have loved me like their own son. I am thankful for my children, who love me and challenge me to be a better man every day. I am also very thankful for my wife, Holly. I do not know how to express this in words, but you mean everything to me. Thank you so much for loving me and being my best friend. You have been a constant source of love and support. I love you.

✻ ✻ ✻

TABLE OF CONTENTS

Dedication 9
1. Saved By Grace 13
2. Eternal Life 19
3. Water Baptism 25
4. Repentance 31
5. The Lord Our Righteousness 35
6. Sinners or Saints? 43
7. What Happens When We Sin? 47
8. The True Nature of God 53
9. The Integrity of God's Word 59
10. The Power of Our Words 65
11. Faith 71
12. The Measure of Faith 77
13. Increase Our Faith 81
14. Activating Faith 87
15. The Heart 93
16. Take Captive Every Thought 99
17. Healthy Thinking (Part 1) 103
18. Healthy Thinking (Part 2) 109
19. Hearing God 115
20. Value and Worth 121
21. Forgiveness 127
22. Spirit, Soul, and Body 133
23. Identity (Part 1) 139
24. Identity (Part 2) 143
25. Holy Spirit 149
26. Baptism in The Holy Spirit 155

TABLE OF CONTENTS Cont.

27. How to Receive the Baptism in the Holy Spirit 159
28. Benefits of Praying in Tongues 169
29. Authority of The Believer 175
30. Biblical Basis for Healing 181
31. Hindrances To Healing 189
32. Deliverance 195
33. The Old Covenant 201
34. The New Covenant 207
35. The Church 213
36. The Sovereignty of God 219
37. Under Law or Under Grace? 225
38. The Purpose of The Law 231
39. The Right Way To Use The Law 237
40. How Jesus Fulfilled The Law 243
41. No More Consciousness of Sin 249
42. Christology 255
43. The Lord's Supper 261
44. Paul's Thorn 269
45. Blessed or Cursed? 277
46. God Wants You Blessed 283
47. When Prayers Seem Unanswered 289
48. Self-Centeredness 295
49. Marriage 301
50. Charismatic Church History 305
51. 1 John 1:9 313
52. The Fruit of Salvation 323
References 329

1
Saved By Grace

Do you know who Kate Middleton is? She married Prince William, whose father is Prince Charles and whose mother was Princess Diana. Prince William is second in line to the throne of Queen Elizabeth II.

Kate did not grow up with a lot of money. She did not come from Royal blood. Her parents were both flight attendants for British Airways. She is the first commoner to marry into the British Royal Family in over 350 years. When she arrived at Westminster Abbey on April 29th, 2011, she arrived in a car with her father. When she left the wedding ceremony, she left in a golden carriage with her husband. She was now a princess of the Royal Family.

This wedding was very expensive. Traditionally, the parents of the bride pay for the wedding. This was not possible for Kate and her family. Kate's gold wedding band was $11,000. Her two wedding cakes were $80,000. Kate's dress cost $434,000. The reception, with their 600 guests, cost $600,000. Their flowers were $800,000, and their security for the event cost $32,000,000.[1] Kate Middleton is now rich beyond her wildest dreams. All the blessings of the Royal Family that William was entitled to through birth, she now receives through marriage.

This love story is very similar to the beautiful love story of Father God toward us. Ephesians 2:8-9 says, *For by grace you have been saved through faith, and that not of yourselves; it is the gift of God, not of works, lest anyone should boast.* Salvation is the gift of God. It is not of yourself. It is not something that can be earned. It is a gift to be received by faith. Romans 4:4-5 (NIV) says, *Now to the one who works, wages are not credited as a gift but as an obligation. However, to the one who does not work but trusts God who justifies the ungodly, their faith is credited as righteousness.*

Again, our salvation is a gift, not an obligation that God has to give us as a reward for our hard work or obedience. This mindset of earning has carried over into the Church. People believe that they deserve to be blessed based on works, their years of service, or on their own merit and track record. They think they can earn the Lord's favor; they can earn answered prayer, or they can earn their healing, but it just doesn't work that way. That is not how the Kingdom of God works.

Luke 17:7-10 says, *"And which of you, having a servant plowing or tending sheep, will say to him when he has come in from the field, 'Come at once and sit down to eat'? But will he not rather say to him, 'Prepare something for my supper, and gird yourself and serve me till I have eaten and drunk, and afterward you will eat and drink'? Does he thank that servant because he did the things that were commanded him? I think not. So likewise you, when you have done all those things which you are commanded, say, 'We are unprofitable servants. We have done what was our duty to do.' "*

This story has always bothered me because I did not understand what God was saying through this parable. The servant worked in the field all day long. When he finished work and returned to his master's house, he was instructed to make supper for everyone. He did all this work and did not receive a simple, "Thank you." That is hard to comprehend. This led me to study this out more. I just knew there had to be more to this story.

Luke 17:10 in the *Weymouth New Testament* says, *"So you also, when you have obeyed all the orders given you, must say, 'There is no merit in our service: what we have done is only what we were in duty bound to do.'"* This tells us there is no merit in our service to God.

Webster's Dictionary[4] defines *merit* as: "character or conduct deserving reward, honor, or esteem. A spiritual credit held to be earned by performance of righteous acts and to ensure future benefits."

There is no merit to our service. We don't earn rewards, honor, esteem, or spiritual credits for our performance. Whether you have done nothing, like the man who buried his one talent, or you have obeyed everything, like the servant in Luke 17:10, you are still an unprofitable servant. God does not owe you anything. You don't deserve anything. You haven't earned His favor, merit, rewards, or anything else. We don't achieve merit, favor, grace, or blessings by what we do. We inherit His favor, grace, and blessings because of what Jesus did for us. This is the recipe for humility and grace. However, thinking we have earned something or that we deserve something is the recipe for bondage and legalism.

The good news of the gospel is that salvation has been provided for us by the power of God; we access this salvation through faith in what Jesus did for us. It is a gift from God that we receive by faith, not a work we can achieve by earning.

Kate did not have to work to be good enough to be a part of the Royal Family. She was loved by a member of the Royal Family and received all the blessings and benefits through their marriage. Kate now has access to every room in the palace. She now has access to the Royal Treasury and can wear whatever jewelry she wants. She now even has access to the presence of the Queen. All these things are available to her because of her marriage relationship.

In the same way, because we are loved by the Royal Family of God, we now have access to this great salvation. It is not based on being good enough or working hard enough. It is based on faith in what He provided for us.

Romans 5:1-2: *Therefore, having been justified by faith, we have peace with God through our Lord Jesus Christ, through whom also we have access by faith into this grace in which we stand, and rejoice in hope of the glory of God.*

Praise God we are saved by faith in the grace that Jesus provided for us.

Questions - Saved By Grace

1. Salvation is the _____ of God.

2. I can earn my salvation by doing good works. T or F

3. I will remain saved if I am good enough. T or F

4. How do I receive the gift of God?

5. I can earn spiritual merits with God by doing good works. T or F

6. When a man works, his wages are credited to him as a gift, or an obligation?

7. There is no _____ in our service.

8. According to Romans 5:1-2, I am justified and have access to God by what?

2
Eternal Life

The most famous verse in the Bible is probably John 3:16. We see this verse posted on billboards and on signs at large sporting events. But many people, even in the Church, do not understand what it really means.

John 3:16 says, *For God so loved the world that He gave His only begotten Son, that whoever believes in Him should not perish but have everlasting life.*

Many have been taught that the reason Jesus came to this earth was to die for their sins, so that they could go to Heaven after they die. This is true; He did die for our sins, and believers will go to Heaven when they die. But this is only part of the story and only part of the verse. It also says: *whoever believes in Him should not perish but have* [or receive] *everlasting life* [bracketed words added]. Some translations say *"eternal life."*

What does this mean? Does this mean that if we receive Christ, we will never die? Obviously, we know this is not the case. Even the great Apostle Paul died a physical death. Besides that, Hebrews 9:27 says,

And it is appointed for men to die once, but after this the judgment ... Unless we experience the rapture of the Church, we will all die eventually.

So, what does "everlasting life" or "eternal life" mean? If you remember, in the Garden of Eden before Adam and Eve sinned, they were eternal, meaning they would live forever. They would still be around today if it was not for the fall. There was no such thing as death. Death was not a part of God's original design and plan.

God told Adam that if he ate of the tree of the knowledge of good and evil, he would surely die. When Adam and Eve disobeyed God by eating from the tree of the knowledge of good and evil, they stopped being eternal. Death entered them, and they started to die physically. It took many years, but they gradually died. Eternal life was gone. Adam and Eve actually experienced two deaths. They physically died over time, and they spiritually died instantly. When they ate from the wrong tree, sin and death entered the world and would impact every person who would ever live.

Not only did Adam and Eve die physically and spiritually, but they gave their dominion and authority over the earth to the devil. When they ate, all authority they had received from God was transferred to the devil. We can see this in Luke 4:5-6, *Then the devil, taking Him up on a high mountain, showed Him all the kingdoms of the world in a moment of time. And the devil said to Him, "All this authority I will give You, and their glory; for this has been delivered to me, and I give it to whomever I wish ..."* All authority that belonged to Adam and Eve was delivered over to Satan when Adam and Eve disobeyed God and obeyed the devil.

Now, if you remember, the Tree of Life was another tree in the Garden of Eden. The Tree of Life is a type of Christ. When God removed Adam and Eve from the Garden, He placed an angel to block the way back to the Garden and eternal life. This was actually an act of mercy because God did not want them to eat from the Tree of Life and live forever in their fallen, sinful condition. Death was, in fact, an act of mercy until sin could be officially taken care of.

John 3:16 reintroduces the thought of everlasting life that has been forgotten about since the days in the Garden. But what is everlasting life, and when does it begin? Does it begin after we receive Christ or after we die? To answer this question, let's first define "eternal life." Jesus said in John 17:3, *And this is eternal life, that they may know You, the only true God, and Jesus Christ whom You have sent.* Eternal life is not living forever on this earth, or even in heaven. Real eternal life is knowing the only true God and His Son, Jesus Christ. This is not a "knowing" like you would know of a famous person or having an intellectual knowing of something. This is a knowing in the way Adam knew his wife (see Genesis 4:1). This is an intimate knowledge of Father God and Jesus Christ. We now have the privilege of intimately knowing God.

So, when does eternal life begin? Is it after we go to Heaven or right now? According to John 3:16, when we believe in Christ, we receive eternal life. Eternal life is knowing God. Since Jesus paid the penalty for sin, those who have faith in Him for their salvation have eternal life. That life begins the moment we place our faith in Christ. We read in 1 John 5:11-12, *And this is the testimony: that God has given us eternal life, and this life is in His Son. He who has the Son has life; he who does nothave the Son of God does not have life."*

Praise the Lord! Christ died not only to forgive us of our sins but to bring us back to the Tree of Life, back to the place of intimate fellowship and relationship with Him, back to the original place where there is no death but only life in Him.

Questions - Eternal Life

1. Memorize and quote John 3:16.

2. In what ways did Adam and Eve die after the fall?

3. What happened to the authority that Adam and Eve had over the earth?

4. Why was it an act of mercy when God set an angel in charge to prevent Adam and Eve from going back to the Garden of Eden?

5. How does Jesus describe eternal life?

6. What does the word "know" mean in John 17:3?

7. When does eternal life begin?

8. What did Father God want to restore?

9. According to 1 John 5:12, he who has the Son has _____.

3
Water Baptism

The practice of water baptism goes back thousands of years to the days of John the Baptist, when our Savior and Lord Jesus Christ was baptized in the Jordan River. "Baptism" in the Greek is the word *baptizo*, which means to immerse, submerge, to make overwhelmed (ex. fully wet).[1] When a believer is baptized, they are submerged in water and brought back up out of the water. This is an outward sign (or action) of their faith. It also indicates an inner work of grace that was accomplished for us and in us, when we put our faith in Christ. This is a work of Holy Spirit, not a work of water.

Some people believe that we are not saved unless we are baptized, but this is not accurate. Was the criminal on the cross baptized? No, he was not. Water baptism does not save our souls from Hell; only the blood of Jesus does that. But water baptism does carry a more significant meaning than we may have fully understood. We can look at two illustrations from Old Testament stories.

Look at 1 Peter 3:18-22 (NIV): *For Christ also suffered once for sins, the righteous for the unrighteous, to bring you to God. He was put to death in the body but made alive in the Spirit. After being made alive, he went and made proclamation to the imprisoned spirits—to those who were disobedient long ago when God waited patiently in the days of Noah while the ark was being built. In it only a few people, eight in all, were saved through water, and this water symbolizes baptism that now saves you also—not the removal of dirt from the body but the pledge of a clear conscience toward God. It saves you by the resurrection of Jesus Christ, who has gone into heaven and is at God's right hand—with angels, authorities and powers in submission to him.*

This is where people get the idea that baptism saves you. Verse 20 says that eight people were saved through water. Another translation says "by means of water." If you think about it, water is not what saved them. Water is what actually killed everyone who was not in the ark. The ark is what saved them. If it had not been for the ark, Noah and his family would have died, too. The ark is a picture of Jesus. The end of verse 21 says: *It saves you by the resurrection of Jesus Christ.* If there was no resurrection of Christ from the dead, we could not be saved. Baptism is therefore a picture of Christ's death, burial, and resurrection. This is what saves us, and baptism is symbolic of this.

The second example is found in 1 Corinthians 10:1-2, *Moreover, brethren, I do not want you to be unaware that all our fathers were under the cloud, all passed through the sea, all were baptized into Moses in the cloud and in the sea ...*

When the Israelites crossed the Red Sea, all of their enemies were literally cut off by the water.[2] One online source said, "... the Red Sea crossing was nine miles long and 300 feet deep.[3] All of their enemies either drowned in the sea or were back on land on the other side. Either death or nine miles of water separated them from all of their enemies.

In both of these stories, we see death by water. Death to everyone outside of the ark, and death to the soldiers who chased the Israelites into the Red Sea. We can imagine many dead bodies floating on the water. We can also see in both stories a direct connection to water baptism. These stories are types and shadows of the work of Holy Spirit Who now separates us from our enemies.

Romans 6:4 says, *Therefore we were **buried** with Him through baptism into death, that just as Christ was raised from the dead by the glory of the Father, even so we also should walk in newness of life [emphasis added].*

When we were buried with Christ in water baptism, our old sinful nature was buried with Him. When this happened, Holy Spirit cut off all of our enemies, the attractions, snares, and powers that the World has to offer us. This is just like when the water fell at the Red Sea and cut them off from the World's system and its power to try and draw them back. In the same way that God wanted His sons and daughters free from slavery to Pharaoh, God wants his sons and daughters free from slavery to sin and to Satan. In the same way that God wanted to show Pharaoh and Egypt who the One True God was, today He wants to show the world who the One True God is through us. Praise God, when we came up out of the water, we were symbolically resurrected from the dead to walk in this newness of life, which we actually received when we made Jesus our Lord and Savior.

Baptism is where we bury our sin nature. This is something that has to be done by faith. If we expect nothing, nothing will happen. If we believe that we still have our sin nature, we will carry around that old rotten, stinky corpse. But if we believe by faith that our old man was crucified with Christ, that it was buried with Christ in baptism so we can now walk in the newness of the Spirit, we will truly live.

Also, Colossians 2:11-12 (NIV) says: *In him you were also circumcised with a circumcision not performed by human hands. Your whole self ruled by the flesh was put off when you were circumcised by Christ, having been buried with him in baptism, in which you were also raised with him through your faith in the working of God, who raised him from the dead.*

This tells us that when we are born again, we encounter a spiritual circumcision where our sinful nature is cut off, much like when flesh is cut away in circumcision. Verse 12 goes on to say that baptism symbolically shows this process of death, burial, and resurrection to new life. Let's walk by faith in the baptism that Jesus provided so we can experience the full, true life that God intended.

Questions - Water Baptism

1. What does the word *baptism* mean?
   a. Immerse
   b. Submerge
   c. Overwhelmed (fully wet)
   d. To wash or make clean
   e. All of the above

2. We are not saved unless we have been baptized in water. T or F

3. Baptism is an outward sign of an inner work of grace that was accomplished for us and in us when we put our faith in Christ.
   T or F

4. Baptism symbolizes Jesus' death, burial, and resurrection? T or F

5. Baptism is symbolic of our death, burial, and resurrection? T or F

6. What part of us died and was symbolically buried through baptism?

7. Our spiritual enemies have now been cut off from our new nature.
   T or F

8. What part of us was resurrected from the dead into newness of life with Christ?
   a. Our spirit
   b. Our soul
   c. Our body
   d. Our new man
   e. All of the above

4
Repentance

Mark 1:14-15: *Now after John was put in prison, Jesus came to Galilee, preaching the gospel of the kingdom of God, and saying, "The time is fulfilled, and the kingdom of God is at hand. Repent, and believe in the gospel."*

Jesus is saying here that the time is fulfilled; the time is now; the Kingdom of God is at hand. But, for us to walk in the Kingdom, we must repent and believe the gospel. And for us to truly believe the gospel, we must truly repent. This is the process of faith.

When I was growing up, I often heard sermons that proclaimed that we needed to "Repent, Repent, Repent." At the time, I did not understand what the word meant. I tried to figure it out by watching those around me. Repentance was modeled for me in a few different ways. One way is when people would go to the altar and cry. They would hear a message that moved them or made them feel guilty, and they would respond by going to the altar. They would cry and cry, sometimes making quite a scene, but there was not always a real change that followed. Those same people would often be back the next week.

Another way I saw repentance modeled was by confession of sins. People would search their hearts and confess everything they had ever done. It was like their faith was in their ability to confess. I am not sure what they believed would happen if they forgot something. Maybe, they believed they would go to Hell. I don't know. I am not saying that there is anything wrong with going to the altar or confessing our sins. I have had encounters with God doing both. But our faith cannot rest on these things. Our faith needs to rest on Him.

Many of us have heard definitions of repentance over the years. For example, a turning away, going from one direction to another, a turning from sin to righteous behavior. Turning away from sin to a righteous lifestyle is wisdom. We should make every effort to move away from sin, but this is not the true definition of "repent" or what Jesus had in mind in our opening Scripture verse. The word "repent" is the Greek word *metanoia*.[1] *Meta* means "to change," and *noia* means "your mind." Jesus was saying to "change how you think, and believe the gospel" and "change how you think, for the Kingdom of God is at hand." This is not just about thinking different thoughts but an entirely new way of thinking. True transformation is going to come by renewing our mind or changing how we think.

Romans 12:2 says, *And do not be conformed to this world, but be transformed by the renewing of your mind, that you may prove what is that good and acceptable and perfect will of God.* The word "transformed" here is the Greek word *metamorphoo*,[2] which is where we get our English word *metamorphosis*. Metamorphosis is the process the caterpillar goes through to become a butterfly. In the same way a caterpillar is transformed into a beautiful butterfly by this process, we are transformed by the process of renewing our minds or changing how we think. Until we think like God, until we agree with what He says, there will not be true transformation. There will also not be true repentance or true Bible-believing faith.

Let me give you a few examples. Firstly, let's say that you struggle with believing that your sins are forgiven. You know what the Bible says, and you mentally agree that it must be true. But for whatever reason, you sometimes struggle with believing this in your heart. If that is the case, then you need to repent (change how you think and agree with God), and then you can truly believe in your heart. You need to find the verses in the Bible that talk about forgiveness, meditate on them, and confess them out loud. Verses like Psalm 103:12, *As far as the east is from the west, so far has He removed our transgressions from us.* Or Hebrews 8:12 which says, *For I will be merciful to their unrighteousness, and their sins and their lawless deeds I will remember no more.* As you meditate on these verses and others like them, confess them over your life, and you will start to believe them. This process will take time, but after you believe them, you will experience true repentance (*metanoia*) and transformation.

Secondly, let's say you struggle with the thought that He dances over us with singing (Zephaniah 3:17).[3] Again, you might agree with this intellectually, but you don't truly believe it in your heart. This is not faith, as real faith is from the heart, not the head. With the heart, man believes unto righteousness (Romans 10:10). You need to repent (change how you think, and agree with God) and then you can believe this in your heart. Jesus said in John 8:32, *And you shall know the truth, and the truth shall make you free.* It is God's truth, God's reality, that will set you free. As you meditate on His truth, despite how you feel, it will bring true transformation, true repentance, and true faith in His Word. So let us truly repent, for the Kingdom of God is at hand.

Questions - Repentance

1. Jesus said to _____ for the Kingdom of God is at hand.

2. True repentance is to go to the altar and cry. T or F

3. Repentance is to confess your sins. T or F

4. The Greek word for "repent" is the word _____.

5. The word "repent" means to _____ _____ _____ or change how you think.

6. The process of metamorphosis is a transformation from immature to mature.   T or F

7. Romans 12:2 says that we are _____ by renewing our minds.

8. Our lives will be transformed as we:
   a. Repent
   b. Meditate
   c. Confess
   d. Agree
   e. All of the above

5
The Lord Our Righteousness

There are seven redemptive names of God scattered throughout the Old Testament. They are:

1. Jehovah-Shammah, the Lord (who) is Present.
2. Jehovah-Rapha, the Lord our Healer.
3. Jehovah-Nissi, the Lord our Banner (or Refuge).
4. Jehovah-Tsidkenu, the Lord our Righteousness.
5. Jehovah-Shalom, the Lord our Peace.
6. Jehovah-Jireh, the Lord our Provider.
7. Jehovah-Ra'ah, the Lord our Shepherd.

Each one of these names point to Christ. He is Ever Present, our Healer, our Refuge, our Righteousness, our Peace, our Provider, and our Shepherd.

In this lesson, I am going to focus on Jehovah-Tsidkenu, the Lord our Righteousness.

"Behold, the days are coming," says the LORD, "That I will raise to David a Branch of righteousness; A King shall reign and prosper, and execute judgment and righteousness in the earth. In His days Judah will be saved, and Israel will dwell safely; now this is His name by which He will be called: THE LORD OUR RIGHTEOUSNESS" (Jeremiah 23:5-6).

Jehovah-Tsidkenu is "the Lord our Righteousness" in Hebrew.

In my experience as a pastor, many people get confused about the subject of righteousness. When they think of righteousness, they usually think of righteous behavior. Righteous behavior is important; we should all try to live right and treat others as we want to be treated. But "righteousness" and "righteous behavior" are two different things. "Righteousness" is the focus of this chapter.

I believe that a lack of understanding about righteousness holds many Christians in bondage. Not understanding righteousness will affect how we view ourselves, others, and God. It will affect how we believe God sees us, how we serve God, how we worship, how we pray, our expectations when we pray, and many other things as well. Our understanding of righteousness is pivotal to our Christian experience.

Hebrews 5:13 says, *For everyone who partakes only of milk is unskilled in the word of righteousness, for he is a babe.* If we don't understand righteousness, we will never grow past the baby stages of Christian living. Many Christians today are not sure what they believe about righteousness, and that is why I want to encourage you with this truth.

The first thing we need to understand is that there are two kinds of righteousness. There is the Righteousness of God and the righteousness of man. The Righteousness of God is referring to His holiness and perfection. The righteousness of man is referring to our behavior, or works.

Isaiah 64:6 says all our righteousnesses are like filthy rags.[1] Romans 3:10 says, ... *There is none righteous, no, not one* ... These verses are referring to our righteousness, our *self*-righteousness. Self-righteousness is man's best effort to try and be good enough before God, which is impossible for any human to do.

Therefore *no one* will be declared righteous in God's sight by the works of the Law; rather, through the Law we become conscious of our sin (see Romans 3:20, emphasis mine).

The best Law-keeper ever will not be declared righteous in God's sight by his good works. Our good works may look righteous in man's sight but never in God's. There is no way for us to obtain right standing with God by obeying the Law or doing good works. If we lived a million years, we could not do enough good to earn right standing with God. There is a way, however, to receive right standing with God, but it is not through our works.

But now the righteousness of God apart from the Law is revealed, being witnessed by the Law and the Prophets, even the righteousness of God, through faith in Jesus Christ, to all and on all who believe ... (Romans 3:21-22)

Paul is saying here that there is now a way for us to become righteous by faith in Jesus Christ and not by our works of observing the Law. So, the truth is that there is a way to become righteous, but it is not through our own works and effort.

How do we become righteous? Romans 10:10 says, *For with the heart one believes unto righteousness, and with the mouth confession is made unto salvation.*

Romans 5:17 (NIV) further explains: *For if, by the trespass of the one man, death reigned through that one man, how much more will those who receive God's abundant provision of grace and of the gift of righteousness reign in life through the one man, Jesus Christ!*

From these verses, we learn that: 1) with the heart, we believe unto righteousness, and 2) righteousness is a gift to be received.

Righteousness means "right standing with God." Therefore, our right standing with God is a gift. Today, we have right standing with

God, not because of anything we have done or ever could do but because of what Jesus Christ has already done for us. We become righteous by believing unto righteousness and receiving the gift of righteousness.

Second Corinthians 5:21 says, *For He made Him who knew no sin to be sin for us, that we might become the righteousness of God in Him.* Praise God, Jesus Christ became sin. He took all our sin and the consequences for our sin upon Himself. When we place our faith or our belief in Christ as our Source of righteousness, we become righteous; we receive the gift of right standing with God. So, it is true that there is no one righteous, not even one who can obtain right standing with God by their own effort. But when we put our faith in Jesus and His finished work on the Cross, we receive the gift of righteousness—the gift of right standing with God—and we become the righteousness of God in Him.

But now the righteousness of God apart from the law is revealed, being witnessed by the Law and the Prophets, even the righteousness of God, through faith in Jesus Christ, to all and on all who believe ... (Romans 3:21-22).

We began this lesson with Jeremiah 23:5-6. Let's remind ourselves of this important Scripture:

"Behold, the days are coming," says the Lord, "That I will raise to David a Branch of righteousness; A King shall reign and prosper, and execute judgment and righteousness in the earth. In His days Judah will be saved, and Israel will dwell safely; now this is His name by which He will be called:

THE LORD OUR RIGHTEOUSNESS."

Has this day come? Has the Righteous Branch come through the lineage of King David and the lineage of Judah? Yes. Who was that verse referring to? Jesus. And what was the name by which He was to be called? *THE LORD OUR RIGHTEOUSNESS.* Jesus is our righteousness. He is our right standing with God. He provided our right standing

CHAPTER FIVE   THE LORD OUR RIGHTEOUSNESS

with God through what He did, not by anything we could ever do.

When we place our faith in Jesus and His finished work on the Cross, we inherit the gift of eternal life and right standing with God. Praise God! If you are born again, you are the righteousness of God. You are righteous. You received this position as a gift. You did not earn it, so it is not self-righteousness. It is the *gift* of righteousness.

Questions – The Lord our Righteousness

1. *Jehovah Tsidkenu* means
   a. the Lord who is Present
   b. the Lord our Healer
   c. the Lord our Banner [or Refuge]
   d. the Lord our Righteousness
   e. the Lord our Peace
   f. the Lord our Provider
   g. the Lord our Shepherd

2. What does the word *righteous* mean?
   a. Right standing with God
   b. My self-righteous position with God
   c. Right standing until I sin.
   d. I'm good enough, I guess

3. In what ways will not understanding righteousness affect our spiritual lives?
   a. How we view ourselves, others, and God
   b. How we believe God sees us
   c. How we serve and worship God
   d. How we pray, and our expectations when we pray
   e. We will remain a spiritual baby
   f. All of the above

CHAPTER FIVE — THE LORD OUR RIGHTEOUSNESS

4. There is no one righteous in God's sight (of themselves), not even one. T or F

5. There are two kinds of righteousness. What are they?

6. Do we become righteous by obeying the Law?

7. Our self-righteousness is like a filthy rag. T or F

8. How do we become righteous?

9. Righteousness is a _____ (Romans 5:17).

6

Sinners or Saints

Romans 5:12 (NIV) says, *Therefore, just as sin entered the world through one man, and death through sin, and in this way, death came to all people, because all sinned—*

In the garden, when Adam and Eve decided to eat from the tree of the knowledge of good and evil, they spiritually died, and they gave up their authority to the enemy. From then on, every person born was born with a sinful nature. We can see this with the very first person born after the fall, Cain, who killed his brother, Abel. You see, we did not become sinners when we committed our first sin. We are all born sinners, just as Cain was, because of Adam's sin. This is important to know.

But are we still sinners after we are born again? Many people are confused by this question. They are not sure what the truth is. I often hear people say, "I'm just an old sinner saved by grace." It is true that we were all born sinners, and it is true that we are now saved by grace through faith, but are we sinners after we are born again? Are we saved and sinners at the same time?

Let's see what the Word has to say. The Bible refers to *believers* as "saints," "holy ones," or "righteous ones," more than 240 times. While *unbelievers* are referred to as "sinners" over 330 times.[1] So, the Bible clearly calls unbelievers "sinners" and believers "saints," "holy ones," or "righteous ones," indicating that we cannot be sinners and saints at the same time. We were sinners when we were unbelievers, but we became saints when we were saved.

I think part of the confusion with this question comes from a misunderstanding about sin and sinners. We often relate sin and sinners with people's behavior. Romans 6:1-2 (NIV) says, *What shall we say, then? Shall we go on sinning so that grace may increase? By no means! We are those who have died to sin; how can we live in it any longer?*

There are two Greek words used for "sin" and "sins" in Romans chapter 6:

- One Greek word is *hamartia*, a noun—a person, place, or thing. It is used 48 times in Romans and 16 times in chapter 6 alone.

- The other Greek word is *hamartano*, a verb—an action word.[2] It is used 7 times in Romans and once in Romans chapter 6 (vs. 15).

Guess which Greek word is used in verses 1 and 2. It is *hamartia*, the noun. The verse should not be translated, "Shall we go on sinning so that grace may increase" because *sinning* is a verb. *Hamartia* is a noun, so it must be a person, place, or thing. Sin is not a person. It is not the devil because the devil is not omnipresent. It also is not a thing, like a rock or a tree. So, by the process of elimination, it must be a place, a spiritual place called *sin*. So, this verse could be translated, "Shall we go on living in the place called *sin*, so that grace might increase?" This changes the whole meaning.

Think about this: Romans 7:14 (NIV) says, *We know that the law is spiritual; but I am unspiritual, sold as a slave to sin* (noun = place). If you live in Texas, you are called a Texan. If you live in the United States of America, you are called an American. If you live in Canada, you are called a Canadian. So, if you live in sin, you are called a sinner. Once we move from the place of sin to the place of righteousness, we have new titles. Colossians 1:13 (KJV) says, *Who hath delivered us from the power of darkness, and hath translated us into the kingdom of his dear Son.* We do not live in darkness anymore, we do not live in sin anymore. We have been translated out of that place and into the Kingdom of God. This new location, or position in Christ, makes us saints, not our behavior.

Misunderstanding the scriptures causes people to be afraid of calling themselves saints. For example, 1 John 1:8-10 says, *If we say that we have no sin, we deceive ourselves, and the truth is not in us. If we confess our sins, He is faithful and just to forgive us our sins and to cleanse us from all unrighteousness. If we say that we have not sinned, we make Him a liar, and His word is not in us.* People read this and think if they call themselves a saint, it insinuates they never sin. Here it says that if we say we have not sinned, we deceive ourselves, and we are calling God a liar. In order to honor the Word in their own minds and appear humble, they call themselves sinners. But as we saw before, the Bible teaches that sinners are unbelievers, and saints are believers. God's reality that brings us personal freedom says we are now saints through Christ. We are not to call ourselves sinners or unbelievers anymore.

Neil Anderson, in his book, *Victory over the Darkness,* writes: "telling Christians that they are sinners and then disciplining them if they don't act like saints seems counterproductive at least and inconsistent with the Bible at worst."[3] I think Neil was being kind in this correction.

Romans 3:23 says that all have sinned and fall short of the glory of God.[4] But once we receive Christ, we are no longer sinners, we are saints who sometimes sin. We don't live in sin, we don't practice sin, we have been translated into a new Kingdom, into a place called righteousness. This new location or place in Christ is what makes us saints, not our behavior.

Questions - Sinners or Saints

1. Every person born after the fall was born with a sinful nature. T or F

2. We became sinners when we committed our first sin. T or F

3. I'm a sinner, saved by grace. T or F

4. Believers are called _____ more than 240 times in Scripture.
   a. Saints
   b. Holy ones
   c. Righteous ones
   d. All of the above

5. The Bible refers to unbelievers as _____ over 330 times.

6. There are two Greek words used for sin and sins in chapter 6 of Romans. T or F

7. If you live in a place called "sin," you are called a _____.

8. Our new location, or place in Christ, makes us _____, not our behavior.

9. Once we receive Christ, we are no longer sinners; we are saints who sometimes _____.^

7
What Happens When We Sin?

One day, I was speaking to a lady in our community about salvation. She believed that we are initially saved by grace through faith, but she also believed it was our job to maintain our salvation through good works. Therefore, if our good works outnumber our bad works, we would be saved. However, if our bad works outnumber our good works, we would go to Hell. She had basically been taught that there is a large scale in Heaven constantly remembering and weighing everything we do or don't do.

I was taught when I was growing up that we could lose our salvation, so I had very little confidence or assurance of my salvation. I remember one day at a youth conference speaking with a young lady during one of the breaks. I mentioned in passing that I had probably been saved 100 times. She looked stunned and said, "You can't get saved 100 times. Either you're saved, or you're not." I walked away thinking that girl didn't know what she was talking about. After much study, however, I now believe that she did.

So, what happens when we sin?

We read in 1 John 3:9, *Whoever has been born of God does not sin, for His seed remains in him; and he cannot sin, because he has been born of God.* And 1 John 5:18 (NAS) says, *We know that no one who has been born of God sins; but He who was born of God keeps him, and the evil one does not touch him.* These verses make it sound like Christians can never sin again. However, we know from experience and from other verses that sometimes we do sin. For example, 1 John 2:1 says, *My little children, these things I write to you, so that you may not sin. And if anyone sins, we have an Advocate with the Father, Jesus Christ the righteous.* Here we see two verses implying that Christians will never sin again and another saying that if we do sin, Jesus will speak to the Father in our defense. So how do we rectify the two as they seem to contradict one another? One way to rectify them is by adding the word "practice." A Christian does not practice sinning anymore. I think this is fair and accurate, but I also believe there is more in these verses.

Notice in the second half of 1 John 5:18, ... *but he who has been born of God keeps himself, and the wicked one does not touch him.* This is referring to Jesus being born of God, and He keeps us. The word "keeps" means *to attend to carefully, to take care of, and to guard.*[1] This says that Jesus carefully attends to us in such a way that He guards us and protects us so that the evil one cannot touch us. But our lives have been touched in one way or another at some point by the evil one, so what does this mean?

Second Corinthians 1:21-22 says, *Now He who establishes us with you in Christ and has anointed us* is *God, who also has sealed us and given us the Spirit in our hearts as a guarantee.* And Ephesians 1:13 says, *In Him you also trusted, after you heard the word of truth, the gospel of your salvation; in whom also, having believed, you were sealed with the Holy Spirit of promise.* Notice you were sealed, past tense, when you believed.

Imagine that I had you over for dinner one evening, and I offered you a big juicy steak. But then I told you I had dropped it in a mud puddle. My dog took it and ran off with it. I chased him all around the yard and finally caught him in the driveway. The steak had gravel, fur, and dog saliva all over it, but I washed it off. Would you still want to eat this steak? I think most people would say no. If the same scenario happened, but the steak was vacuum sealed in thick plastic, most people would still eat it.

This is a picture of our born-again spirit. It has been vacuumed sealed by the Holy Spirit, and sin can no longer penetrate our spirit. Jesus keeps us safe, and the evil one cannot touch our spirit. When Adam sinned one time, he died spiritually, and his nature changed. He then had a sin nature and was totally contaminated and defiled. When we sin today, because we have been made righteous, because we are born again with a divine nature, because we have been sealed by the promised Holy Spirit as God's purchased possessions, the evil one cannot touch us. He cannot get to our perfected-forever spirits. He cannot change our divine nature. Just like that vacuumed-sealed steak, our spirits have been preserved by the Holy Spirit forever.

So, are we only sealed until the next time we sin? No! Ephesians 4:30 (KJV) says, *And grieve not the Holy Spirit of God, whereby ye are sealed unto the day of redemption.* Our spirit is sealed until the day of redemption, until the final day of judgment. That is why 1 John 4:17 says, *Love has been perfected among us in this: that we may have boldness in the day of judgment; because as He is, so are we in this world.* We can have confidence, boldness, and assurance today of our salvation because our spirit has been sealed, protected from sin's contamination, never to be touched by the evil one again. We are saved, and Jesus keeps us safe in Him.

Questions - What Happens When We Sin?

1. Who or what maintains my salvation?
   a. Jesus
   b. My good works
   c. My good works outnumbering my bad works
   d. All of the above

2. We are only saved until the next time we sin. T or F

3. After we are born again, it is impossible for us to ever sin again. T or F

4. According to 1 John 2:1, who speaks to the Father in our defense if we sin?

5. Who establishes us in Christ, according to 2 Corinthians 1:21?

6. Who sealed us, and placed Holy Spirit in our hearts (spirit) as a guarantee, according to 2 Corinthians 1:21-22?

7. Our born-again spirit has been sealed until:
   a. We die
   b. We sin
   c. God gets angry with us
   d. The day of redemption

8. We can have confidence, boldness, and assurance of our salvation because …
   a. Our spirit has been sealed
   b. Our spirit is protected from sin's contamination
   c. Our spirit will never to be touched by the evil one again
   d. All of the above

8
The True Nature of God

It is hard for people to relate to God when they don't know what He is like. Many people have opinions about Him. They think He is angry, that He is hard to please. They say things like "God is going to get you," as if He is looking for a reason to punish you. They think that God is violent, wanting to send judgment. They think He causes storms, hurricanes, and floods. They think He sends sickness and disease to punish people or to teach them a lesson. They believe that He causes everything to happen in their lives due to His sovereign, perfect will. But do they understand the true nature of God?

Looking at the stories of war in the Old Testament, people often think that God is angry and that He likes punishment and death. But that could not be farther from the truth.

Let's think about the USA, for example. As a nation, America is approximately 239 years old. Research shows that as of 2015, the USA had been involved in war 222 years out of its 239 years of existence. This means that in 93% of its existence, America has been at war.[1] More than 1.1 million American lives have been lost in these 239 years.[2]

If you were to judge America by those numbers, some people might conclude that Americans love to fight and kill and that they are angry and mean. People from other countries who do not know or understand the culture, the Constitution, or the reasoning behind some of these wars may think that we are money-hungry, greedy, evil people who should mind their own business. Those people would be getting a completely wrong impression of the USA as a whole.

It is the same way with God. We are judging events that happened over the course of 4,000 years (not 239) that happened in different countries, in different cultures, and under a different covenant. We read these stories through our outside perspectives and judge without a full understanding of the people and God. We read these stories and instantly concluded that God is mean, cruel, angry, hateful, and hard to please.

I believe that in the same way that people can have a wrong impression of America and Americans, people, even good church-going people, can have a wrong impression of God. These misunderstandings have marred people's view of the true nature of God.

The most important relationship is our relationship with God. How you perceive Him, you will receive Him. Who He is to you is who He will be through you. So, understanding His true nature is pivotal to our relationship with God.

Psalm 86:15 (NIV): *But you, Lord, are a compassionate and gracious God, slow to anger, abounding in love and faithfulness.*

Psalm 106:1 *Praise the Lord! Oh, give thanks to the Lord, for He is good! For His mercy endures forever.*

From these two verses alone, we can see that God is compassionate, gracious, slow to anger, abounding in love, faithful, good, and merciful.

CHAPTER EIGHT — THE TRUE NATURE OF GOD

This is the true nature of God.

In Hebrews 1:3 (NIV), we see that, *The Son is the radiance of God's glory and the exact representation of his being ...* This means that Jesus the Son is exactly like Father God. If you want to know what God the Father is like, look at the life of Jesus. Jesus came to reveal the Father heart of God toward mankind.

Was Jesus violent? Was He angry? Was He hard to please? Did He desire to bring judgment on sinners? Did Jesus cause storms? Did He make people sick with diseases? No, He did not! He was patient and kind. He was gracious and forgiving. This can be seen in the verses of the woman caught in the act of adultery[3] or the woman at the well[4] or Peter after he denied knowing Jesus three times.[5] Jesus said that He did not come to judge the world but to save the world through Him. He rebuked storms, and He healed sicknesses and diseases.

Acts 10:38 says, *... how God anointed Jesus of Nazareth with the Holy Spirit and with power, who went about doing good and healing all who were oppressed by the devil, for God was with Him.*

This is the true nature of God.

In the same way that people could have a wrong impression about the United States due to our history of war, it is possible that people could have a wrong impression about God. If you want to know what Father God is like, study the life of Jesus. Jesus is the revelation of the true nature of Father God.

Questions - The True Nature of God

1. Is it possible that you have a wrong impression of God? Explain.

2. How you perceive Him, you will _____ Him.

3. Who He is to you, He will be _____ you.

4. The Son is the radiance of God's glory and the exact representation of his being.   T or F

5. What does this mean to you?

6. According to Psalm 106:1, God is _____.

7. Did Jesus cause sickness, disease, or storms?   Y or N

8. According to Acts 10:38, Jesus was anointed by God to do _____ works.

9. Jesus went around healing all who were oppressed by the devil. Therefore, healing is _____ and the will of God.

CHAPTER EIGHT THE TRUE NATURE OF GOD

10. What is the true nature of God?

9
The Integrity of God's Word

In Matthew 5:18 Jesus says, *For assuredly, I say to you, till heaven and earth pass away, one jot or one tittle will by no means pass from the law till all is fulfilled.* "Jot or tittle" is a phrase that means a very small amount. "Jot" comes from the Greek letter iota, which is the smallest letter in the Greek alphabet. A "tittle" is a small dot or mark that helps identify one letter from another,[1] similar to the dots in our i's or j's, or an apostrophe in English. Jesus is saying in this text that everything will be fulfilled right down to the smallest, finest detail, even things that appear to be insignificant.

Henry Liddon, an English theologian, said that in the Old Testament, there are 332 distinct predictions (prophecies) that were literally fulfilled through Christ.[2] Amazingly, these scriptures were written 400 to 1,000 years before Jesus was even born. In this lesson, we will see the wonder of this by looking at a mere 15 of the 332 prophecies.

Prophecies about the Birth of Jesus

Isaiah 7:14: *Therefore the Lord Himself will give you a sign: Behold, the virgin shall conceive and bear a Son, and shall call His name Immanuel.*

Hosea 11:1: *"When Israel was a child, I loved him, and out of Egypt I called My son."*

Psalm 72:10: *The kings of Tarshish and of the isles will bring presents; the kings of Sheba and Seba will offer gifts.*

Prophecies about the Life of Jesus

Psalm 78:2: *I will open my mouth in a parable; I will utter dark sayings of old.*

Isaiah 35:5-6: *Then the eyes of the blind shall be opened, and the ears of the deaf shall be unstopped. Then the lame shall leap like a deer, and the tongue of the dumb sing. For waters shall burst forth in the wilderness, and streams in the desert.*

Zechariah 9:9: *"Rejoice greatly, O daughter of Zion! Shout, O daughter of Jerusalem! Behold, your King is coming to you; He is just and having salvation, Lowly and riding on a donkey, A colt, the foal of a donkey."*

Prophecies about the Betrayal of Jesus

Psalm 41:9: *Even my own familiar friend in whom I trusted, who ate my bread, has lifted up his heel against me.*

Zechariah 11:12-13: *Then I said to them, "If it is agreeable to you, give me my wages; and if not, refrain." So they weighed out for my wages thirty pieces of silver. And the LORD said to me, "Throw it to the potter"—that princely price they set on me. So I took the thirty pieces of silver and threw them into the house of the LORD for the potter.*

Prophecies about the Flogging and Crucifixion of Jesus

Isaiah 50:6: *I gave My back to those who struck Me, and My cheeks to those who plucked out the beard; I did not hide My face from shame and spitting.*

Psalm 22:16: *For dogs have surrounded Me; the congregation of the wicked has enclosed Me. They pierced My hands and My feet.*

Psalm 34:20: *He guards all his bones; Not one of them is broken.*

Psalm 22:18: *They divide My garments among them, and for My clothing they cast lots.*

Psalm 22:7-8: *All those who see Me ridicule Me; They shoot out the lip, they shake the head, saying, "He trusted in the LORD, let Him rescue Him; Let Him deliver Him, since He delights in Him!"*

Psalm 69:21: *They also gave me gall for my food, and for my thirst they gave me vinegar to drink.*

Psalm 22:1: *My God, My God, why have You forsaken Me? Why are You so far from helping Me, and from the words of My groaning?*

This doesn't even include Isaiah 53.

Peter Stoner, M.S. Chairman of the Departments of Mathematics and Astronomy at Pasadena City College and Robert Newman, Ph.D. in Astrophysics, Cornell University, also Professor of Physics and Mathematics, wrote the book titled *Science Speaks, Scientific Proof of the Accuracy of Prophecy and the Bible.* In this book, they took eight of the 332 prophecies fulfilled by Christ and determined the odds of one person fulfilling those eight. The results were amazing! They calculated the odds to be 1 in 10 to the 17th power or 1 in 1.7 sextillion.[3] Dr. Stoner said, "Suppose we take 1.7 sextillion silver dollars and lay them on the face of Texas. They will cover all of the state two feet deep. Now mark one of these silver dollars and stir the whole mass thoroughly, all over the state. Blindfold a man and tell him that he can travel as far as he wishes, but he must pick up one silver dollar and say that this is the right one. What chance would he have of getting the right one? Just the same chance that the prophets would have had of writing these eight prophecies and having them all come true in any one man, from their day to the present time, providing they wrote using their own wisdom."[4]

Well, that is what Jesus did, except Jesus did not fulfill only eight prophecies, or fifteen, but over 300. The odds of one man doing all of these would be almost incalculable.

God honors His Word right down to the smallest jot or tittle. This should give us great assurance and comfort to know that the God who was faithful over these 332 prophecies will be faithful over every Word and promise that He has ever made. We can have confidence in the integrity of God and His Word. For God truly does watch over His Word to carry it out until completion (Jeremiah 1:12).

CHAPTER NINE   THE INTEGRITY OF GOD'S WORD

Questions - The Integrity of God's Word

1. What is a jot or a tittle?
   a. A phrase that means a small amount
   b. Smallest letter in the Greek alphabet
   c. A small dot on a letter
   d. All of the above

2. What does this say about the Word of God?
   a. Every word that God has ever spoken will be fulfilled
   b. The smallest details will be fulfilled
   c. Even things that appear to be insignificant will be fulfilled
   d. All of the above

3. The 332 prophecies were written 400-1000 years before Jesus was born. T or F

4. There were prophecies about the birth of Jesus. T or F

5. There were prophecies that named all 12 of the disciples. T or F

6. There were prophecies about His friends betraying Him. T or F

7. There were prophecies about His whipping and crucifixion. T or F

8. What are the odds of Jesus fulfilling all 332 prophecies?
   a. 1 out of 332
   b. 1 out of 100 billion
   c. 1 out of 1.7 sextillion
   d. A number incalculable

9. What are the odds of another person (messiah) coming and fulfilling all of these again?
   a. Likely
   b. Not likely
   c. Probable
   d. Impossible

10. God's Word can be trusted right down to the smallest detail.
    T or F

11. Can you trust God today?

10
The Power of Our Words

I grew up hearing the phrase that "sticks and stones may break my bones, but names will never hurt me." I have found from experience, however, that this is just not true. Sometimes words that are spoken have a lasting impact on our lives. What is it about words that cause them to cling to us and cause us pain?

The Word of God teaches that there is power in our spoken words. Proverbs 18:21 (NIV) says, *The tongue has the power of life and death, and those who love it will eat its fruit.* The Amplified Bible expands the translation: *...And those who love it and indulge it will eat its fruit and bear the consequences of their words.* So, we see that there is power and there are consequences in our words.

Proverbs 6:2 (KJV) says, *Thou art snared with the words of thy mouth, thou art taken with the words of thy mouth.* Proverbs 13:3 (AMP) says, *The one who guards his mouth [thinking before he speaks] protects his life; the one who opens his lips wide [and chatters without thinking] comes to ruin.* Proverbs 12:14 (KJV) says, *A man shall be satisfied with good by the fruit of his mouth...* Proverbs 12:18 (NASB) says, *There is one who speaks rashly like the thrusts of a sword, but the tongue of the wise brings healing.*

When some people speak rashly or harshly, it's like they are jabbing a sword into someone and cutting them, damaging them, or damaging themselves. Our words are not just words; they carry power. They create the environment and the atmosphere in which we live.

From the Proverbs listed, we see on the negative side that:

1) Our tongue has the power of death.
2) We are snared by our words.
3) When we talk too much, we will come to ruin.
4) When we speak rashly, we hurt people, as with a sword.

But we also see on the positive side that:

1) Our tongue has the power of life.
2) Our tongue produces satisfying good fruit.
3) If we guard our tongue, we keep our life.
4) The tongue of the wise brings healing.

You can see from these lists that there is power in our words.

Matthew 12:36 (NASB) says, *But I tell you that every careless word that people speak, they shall give an accounting of it in the day of judgment.* If God hears every careless word that we speak, I would assume that He also hears all of the other words that we speak, so He can determine which words are careless and which words are not. In fact, Psalms 139:4 (NIV) says, *Before a word is on my tongue you, Lord, know it completely.* Believing this should change how we speak to each other and how we talk in general. Matthew 12:37 goes on to say, *For by your words you shall be acquitted, and by your words you will be condemned.* What we say to each other and to God is important. Therefore, we need to choose wisely what we are saying.

Many people talk to God like it is a telephone conversation. Once they have said everything they need to say, they mentally hang up. To them, the conversation is over, and they assume that God is not listening to them anymore. They have their prayer time, their devotional time, and then they hang up. Their life and their time with God are completely compartmentalized like they are punching their timecard at work. But is this an accurate picture of our prayer time, our communication with God? What if God hears every word we say just like it is a prayer?

Remember the Book of Job? For almost 36 chapters, Job and his three friends are talking, and his friends are trying to convince Job that he has sinned and that he needs to repent. But then in the last four chapters, God starts speaking to Job and his friends, correcting them for some of the things that were said. You may remember this verse from the story where God said to Job, *"Where were you when I laid the foundations of the earth? Tell Me, if you have understanding."*[1] So even though these four men were talking with each other and not to God specifically, He still heard them and had some things to say about their conversation.

Another example is after the 12 spies investigated the land of Canaan. Numbers 14:26-28 (NIV) records, *The Lord said to Moses and Aaron: "How long will this wicked community grumble against me? I have heard the complaints of these grumbling Israelites. So, tell them, 'As surely as I live, declares the LORD, I will do to you the very thing I heard you say.'"*

Were these people who were grumbling and complaining praying? I don't believe they were. With God there is no difference between spoken prayer and casual conversation. He hears it all, every spoken word. Notice God said that *"I will do to you the very things I heard you say."* We are responsible for everything we say.

Clearly, our words are especially important to God. The words that we speak flow from our hearts and are important to Him. Jesus said that out of the abundance of the heart the mouth speaks.[2] So if you want to know what is in your heart, listen to what you are saying. Don't deny it, don't suppress it, just listen. Then acknowledge what you are saying, and let the Lord help you deal with the root issues behind your words, such as fear, trauma, unbelief, ignorance, etc. By owning what you are saying and taking responsibility for it, you can receive grace, mercy, forgiveness, and help to change what you have been saying and begin to speak life because there is power in your words.

Deuteronomy 30:19 (NIV) says: *This day I call the heavens and the earth as witnesses against you that I have set before you life and death, blessings and curses. Now choose life, so that you and your children may live.*

We have all been given a choice in what we say. One way leads to life, and the other leads to death. Which one will you choose? This is a choice we will need to make over and over every single day. If you love life, speak life, and your words will work for you, but if you speak death, your words will work against you. Life and death truly are in the power of the tongue. Therefore, we need to be speaking life because there is power in our words.

2 Corinthians 4:13 says, *It is written: "I believed; therefore I have spoken." Since we have that same spirit of faith, we also believe and therefore speak.*

CHAPTER TEN   THE POWER OF OUR WORDS

Questions - The Power of Our Words

1. Life and death are in the power of our words. T or F

2. Our words create the atmosphere in which we live. T or F

3. According to Proverbs 6:2 we are _____ by the words of our mouth.

4. God hears _____ word that we say.

5. To God, there is a difference between prayer time and just talking. T or F

6. God heard and commented on the private conversations between Job and his friends. T or F

7. God heard the private grumblings and complaining of the Israelites. T or F

8. Deuteronomy 30:19 says that God has given us a choice—life and death, blessings and curses. T or F

11
Faith

When we speak of faith, we are not talking about religion. You hear people ask, "What faith are you?" And you hear answers like, "Catholic, Protestant, Baptist, Methodist, etc." But that is not the meaning of faith. We are not looking at religion or denominations. We are looking at belief. In this lesson, we will look at what faith is, where faith comes from, and how we receive faith.

What is faith?

Hebrews 11:1 says: *Now faith is the substance of things hoped for, the evidence of things not seen.* The word *substance* here means "confidence, firm trust, and assurance."[1] The word *evidence* means "conviction or proof."[2] This verse says that *faith is*, but this verse is not telling us what faith *is*; this verse is telling us what faith *looks like*. Faith is "believing God." Faith is "trusting God."

Hebrews 11:2 says: *For by it* [faith] *the elders obtained a good testimony* (bracketed words added). Faith *looks like* confidence, firm trust, an assurance, a conviction that we have received the unseen thing that we are hoping for or anticipating. Faith is particularly important. Hebrews

11:6 (NIV) says: *And without faith it is impossible to please God, because anyone who comes to him must believe that he exists* [is] *and that he rewards those who earnestly seek him* [bracketed word added for explanation]. It is impossible to please God without faith. The phrase *please God* in the Greek language means to "gratify entirely."[3] So, it is impossible to gratify God entirely without faith. Faith pleases God, and faith gratifies God entirely.

Where does faith come from?

Romans 10:17 (KJV) says: *So then faith cometh by hearing, and hearing by the word of God.* There are two different terms for "word" in the Bible. They are *logos* and *rhema*. *Logos* is the **written** Word of God. *Rhema* is the **spoken** Word of God.[4] The word used in verse 17 is *rhema*, the **spoken** Word of God.

There is also a translation error here. The original word for *God* in the Bible is *Theos*,[5] which is where we get the word "theology." Theology is the "study of God." The original language word in this verse is not *Theos*; it is *Christos*, which means "Christ." This is the only place in the whole New Testament where the word "God" is used where "Christ" is supposed to be used. So then, faith comes from hearing the spoken word of Christ. You might think, *What is the difference? Isn't Jesus God, the Trinity, and all of that?* Yes, He is. But when people see "word of God" written here, they immediately think about reading the Word of God, the Bible. How many people do you know who read their Bibles every day and have whole sections memorized, but they don't appear to have much in the area of faith?

All Scripture is God-breathed and is useful for teaching, rebuking, correcting and training in righteousness, 2 Timothy 3:16 (NIV). All of the Scriptures were spoken by God. But that doesn't mean that the Bible recorded everything that God had to say. Jesus said in John 16:12, *"I still have many things to say to you, but you cannot bear them now."* Paul said that he would address other things when he arrived in person.⁶ He also said that he heard inexpressible things that he was not permitted to share.⁷

Even though you can get faith from reading your Bible, that is not what Romans 10:17 is referring to. It says that faith comes by hearing the spoken word of Christ. Remember, Jesus said in Matthew 4:4 (NIV), *"It is written: 'Man shall not live on bread alone, but on every word that comes from the mouth of God.'"* Jesus only said what He heard the Father say.⁸

Could this be a key to activating the faith He gave us? Think of a time when God spoke to you, and you know that you know He did. How much faith did it feel like you needed to exercise to believe it? None, right? Because faith was activated when you heard the *rhema* word of Christ.

How do we receive faith?

Romans 10:10 says, *For with the heart one believes unto righteousness, and with the mouth confession is made unto salvation.* We receive what we asked for in prayer in our hearts. It is with our hearts that we believe, not with our heads. This is what Jesus said in Mark 11:24, *Therefore I say to you, whatever things you ask when you pray, believe that you receive them, and you will have them."*

Again, we receive in our heart, our spirit, not in our mind. This is where people miss it. They do well logically agreeing with the Word. That is a good place to start. We can't have faith without agreement. But the logical agreement never moves from the mind to the heart.

John Wesley said that the devil has given the Church a substitute for faith, one that looks and sounds so much like faith that few people can tell the difference. He called this substitute "mental assent."⁹ I believe mental assent is keeping many people from receiving the blessings of answered prayer. It is keeping some people from truly being born again. They are mentally agreeing with the Word, but they are not believing the Bible way. Faith is not of the mind. It is with the heart, the spirit, that one believes unto righteousness. Agree with God's Word today and let the truths of God move from mental knowledge to your heart as absolute truth.

CHAPTER ELEVEN — FAITH

Questions - Faith

1. Hebrews 11:1 says, *Now faith is the substance of things hoped for, the evidence of things not _____.*

2. Hebrews 11:1 is not telling us what faith is; it is telling us what faith looks like. T or F

3. Faith looks like confidence, firm trust, an assurance, a conviction, that we have received the unseen thing that we are hoping for or anticipating. T or F

4. Hebrews 11:6 says that, without faith, it is _____ to please God, because anyone who comes to him must believe that he exists and that he rewards those who earnestly seek him.

5. Romans 10:17 (KJV), *So then faith [cometh] by hearing, and hearing by the _____ of God.*

6. Romans 10:17 should be translated, "faith comes from hearing the spoken word of Christ." T or F

7. Mental assent and faith are the same things. T or F

8. We are to believe from our _____.

12

The Measure of Faith

We sometimes hear people say, "I wish I had more faith," or "I wish I had his faith or her faith." For some reason they believe that their faith isn't good enough, or that they don't have enough. Therefore, when they pray, they don't expect anything to happen, and unfortunately, that is what often happens, nothing. We see this in James 1:6-7 (NIV): *But when you ask, you must believe and not doubt, because the one who doubts is like a wave of the sea, blown and tossed by the wind. That person should not expect to receive anything from the Lord.* In order to receive answered prayers from the Lord, we must ask in faith, and believe.

People often think that a particular person, pastor, or leader was blessed with great faith, but they themselves only have a small amount of faith. But is this biblically accurate? Romans 12:3 (KJV) says that … *God hath dealt to every man the measure of faith.* God did not give one person a large amount of faith and another a tiny portion. We all receive **the** measure of faith.

If I were serving soup to a group of people, and I used the same ladle to serve each person, then that ladle would be the measure. Everyone would receive the same amount of soup because I used the same measure each time. That's the way it is with faith. God used the same measure with each of us. All believers receive the same amount of faith.

Apostle Peter confirmed this in 2 Peter 1:1, *"Simon Peter, a servant and an apostle of Jesus Christ, to them that have obtained **like precious faith** with us through the righteousness of God and our Savior Jesus Christ ..."* (emphasis added). The Greek word for "like precious" in this verse is *isotimos*, which means "of equal value or honor."[1] Now since the group of people Peter was addressing had an equal value or amount of faith as he had, and since we have all been given the same measure of faith, we can conclude that we have an equal amount of faith as Peter. That means we have the same faith that Peter had when he raised Dorcas from the dead.[2] We would also have the same measure of faith that Paul had when he healed the crippled man.[3] The measure of faith that Peter and Paul had was the same measure that Jesus had because there is only one measure of faith. Therefore, we also have the faith of Jesus. Since we have the same measure of faith that Jesus has, we can do the same works that Jesus did.[4]

Paul said in Galatians 2:20 (KJV): *I am crucified with Christ: nevertheless I live; yet not I, but Christ liveth in me: and the life which I now live in the flesh I live by the faith of the Son of God, who loved me, and gave himself for me.* Paul said that he is spiritually alive because of the faith of the Son of God that now lives inside of him. Paul did not say that he lived by faith **in** the Son of God but by the faith **of** the Son of God.

In Ephesians 2:8, Paul said: *For by grace you have been saved through faith, and that not of yourselves; it is the gift of God.* The faith we have received is a gift from God, and we have all been given the same measure of faith, the faith of the Son of God.

Many Christians have not understood this and, as a result, have spent a lot of time asking God for more faith. We do not need to pray and ask God for more faith. We already have enough. We have been given the measure of faith. It would be like praying and asking God for more muscles. He has already given us muscles. If we want our muscles to be stronger, we must exercise them. We must put them to work. We must stretch them and push them to new limits.

Now Jesus did say that He had not seen such great faith as the centurion had,[5] and He also spoke about the disciple's little faith in Matthew 8:26. Andrew Wommack says in reference to this that Jesus was speaking about how much faith He saw them expressing and that none of us use all the faith we've been given all the time. So, in that sense, some of us do have more or less faith than others, but technically, it is more faith that is being expressed or exercised in our lives.[6]

It is like the parable of the soil. Only the good soil produced a harvest, even though the same seed was sown in all four. We are responsible for stewarding the faith that God has given us. We have been given the same seed and the same measure of faith, but now we have to tend the garden of our hearts so that His faith that He has given to us will grow and be more effective.

The more we tend our garden, uprooting the weeds of doubt and unbelief, agreeing with God and His Word, the more fruit we are going to bear. The more we renounce lies of the enemy and agree with God's Word, the more effectual His faith will be in us and through us.

That is what Paul said in Philemon 1:6 (KJV) which says, *That the communication of thy faith may become effectual by the acknowledging of every good thing which is in you in Christ Jesus."* The truth is, the Lord has given us everything we need for life and godliness,[7] including all the faith we need.

Questions - The Measure of Faith

1. But when you ask, you must believe and not _____ because the one who _____ is like a wave of the sea, blown and tossed by the wind. That person should not expect to receive _____ from the Lord. James 1:6-7.

2. Some people have been given more faith than others? T or F

3. All born-again Christians were given the same _____ of faith.

4. We were given the same measure of faith as Peter. T or F

5. We were given the same measure of faith as Paul. T or F

6. We were given the same measure of faith as Jesus. T or F

7. Our faith we received from God is a _____.

8. The more we _____ our garden, the more we pull out the _____ of doubt and unbelief, the more we agree with God and His Word, the more fruit we are going to see.

9. Philemon 1:6, that the communication of thy faith may become _____ by the acknowledging of every good thing which is in you in Christ Jesus.

13
"Increase Our Faith"

In Luke 17:3-6 (NIV), *Jesus said to his disciples: ... "If your brother or sister* [fellow disciple] *sins against you, rebuke them; and if they repent, forgive them. Even if they sin against you seven times in a day and seven times come back to you saying 'I repent,' you must forgive them." The apostles said to the Lord, "Increase our faith!" He replied, "If you have faith as small as a mustard seed, you can say to this mulberry tree, 'Be uprooted and planted in the sea,' and it will obey you"* [bracketed words added].

The context here is forgiveness. The Old Testament taught "an eye for an eye, a tooth for a tooth." The Rabbis and Pharisees of their day taught that people were required to forgive a person three times, and after that, they could have nothing to do with them. But the Lord had instructed the disciples to forgive someone even if they sinned against them seven times in the same day. The thought of forgiving someone seven times in the same day stretched the disciples so severely that they cried out, *"Lord, increase our faith,"* or "give us more faith." They did not believe they could do this without help.

Notice Jesus' response to their request for more faith from verse 6:

He replied, "If you have faith as small as a mustard seed, you can say to this mulberry tree, 'Be uprooted and planted in the sea,' and it will obey you." After their request for more faith, Jesus instructed them to speak to a tree. This is a strange request. Jesus told them to speak specifically to a mulberry tree. Most likely, He was standing right beside one of these trees to illustrate what He was trying to teach. Now remember, He was teaching them how to strengthen their measure of faith in the area of forgiveness. It is interesting that mulberry trees are fast growing trees with an aggressive root system, just like bitterness and unforgiveness can be in our lives.

Hebrews 12:15 (NIV) says, *See to it that no one falls short of the grace of God and that no bitter root grows up to cause trouble and defile many.* Jesus was telling His disciples to speak to the tree of bitterness and unforgiveness to come up by the roots, and it would obey. By doing so, their faith would be strengthened to forgive those who hurt them.

It is hard to forgive sometimes, especially when the same person hurts us over and over again. I suspect that is why the disciples asked the Lord to increase their faith. They did not believe they could do it. I find it hard to even imagine being hurt by the same individual seven times in the same day and forgiving them all seven times. But that is exactly what Jesus asks us to do. If you are finding it hard to forgive someone, speak to the mulberry tree, the tree of bitterness and unforgiveness, to come up by the roots and be thrown into the sea. You will see that it will obey you, and then you will be able to forgive from your heart much easier.

Another thing I want to highlight is from Luke 17:6 (NIV). *He replied, "If you have faith as small as a mustard seed ..."* In the original Greek language, the word "small" is not there. The King James Version says, *"If ye had faith as a grain of mustard seed ..."* The point of the verse is not about the size of the seed. It is about having faith like a mustard seed. There are characteristics in a mustard seed that Jesus is comparing to faith. When Jesus spoke these words, He was speaking to an agricultural society who would be familiar with seeds. The mustard seed comes from the weed family. They are very tenacious and will grow almost anywhere. They will grow where most seeds cannot survive. If they are sown among rocks, they will still grow. They will push and push until the rocks are moved out of the way to let the sunlight in.

This is a picture of faith that Jesus wants us to see. It has nothing to do with the size of the seed or the size of our faith because He has already given us the measure of faith that is needed for anything. It has to do with us being tenacious with the faith He has given us. We need to push and push until those rocks are moved out of our way. This is not a passive faith but an active faith. We already have enough faith. We just need to exercise our faith by speaking to the tree until it submits. Everything we need is in the seed that has been planted!

Is His speaking to an object, like a tree, a one-time teaching by Jesus? No, it is not. Matthew 17:14-20 states: *And when they had come to the multitude, a man came to Him, kneeling down to Him and saying, "Lord, have mercy on my son, for he is an epileptic and suffers severely; for he often falls into the fire and often into the water. So, I brought him to Your disciples, but they could not cure him." Then Jesus answered and said, "O faithless and perverse generation, how long shall I be with you? How long shall I bear with you? Bring him here to Me." And Jesus rebuked the demon, and it came out of him; and the child was cured from that very hour. Then the disciples came to Jesus privately and said, "Why could we not cast it out?" So Jesus said to them, "Because of your unbelief; for assuredly, I say to you, if you have faith as a mustard seed, you will say to this mountain, 'Move from here to there,' and it will move; and nothing will be impossible for you."*

Think about this for a moment. What were the disciples asking? They were saying, "Why couldn't we cast out the demon? Why could we not heal the boy? What is wrong with our faith? We tried, but it didn't work?" They probably thought that they needed more faith to get the job done. But that is not what Jesus said to them. He said the reason the boy was not healed had nothing to do with the will of God, or their faith. It was because of their unbelief. This is the only time the word "unbelief" is used in the New Testament, and it means "littleness of faith." They had faith, but it was not strong yet. It was still small. They needed to exercise their faith to make it grow strong.

Jesus continued to teach the disciples how to exercise their faith, in verse 18. Jesus instructed the disciples to speak to the mountain to move from here to there, and it would obey. The reason for their failure to heal the boy was not the demon. Jesus did not say the demon was too powerful. The obstacle was their personal unbelief. Their unbelief was stronger than their faith. Jesus told them to speak to that mountain of unbelief, with mustard seed-like faith, and to command it to be cast into the sea, and it would obey. This is something I think we can all practice.

Another example is found in Mark 11. Verses 12-14 say, *"Now the next day, when they had come out from Bethany, He was hungry. And seeing from afar a fig tree having leaves, He went to see if perhaps He would find something on it. When He came to it, He found nothing but leaves, for it was not the season for figs. In response Jesus said to it, "Let no one eat fruit from you ever again." And His disciples heard it."* Skip ahead to verses 20-24, *"Now in the morning, as they passed by, they saw the fig tree dried up from the roots. And Peter, remembering, said to Him, "Rabbi, look! The fig tree which You cursed has withered away." So Jesus answered and said to them, "Have faith in God. For assuredly, I say to you, whoever says to this mountain, 'Be removed and be cast into the sea,' and does not doubt in his heart, but believes that those things he says will be done, he will have whatever he says. Therefore I say to you, whatever things you ask when you pray, believe that you receive them, and you will have them."*

In this story, Jesus was hungry, and he went looking for fruit on a tree that was not in season. The time for figs had not yet come. I'm sure Jesus would have known what season figs grow, but He looked anyway. He then curses the fig tree because it did not have fruit, even though it was not the right season. Why would Jesus do this? Some have suggested in fun that He was still upset with the fig tree from the time of the Garden of Eden when Adam and Eve hid behind it after the fall. This is funny, but unlikely. I believe it was to teach the disciples this same lesson once again.

They asked Jesus how the fig tree withered so quickly. Jesus responded, *"Have faith in God."* Other translations say, *"Have faith of God."* Then He told them that if they had faith, and not doubt, they could speak to the mountain, and it would move into the sea.

These are three different occasions, three different stories with the same teaching. First, the forgiveness of sins, the healing of the epileptic boy, and the cursing of the fig tree that did not produce fruit. Three different times they asked Jesus about faith, and three different times He told them to speak to the circumstance. Speak to the tree of unforgiveness. Speak to the mountain of unbelief. Speak to the mountains in your life, the areas in your life that are not producing fruit. He told them to speak to them, and they would be uprooted and cast into the sea. By doing so, their faith would grow. And our faith will grow as well, if we do the same.

You, like the disciples, may feel like you don't have enough faith. The truth is that the Lord has given us everything we need for life and godliness,[1] including all the faith we need. We just need to acknowledge what we already have and speak to the mountains in our lives. I believe the Lord would like to encourage you today by saying that you already have enough faith; you just need to exercise what you have. Why not start today by speaking to the mountains in your life in Jesus' name.

Questions – Increase Our Faith

1. How many times are we to forgive our brother in the same day if he sins against us?

2. When the disciples asked Jesus to increase their faith, He told them to speak to a _____.

3. If you are having trouble forgiving someone, you should speak to the _____ of unforgiveness to be uprooted and cast into the sea.

4. When the disciples asked Jesus why they couldn't heal the epileptic boy, Jesus told them to speak to the _____ of unbelief.

5. If you are having trouble believing for a breakthrough, you should speak to the _____ of unbelief to be uprooted and cast into the sea.

6. When the disciples asked Jesus how the fig tree withered so quickly, Jesus told them to speak to the _____.

7. Mark 11:23 says, "For assuredly, I say to you, whoever says to this _____, 'Be removed and be cast into the sea,' and does not doubt in his heart, but believes that those things he says will be done, he will have _____ he says."

8. Mark 11:24 says, "Therefore I say to you, whatever things you ask when you pray, believe that you _____ them, and you will _____ them."

14
Activating Faith

Romans 10:10 says, *"For with the heart one believes unto righteousness, and with the mouth confession is made unto salvation."* In this verse, we see two parts of faith. Part one is believing from the heart. Part two is, with the mouth, confession is made unto salvation. This is not talking about the confession of our sins. Verse 9 says, *"that if you confess with your mouth the Lord Jesus and believe in your heart that God has raised Him from the dead, you will be saved."* So, with your heart, you believe Jesus is Lord. With your heart, you believe that God raised Him from the dead. With the heart, you believe unto righteousness. This is faith in our hearts in what Jesus did, and through it, we receive the gift of righteousness.

But it is with our mouths that we confess unto salvation. This can be a bit confusing. So, we believe to receive righteousness, but we confess to receive salvation? You might say, "Well preacher, I thought righteousness and salvation were the same things." Apparently, they are not the same, or there would not be a distinction here. Righteousness is our right standing with God. Our salvation is the benefits we are to receive because of our right standing with God.

The word "salvation" comes from the Greek word *Sozo* and is used 110 times in the New Testament.[1] Sozo, or salavation, means "to save, to keep safe and sound, to save from injury or peril, to save from suffering, ex: to save from disease, to save from our sin, to save from the penalties of judgment (Hell)."[2] The word also means "to heal, to make well or whole, to restore to health, to deliver, to protect, to rescue from danger or destruction."[3] The writers of the New Testament showed the fullness of the word *"Sozo"* by using it in its many different forms, displaying the other aspects of our salvation. For example, Luke 19:10 (NIV) says, *"For the Son of Man came to seek and to save what was lost."* The word "save" is *Sozo*. In Mark 6:56 (NIV), *"And wherever he went—into villages, towns or countryside—they placed the sick in the marketplaces. They begged him to let them touch even the edge of his cloak, and all who touched it were healed."* Here the word "healed" is *Sozo*. Luke 8:36 (NAS) says, *"Those who had seen everything reported to them how the man who had been demon-possessed had been made well."* And here, *"made well,"* referring to the man's deliverance, is the word *Sozo*. *Sozo* means "saved, healed, and delivered." Therefore, "salvation" means "saved, healed, and delivered."

These are all part of our salvation benefits that we now have access to because we are in right standing with God. We now have access to the forgiveness of all our sins, and we now have access to the healing of all our diseases. We now have access to deliverance from any demon. But we receive these benefits by the confession of our mouth. You can believe these things all day, but unless you confess it with your mouth, you will not receive the benefits of your salvation.

Let me show you this in another verse. 2 Corinthians 4:13, *"And since we have the same spirit of faith, according to what is written, 'I believed and therefore I spoke,' we also believe and therefore speak ..."* There are so many Christians today who are living below their salvation privileges. They believe they are saved, but they don't believe they are righteous when salvation is a benefit of righteousness. Many are not even sure if they are righteous *or* saved.

Guess what? They say so with their mouths. According to their faith, it is done unto them. By their words, they are acquitted, and by their words, they are condemned. They don't know what to confess because they don't know what they believe. All they have been taught is to confess their sins, not how to confess unto the benefits of salvation. Because they have not been taught, they are living below their salvation benefits.

I want you to notice something about Romans 10:9-10 ... *"that if you confess with your mouth the Lord Jesus and believe in your heart that God has raised Him from the dead, you will be saved. For with the heart one believes unto righteousness, and with the mouth confession is made unto salvation."* Notice in verse 9 that it first says if you confess with your mouth and then believe in your heart. Then in verse 10, it says believe first and then confession. This is the process of faith. Let's say, you believe Jesus is Lord. You believe that God raised Jesus from the dead. But you are struggling with believing that you are righteous or that you are born again. Confession needs to come first to help you believe. Confession brings possession. Confession will remove doubt and unbelief that tries to steal the truth from you. Confession will bring feelings to your soul. Sometimes we are believing first and then confessing, and other times we are confessing first and then believing. This is the process of faith.

Holiness preacher George Watson said, "I have seen hundreds and hundreds who didn't have one bit of feeling or emotion stand and say, 'Well, I will dare say it; the blood cleanses.' They kept saying it, and it wasn't five minutes before their faith had brought consuming fire down from heaven. Why? Because your faith is not perfect until that faith comes out of your mouth."[4]

Another quote by George Watson effectively summarizes this chapter well: "An inner faith and an audible confession are the two wings of religious life. God has, in infinite wisdom, ordained them both as conditions of His blessing. Faith in the heart is the condition by which we obtain the fact of God's blessing, and confession with the mouth is the condition by which we obtain the experience or emotion of God's blessing. Heart faith and mouth confession are twin-born of the Holy Spirit, and that which God has joined together, we dare not put asunder."[5]

CHAPTER 14 ACTIVATING FAITH

Questions - Activating Faith

1. Romans 10:10, For with the heart one believes unto righteousness, and with the mouth, confession is made unto _____.

2. Romans 10:9, that if you confess with your mouth the Lord Jesus and believe in your heart that God has raised Him from the dead, you will be _____.

3. We believe to receive righteousness, but we confess to receive salvation.   T or F

4. Salvation is a benefit of right standing with God.   T or F

5. The word Salvation means: Saved, Healed, Delivered, Forgiven.   T or F

6. 2 Corinthians 4:13, "And since we have the same spirit of faith, according to what is written, 'I believed and therefore I _____,' we also believe and therefore _____."

7. If you are struggling to believe that you're righteous or that you're born again, you need to confess what the Word says first, to help you believe.   T or F

8. Confession brings _____.

9. Confession will _____ doubt and unbelief that tries to steal the truth from you.

10. Sometimes we are _____ first and then _____ and other times we are _____ first and then _____. This is the process of faith.

15
The Heart

Often, people read the Old Testament and don't translate it through the Cross. They read it as if it carried the same meaning today as it did back then. But there has been a change. The resurrection of Jesus changed everything. Failure to understand these changes can keep us in bondage. For example, Jeremiah 17:9 says, *"The heart is deceitful above all things, and desperately wicked; Who can know it?"* Now is this the condition of our born-again hearts or spirits today? Can our hearts be trusted? Or are they still desperately wicked?

Ezekiel 36:26 says, "I will give you a new heart and put a new spirit in you; I will remove from you your heart of stone and give you a heart of flesh." Ezekiel prophesied about a day coming when hearts would change from stone to flesh; from hard to soft. The question is, has that day already happened? Or is this talking about once we get to heaven? In this lesson, I want to show you that this day has already taken place.

2 Corinthians 5:17 says, "Therefore, if anyone is in Christ, he is a new creation; old things have passed away; behold, all things have become new." Praise God, the old heart of stone is gone, and we have

been given a new heart, a new spirit. Galatians 4:6 tells us that, "Because we are sons, God sent the Spirit of his Son into our hearts, the Spirit who calls out, "Abba, Father." And Romans 8:14 says, "The sons of God are led by the Spirit of God." Now, where is the Spirit of His Son? In our hearts, right? So, the Sons of God are led from their hearts. Then how could our hearts still be deceitful and wicked if Jesus Himself lives there? They can't be. They have been made new.

Let's look at another example. David said in Psalm 51:10-11 (KJV), "Create in me a clean heart, O God; and renew a right spirit within me. Cast me not away from thy presence, and take not thy holy spirit from me." These verses were true for King David, but they are not applicable in the same way for us today. There has been a change in the New Testament. There has been a change because of the Cross. Now I just showed you that our hearts/spirits have been changed and made new when we were born again. If Jesus himself is living in our hearts, wouldn't that mean they are clean? I have heard people say that "God doesn't live in a dirty vessel," and you know what? They are correct. God cleansed the house and gave us a new spirit that is absolutely clean, recreated in Christ Jesus. In fact, Ephesians 4:24 says that our spirits were recreated righteous and truly holy. Hebrews 12:23 says that our spirits are righteous and made perfect. Hebrews 10:14 says they are perfected forever. We no longer need to pray for God to create in us a clean heart because He has already done it. It is perfected forever.

The first half of Psalm 51:11 says, "Cast me not away from thy presence." But John 6:37 says, "All that the Father gives Me will come to Me, and the one who comes to Me I will by no means cast out." Praise God, He is not going to cast us out of His presence today. That is one of the reasons why He came, so that we could live with Him forever. The second half of the verse says, "and take not thy Holy Spirit from me." Well, John 14:16 says, "And I will ask the Father, and He will give you another Counsellor to be with you forever." If the Counsellor, the Holy Spirit, is going to be with us forever, how could he leave? Forever is forever, meaning without a break. You see, there has been a change. Today, because of the resurrection of Jesus Christ from the dead, because our sins have been taken away, because our spirits have been recreated righteous and truly Holy, He won't leave us. In fact, Hebrews 13:5 says, "Never will I leave you, never will I forsake you." Today, it isn't appropriate for us to pray those kinds of prayers because Jesus has already solved the heart problem by giving us a new one, a new, born again heart that was recreated in Christ Jesus.

Years ago, I was praying, and the Lord spoke to me. He said, "To the pure, all things are pure." (Titus 1:5) I quickly responded, "Yes Lord, I know that verse." Then He said it again, "To the pure, all things are pure." But He added, "I see you pure." This shocked me. I was still seeing myself after my flesh, after my failures, and shortcomings. But God didn't see me that way. He is pure and to the pure all things are pure. So, He sees me pure. He sees you pure. He sees us pure, because of the finished work of Jesus on the Cross. In fact, 1 John 3:3 says, "everyone who has this hope in Him purifies himself, just as He is pure." Think about this. Everyone who has placed their hope in Jesus for their salvation is NOW pure and just as pure as Jesus is. How can this be? It is true because there has been a change. God took out the heart of stone and gave us a new heart that was recreated pure, righteous, and holy. He gave us a new spirit that was born again, recreated in Him. A new heart that has been made perfect forever through the sacrifice of Himself. Praise God, that is what our new hearts looks like today because we are in Him.

Questions - The Heart

1. When we are applying Scriptures from the Old Testament, we need to translate them through the Cross. T or F

2. Jeremiah 17:9, "The heart is deceitful above all things, and desperately wicked; who can know it?" Does this apply to us today? Y or N

3. I will give you a new _____ and put a new _____ in you; I will remove from you your heart of stone and give you a heart of flesh.

4. Since our spirits have been made new:
    a. Old things have passed away
    b. Our heart of stone is gone
    c. God sent the Spirit of his Son into our hearts
    d. The sons of God are led from their hearts through the Spirit of God.
    e. All of the above

5. Psalm 51:10-11, "Create in me a clean heart, O God; and renew a right spirit within me. 11 Cast me not away from thy presence and take not thy holy spirit from me." Does this apply to us today? Y or N

6. Our new, born again spirits are:
    a. Righteous and truly Holy
    b. Righteous and made perfect
    c. Perfected forever
    d. All of the above

7. After we are born again, do we need to pray for God to create in us a clean heart?   Y or N

8. John 14:16 says, And I will ask the Father, and he will give you another Counsellor to be with you _____.
   a. Forever
   b. Once in awhile
   c. Sometimes
   d. Until the next time that you sin

9. To the pure, all things are _____.

10. According to 1 John 3:3, everyone who has placed their hope in Jesus for their salvation is NOW pure and just as pure as Jesus is.   T or F

16
Take Captive Every Thought

A few summers ago, my family and I were in New Brunswick, Canada, visiting my mom and dad. My wife and I decided to take our children out for the day to show them some of my old stomping grounds—my old high school, my old home, our Bible College, different places I had worked, etc. After touring the town, we spontaneously decided to go see a movie. With no theater in my hometown, it was an hour and a half drive to the destination. We had a wonderful day out but didn't get home until after midnight.

When we returned home, we found my mother was frantic. Our cell phones had been turned off, so she could not contact us. She confessed that she had expected us home much earlier, and so, as time passed, she had fearfully imagined that we had been in a horrible car accident and were possibly dead. She envisioned us stranded on the side of the road, where no one knew our identities or how to contact her. She got so worked up that she started calling my friends and former Bible College asking if they had seen us. She even considered calling the police. She had imagined this whole scenario and got herself completely worked up when, in reality, we were all safe and having a great time.

The Bible teaches that we are to control what we think about. 2 Corinthians 10:5 says, *"casting down arguments and every high thing that exalts itself against the knowledge of God, bringing every thought into captivity to the obedience of Christ."* Either we bring those thoughts that are contrary to the knowledge of God into captivity, or they take us captive.

Fear, worry, and anxiety have a way of negatively affecting our imaginations, just like they did with my mother. They can alter our view of reality. Once we imagine something enough, it can feel like reality to our emotions. It is like going into the hall of mirrors at the fair. One mirror makes you look tall, another mirror makes you look short, then another mirror makes your head look big and the rest of you look small. The distortion of the mirror changes the image of what you truly look like. That is what the devil wants to do in our lives. If he can distort that mirror with fear, if he can distort how we see ourselves, how we see God, and how we see others, it will change our view of reality and potentially alter our lives in many different ways.

For example, if you see yourself as a sinner versus seeing yourself as a saint who sometimes sins, that will affect your spiritual reality. If you see God as angry, this is going to alter your spiritual reality. If you see God as hard to please, you are going to live under a legalistic, must-try-harder perspective. If you are critical, judgmental, or accusatory toward others, it will affect every relationship in your life. This will also affect your relationship with yourself. That might sound weird, but how you relate to yourself is filtered through your view and perspective of reality. And how you judge others, you will also judge yourself. Who God is *to* you, He will be *through* you. So, having godly perspectives and godly realities is particularly important to enjoying a good and healthy life.

In John 8:32 Jesus said, *"And you shall know the truth, and the truth shall make you free."* This says that you will know the truth. The truth that you do not know will not set you free. It is the truth that you do know that will set you free. So, the more truth that we know, the more freedom we can experience. One of the definitions of "truth" from this verse is *reality*.[1] So, Jesus is saying that you will know His reality and His reality shall make you free. Alternate realities will put you in bondage. But God's reality, God's perspective, will set you free.

This makes me think of what Amos 3:3 says, *"Can two walk together, unless they are agreed."* A major key to walking in Jesus' reality and freedom is to agree with what He says. If you don't agree with Him, you won't walk with Him in that area of your life. These areas where we don't yet fully agree need to be cast down because they are against the knowledge of God. Those thoughts need to be taken captive or placed in prison. Then we need to agree with thoughts that are obedient or in agreement with Christ's. The agreement with Christ's realities brings freedom. That is why it is vital to take captive every thought that is contrary to the Word of God. This process will take time, but if you are determined and consistent, you will experience the ever-increasing freedom that Jesus promised.

Questions - Take Captive Every Thought

1. We need to bring thoughts that are contrary to the knowledge of God into captivity, or they will take us _____.

2. Fear, worry, and anxiety have a way of negatively affecting our imaginations.   T or F

3. Entertaining thoughts that are contrary to God's will distort how we see _____, how we see _____, and how we see _____.

4. How you judge others, you will judge yourself. And how you judge yourself, you will judge others.   T or F

5. Who God is to you, He will be _____ you.

6. The truth that you _____ know will not set you free. It is the truth that you _____ that will set you free.

7. One of the definitions for truth from John 8:32 is _____.

8. Amos 3:3 says, "Can two walk together unless they are _____?

9. A major key to walking in the reality of Jesus and freedom that He promised is to _____ with what He says.

17
Healthy Thinking (Part 1)

You are an amazing creation. You are fearfully and wonderfully made. Of all the works of God's hand, you are His masterpiece. Did you know that in the average lifespan, the human heart beats more than 3 billion times?[1] The human eye is capable of seeing 7,000,000 colors?[2] The human nose can detect 1 trillion smells?[3] There are 100 billion neurons present in the brain. The blood vessels that are present in the brain are approximately 100,000 miles long.[4] That is a greater distance than 4 trips around the earth.

We are an amazing creation, and we were created in the very image of God. 2 Timothy 1:7 says: *"For God has not given us a spirit of fear, but of power and of love and of a sound mind."* We have a powerful, sound mind given to us by God.

It is important to understand that our minds and our brains are not the same things. If we compare our brains and our minds to a computer, our brains would be like the computer processor that calculates and processes information, and the hard drive would be like the storage of our memories. Our minds would be comparable to a computer's operating system, like Linux, Windows, or Mac. Whatever operating system you are running will determine how that computer works and processes information. If we try to use an operating system that is not designed for a particular computer, there are going to be many system failures and vulnerabilities to the computer's overall function and ability. For example, if you format a MacBook and try to install Windows on it, there will be many problems. Although it is possible, it will not function as originally designed.

Our bodies, our minds, our brains work best when we apply God's original design. His software with our hardware will work best and produce the best results. So, we must reformat the sin corrupted software of the old man and install a new operating system that is compliant with our new creation spirits. Romans 12:2 says, *"And do not be conformed to this world, but be transformed by the renewing of your mind, that you may prove what is that good and acceptable and perfect will of God."* God wants us to experience transformation in our lives, but He will not make that happen. We must partner with His thoughts to experience the renewal of our minds and lives. Then we can understand His will and plans for us.

There is a certain way that God wants us to think. Philippians 4:8 says, *"Finally, brethren, whatever things are true, whatever things are noble, whatever things are just, whatever things are pure, whatever things are lovely, whatever things are of good report, if there is any virtue and if there is anything praiseworthy—meditate on these things."* This is a healthy way to think, and it will produce healthy emotions, healthy relationships, and healthy lives.

But when we think about other things, it can be very unhealthy. Romans 1:28 (NIV) says, *"Furthermore, just as they did not think it worthwhile to retain the knowledge of God, so God gave them over to a depraved mind, so that they do what ought not to be done."* These people did not think the knowledge of God was worthwhile. They started to have thoughts that were contrary to His, and they partnered with those thoughts. So, God gave them over to a depraved mind, and they did things that should not be done. Romans 1:21-23 says, *"because, although they knew God, they did not glorify Him as God, nor were thankful, but became futile in their thoughts, and their foolish hearts were darkened. Professing to be wise, they became fools, and changed the glory of the incorruptible God into an image made like corruptible man—and birds and four-footed animals and creeping things."* In these scriptures, we see the process of a depraved mind. First, they did not glorify God as God. Second they were not thankful. Third, they became futile in their thoughts. Fourth, their foolish hearts were darkened. Fifth, they became fools. And finally, they did things that ought not to be done.

A major sign of a depraved mind is idol worship. This doesn't have to look like someone bowing down and worshipping a statue. Idol worship is worshiping anything over God. In the above Scriptures, they knew about God, but they did not honor Him as God. They did not give God the final say in their lives. They honored their own thoughts and ideas above His, and when they did that, they made themselves out to be gods. We can see this a lot today. People take bits and pieces of the Bible, maybe parts that they like, maybe parts that are easy for them to follow, but the other parts that are harder for them or that others disagree with, they ignore and honor their own thoughts and ideas instead. This is idol worship. This is saying that God is God in certain areas, but I am god in these other areas. We have no right to do this. Either He is Lord of all, or He is not Lord at all. These thoughts that don't agree with God need to be cast down. His thoughts need to have the final authority in our lives.

When we have serious trouble with our vehicles, we often need to take it to the dealership to find out what is wrong. They know more than the average mechanic because they know the specific design of the automobile. It is the same way with God. God is our Creator. We are His masterpiece. He knows how we are designed to operate. Like the computer, your spirit, soul, and body are going to function at their best with the correct operating system. That operating system looks like doing things God's way and giving Him the final say and authority in our lives.

CHAPTER 17   HEALTHY THINKING (PART I)

Questions - Healthy Thinking (Part 1)

1. 2 Timothy 1:7: For God has not given us a spirit of fear, but of power and of love and of a sound _____.

2. Romans 12:2: And do not be conformed to this world, but be _____ by the renewing of your _____, that you may prove what is that good and acceptable and perfect will of God.

3. Philippians 4:8: Finally, brethren, whatever things are _____, whatever things are _____, whatever things are _____, whatever things are _____, whatever things are _____, whatever things are of _____, if there is any _____ and if there is anything _____ —meditate on these things.

4. When people think it is not worthwhile to retain the knowledge of God, God will give them over to a depraved mind.   T or F

5. Once this happens, they will do things that ought not to be done.   T or F

6. The process of a depraved mind found in Romans 1:21-23: (number them 1-6)
   _____ They did things that ought not to be done.
   _____ They did not glorify God as God.
   _____ Their foolish hearts were darkened.
   _____ They became fools.
   _____ They were not thankful.
   _____ They became futile in their thoughts.

7. Idol worship is worshiping anything over _____.

8. Thoughts that don't agree with God's thoughts, need to be cast down, and His thoughts need to have the final authority in our lives.   T or F

18
Healthy Thinking (Part 2)

Second Corinthians 10:3-5: *For though we walk in the flesh, we do not war according to the flesh. For the weapons of our warfare are not carnal but mighty in God for pulling down strongholds, casting down arguments and every high thing that exalts itself against the knowledge of God, bringing every thought into captivity to the obedience of Christ.*

We know from these Scriptures that we are supposed to take captive every thought. We know that we have the power to pull down strongholds in our minds. We also know from Romans 12:2 that by doing so, it will bring transformation to our lives. But how do we do that? How do we take captive every thought? How do we make it obedient to Christ? How do we move our minds away from one thing and onto another?

A thought plus an attached emotion equals an attitude.[1] Attitudes influence what we do and say. Once we recognize a thought or attitude that is against the truth of God or the reality of God, we must stop it, grab it, and put it in prison. It really does not matter where the prison is. You are moving it out of your thought life. One way to help discover our bad thoughts is by listening to what we say, for out of the abundance of our hearts our mouths will speak (see Luke 6:45).[2]

Our imaginations are immensely powerful. When we see something in our minds, it can trigger the same type of emotions as it would if we saw it happen in real life.[3] For example, a movie can excite us, inspire us, scare us, make us sad, etc. Having a bad dream can cause our hearts to race, just like it would if it happened while we were awake. Daydreaming about something negative will cause negative emotions and reactions. These negative daydream-type thoughts need to be cast down.

Since our imaginations are so powerful, I try to use mine in a positive way. When I have a thought that is not from God, however, like a negative thought, a fearful thought, a perverse thought, a judgmental or critical thought, etc., I first recognize that this is not *my* thought. It might feel like mine, but it came from the evil one. Kenneth Hagin used to say, "We can't stop a bird from flying over our heads, but we can stop it from making a nest in our hair." We need to actively take captive these thoughts.

When these types of thoughts come to me, I close my eyes and use my imagination to picture a crane grabbing that thought and lifting it out of my brain and setting it down inside of a prison. I often use my arm and hand as if it were the crane and go through the motions of grabbing that thought, lifting it up and out, and setting it down in my imaginary prison. I sometimes even make a *beep, beep, beep* sound like a big crane does when it is moving. This always helps me.

You can also imagine that thought disappearing like a puff of smoke after an explosion. Or, you could pretend to dig a hole and bury it.[4] Doing this type of thing helps create triggers in your brain to not allow such thoughts.

Once we remove the thought, we need to introduce a new thought that agrees with God's perspective and meditate on that truth. A new thought could be a Scripture verse, a creative song, a good memory, or anything Holy Spirit inspired. If you are not sure what that truth is, you can ask Holy Spirit, and He will help you. He will not make you change your thoughts,. That is your job. But He will help you with new thoughts when you ask Him.

Another way to quickly remove a negative thought is by singing. Let's say you have a negative thought or perhaps a negative accusation against a family member or a friend. You know that you should not be thinking this way, but what do you do? Well, you can start singing. I have done this, and it really helps. One time, I was really struggling with my thoughts. It felt like I was being bombarded from every direction with one negative thought after another. I started to sing something like, "I don't have to think about these things, I can choose to bring an offering." I made up my own lyrics and worshipped Jesus. The thoughts instantly went away, and my peace was restored.

The left side of the brain deals with logic and reasoning, like science and math. The right side of the brain handles creativity, like art and music.[5] By singing the song, you are taking your thoughts from one side of your brain and focusing them on the other, which brings relief. My wife does this in her elementary classroom. When her children are distracted and not paying attention to her instructions, she starts singing the instructions. Before she knows it, the kids are singing the instructions along with her and doing what she asked them to do. This act switched their thoughts from one side of their brains to the other, and it helped them follow instructions.

This process will help you, too, but using this process must be intentional. You must do these things on purpose and for a purpose. The purpose is for a transformed life. Use your imagination for good. God gave it to you. Think about the things of God, and experience His presence and peace. Philippians 4:8 says, *"Finally, brethren, whatever things are true, whatever things are noble, whatever things are just, whatever things are pure, whatever things are lovely, whatever things are of good report, if there is any virtue and if there is anything praiseworthy—meditate on these things."* And Joshua 1:8 says, *"This Book of the Law shall not depart from your mouth, but you shall meditate in it day and night, that you may observe to do according to all that is written in it. For then you will make your way prosperous, and then you will have good success."*

Casting down negative thoughts, meditating on the right thoughts, and speaking the right things will make your way prosperous, and you will have good success.

CHAPTER 18 — HEALTHY THINKING (PART 2)

Questions - Healthy Thinking (Part 2)

1. The weapons of our warfare are not _____.

2. The weapons of our warfare are mighty in God for:
   a. Pulling down strongholds
   b. Casting down arguments
   c. Casting down every high thing that exalts itself against the knowledge of God
   d. Bringing every thought into captivity to the obedience of Christ
   e. All of the above

3. A thought, plus an attached emotion equals an attitude and influences what we do and say. T or F

4. Negative daydreaming-type thoughts need to be cast down. One way to take captive every thought is by:
   a. Using an imaginary crane
   b. Blowing up the thought with an imaginary explosion
   c. Digging an imaginary hole and burying it
   d. Singing a song
   e. All of the above

5. Once we remove the thought, we need to introduce a new thought that agrees with God's perspective and _____ on that truth.

6. The left side of your brain deals with logic and reasoning, like science and _____.

7. The right side of the brain handles creativity, like art and _____.

8. Your imagination is _____ and was given to you by God.

9. Meditating on the right thoughts and speaking the right things will make your way prosperous, and you will have good success.
   T   or   F

19
Hearing God

We learn and experience life through our five senses. In fact, everything we learn is through our five senses—seeing, hearing, touching, tasting, and smelling. Now, imagine a blind man who has never seen anything in his life. He also had never met anyone else who could see. He would believe through his four active senses that he had a true picture of reality. Sadly, he would never know about light, color, and the beauty of a rainbow or a sunset. Now imagine a man who never possessed the ability to hear, and he never encountered anyone else who could hear. He would believe that he had an accurate view of reality through his four working senses. He would never know that the world is full of sounds, beautiful music, and conversation.

We don't experience God the way we do the world around us. We don't perceive Him the same way we do our family and friends. Job 9:11 (NIV) says, *"When he passes me, I cannot see him; when he goes by, I cannot perceive him."* We typically cannot perceive God through our natural senses. Our natural senses help us interact with people and things around us. John 4:24 says, *"God is Spirit, and those who worship Him must worship in spirit and truth."* God is Spirit, so we must interact with God through our spirit. This is not one of our five natural senses but a sixth sense that is spiritual.

There are several ways that God speaks to us today. One of the main ways is through the Word of God. The Bible is not a normal book. It is a spiritual book that is active and alive, one that He wrote with the help of His children. 2 Timothy 3:16 (NIV) says that *"All Scripture is God-breathed and is useful for teaching, rebuking, correcting and training in righteousness."* This spiritual book can help teach and train us in every season of our lives.

Another way that God speaks with us is from His still small voice. 1 Kings 19:12 says, *"and after the earthquake a fire, but the Lord was not in the fire; and after the fire a still small voice."* We see this in the New Testament as well. In Acts 11:12 (NIV) Peter says, *"The Spirit told me to have no hesitation about going with them …"*

There is also the audible voice of God. John 12:28 (NIV), *"'Father, glorify your name!' Then a voice came from heaven, 'I have glorified it, and will glorify it again.'"*

Angels can give us messages from God. We know angels spoke to Mary and Joseph. They also spoke with Paul as recorded in Acts 27:23-24 (NIV), *"Last night an angel of the God to whom I belong and whom I serve stood beside me and said, 'Do not be afraid, Paul. You must stand trial before Caesar; and God has graciously given you the lives of all who sail with you.'"*

God speaks through dreams and visions. In Matthew 1:20 (NIV), it says, *"But after he had considered this, an angel of the Lord appeared to him in a dream and said, 'Joseph son of David, do not be afraid to take Mary home as your wife, because what is conceived in her is from the Holy Spirit."*

God also often speaks to us through his servants, like pastors and prophets, or through ministry gifts, like prophecy, tongues, and interpretation.

Another way that God speaks to us is through inner unrest or inner peace. When you are making decisions, be sure you check how you are feeling. The sons of God are led by the Spirit of God.[1] You might feel a check or an uneasiness in your spirit. Kenneth Hagin used to say that it felt like something was scratching down in his belly. He just didn't have peace about it. If you do not have peace about something, do not proceed until you do. We can be led by our peace or our lack thereof.

The ways I hear God the most are through the Word of God, His still small voice, and inner unrest vs. inner peace. All of these ways are good, but the Bible should always be the number one source. This insures that if someone gives us poor council or an inaccurate prophecy, we will know it is wrong from the wisdom we have learned from God's Word.

Learning to hear and know God's voice takes time and practice. We need to learn how He speaks and how to discern whether we are hearing God, ourselves, or the devil. The best way to practice hearing the still small voice of God is by quieting yourself down. Get really quiet. If responsibilities come to mind, write them down. God is trying to help you. Peaceful music or praying in tongues may help you quiet down.

Second, write down what you hear God say. I started a prayer journal in 1999. Since then, I have filled many notebooks with journaling what God has spoken to me in my quiet times. Go with the flow of what you are hearing in your spirit. You can go back and analyze it later. Stay tuned to the flow of God's Spirit speaking to you.

Over the years, I noticed that when I missed it the most was when I was praying about something that I really wanted. Later, I found Scriptures that showed me why. Ezekiel 14:4 (NASB1995): *"Therefore speak to them and tell them, 'Thus says the Lord GOD, "Any man of the house of Israel who sets up his idols in his heart, puts right before his face the stumbling block of his iniquity, and then comes to the prophet, I the LORD will be brought to give him an answer in the matter in view of the multitude of his idols."'"* This is basically saying that God will allow us to hear what we want to hear when we are praying through an idol. This is what happened to Balaam in

Numbers 22:4-33. If you read the story, you will see that his idol was money. So, it is important when you are praying and journaling about something that you really desire, to be patient and not rush into anything.

It is also helpful to have others read what you have written and see if it bears witness with their spirit. Two are better than one. "And a threefold cord is not quickly broken" (Ecclesiastes 4:12). Over the years, I have improved a lot in hearing God's voice, but it took time and practice. Be patient with yourself, and try not to get discouraged when you miss it. It is part of the process.

Mark Virkler[2] has a great book titled, *How to Hear God's Voice*. In his book, he gives four keys for hearing God. They are, 1) quiet yourself down, 2) fix your eyes on Jesus, 3) tune to spontaneous thoughts, and 4) journaling. This is an excellent resource to help you develop further in hearing God for yourself.

Questions - Hearing God

1. Job 9:11 says, "When he passes me, I cannot see him; when he goes by, I cannot _____ him."

2. We typically perceive God through our natural senses. T or F

3. John 4:24 says, "God is _____, and his worshippers must worship in the Spirit and in truth."

4. God is _____, so we must interact with God through our _____.

5. 2 Timothy 3:16 says, "All Scripture is God-breathed and is useful for _____, _____, _____, and _____ in righteousness."

6. This lesson showed seven ways we can hear God's voice:
    a. His still small voice
    b. God's audible voice
    c. Angels deliver a message
    d. Dreams and visions
    e. Ministry gifts and spiritual gifts
    f. Inner peace vs. inner unrest
    g. _____

7. What is the best way to hear God's voice?

8. God will allow you to hear what you want to hear when you are praying through an idol. T or F

9. Two-way journaling: Find a quiet place and ask the Lord these questions. Write down His answer as well as your response without filtering them.

    "Lord, how do you see me?"

    "Lord, what would you like to say to me?"

20
Value and Worth

A number of years ago, my wife and I visited a friend who was really struggling with depression. In fact, he was struggling so much that he considered committing suicide. He had a life insurance policy, and he thought that he was worth more dead than he was alive. So, how is worth determined? And how much are *you* worth?

In 1996, the Tickle-Me-Elmo doll sold in stores for $28.99.[1] By the time Christmas came, supplies ran out. One parent sold their doll for $7,100.[2] In 2008, the Boston Celtics won the NBA championship, and during the celebration, the players dumped Gatorade on their coach, Doc Rivers. He later sold that shirt in an auction for $35,000.[3] When Barry Bonds broke the Major League Baseball home run record, his record-setting baseball sold for over $752,000.[4] Leonardo da Vinci painted the famous picture called the Mona Lisa. Approximately 10 million people go to France to see his painting every year.[5] In 1962, his picture was valued at $100 million dollars, which today would be worth more than $830 million dollars.[6]

How do people decide what something is worth? I can't go to a closet, for example, take out a pair of shoes, and sell them for $100,000.

It does not work that way. Worth is not determined by the seller but by the buyer. The seller does not get to set the value. The buyer determines what something is worth by what they are willing to pay for it. How much the buyer is willing to pay is determined by how badly they want it. The more they want it, the more they are willing to pay.

Now let's think about this from God's perspective. Romans 7:14 (NIV) says, *"We know that the law is spiritual; but I am unspiritual, sold as a slave to sin."* We were sold as slaves to sin the moment Adam sinned in the garden. The only way for us to be redeemed back from slavery was for a very costly ransom to be paid. We did not have the ability to pay our own ransom. The price was way too high.

Romans 5:8 says, *"But God demonstrates His own love toward us, in that while we were still sinners, Christ died for us."* A lot of people can say that they love us. But do they show it? Do they demonstrate their love with actions? Well, God did. He proved His love for us by coming to this earth and dying in our place. He proved His love with His actions.

1 Corinthians 6:19-20 (NASB1995) says, *"Or do you not know that your body is a temple of the Holy Spirit who is in you, whom you have from God, and that you are not your own? For you have been bought with a price: therefore glorify God in your body."*

You were bought with a price. Christ paid your ransom. But how much did you cost? 1 Peter 1:18-19 (NIV) says, *"For you know that it was not with perishable things such as silver or gold that you were redeemed from the empty way of life handed down to you from your ancestors, but with the precious blood of Christ, a lamb without blemish or defect."* You were bought with a price. The price for your freedom was the blood of Jesus Himself. You see, you could not redeem yourself. The cost was more than you could afford. The price was too high. It required blood, but your blood was stained by Adam's sin. The cost for your pardon was the perfect, sinless, spotless blood of Jesus.

You might at times feel like you are unworthy. You, like my friend mentioned earlier, might not feel like you are worth very much. But you don't get to determine your value. The buyer determines the value by what He is willing to pay. The more they want something, the more they are willing to pay. So, what am I saying? To someone, the Tickle-Me-Elmo doll was worth $7,100. To someone else, a stained Gatorade shirt from the NBA Playoffs was worth $35,000. Barry Bonds' baseball was worth three-quarters of a million dollars. And the Mona Lisa, to someone, is worth more than $830 million dollars.

So how much are you worth to God? Matthew 10:29-31 says, *"Are not two sparrows sold for a penny? Yet not one of them will fall to the ground outside your Father's care. And even the very hairs of your head are all numbered. So don't be afraid; you are worth more than many sparrows."* To God, you are worth more than many sparrows. You are worth more than anything on this earth. You see the buyer, Jesus, determined your worth and your value by what He was willing to pay for you. What was he willing to pay for you? His own blood. The blood of Christ. You are worth the blood of Jesus Christ.

Questions - Value and Worth

1. Who determines what something is worth?
   a. The Buyer
   b. The Seller
   c. The Owner
   d. The Public
   e. The Government

2. When Adam sinned, we were sold as slaves to sin. Romans 7:14. T or F

3. The only way for us to be redeemed back from slavery was for a _____ to be paid.

4. Romans 5:8 says, But God _____ His own love toward us, in that while we were still sinners, Christ died for us.

5. 1 Corinthians 6:19-20 says, "Do you not know that your body is the temple of the Holy Spirit who is in you, whom you have from God, and you are not your own? For you were bought at a _____; therefore glorify God in your body and in your spirit, which are God's.

6. 1 Peter 1:18-19 (NIV) says, "For you know that it was not with perishable things such as silver or gold that you were _____ from the empty way of life handed down to you from your ancestors, but with the _____ _____ of Christ.

CHAPTER 20   VALUE AND WORTH

7. You are worth more than many _____. (Matthew 10:31)

8. You are worth the blood of Jesus Christ. T or F

21
Forgiveness

In 3 John 1:2 (KJV), we read: *"Beloved, I wish above all things that thou mayest prosper and be in health, even as thy soul prospereth."* This Scripture makes a direct connection between our physical health and our emotional health. One of the most important aspects in soul prosperity is how are we doing in forgiveness. Even the most spiritual people can sometimes get caught off guard. They get too busy and forget to take time to process what happened and forgive.

Many years ago, a pastor friend called me. He was going through a difficult time at his church. Someone had spread a rumor around that was totally one-sided and untrue. By the time it got back to him, people were already leaving the church. The story was completely blown out of proportion. Some of the mature believers did what the Bible says and went to him directly asking for his side of the story. They knew him. They knew that this could not be true, and they were right. By the time he called me, he was deeply hurt and felt betrayed. I asked him if he needed to forgive anyone. He said as far as he knew he had already forgiven everyone. I suggested we ask the Holy Spirit just to be sure. The Holy Spirit instantly brought to mind someone's face, then another, and another, totaling seven or eight people, some from that church, and even some from his past. Here is this pastor whom I greatly respect. He walks closely with the Lord. He is very dedicated in his prayer time and devotional life. If he had seven or eight people he needed to forgive, it is possible that you may have people to forgive as well.

Matthew 18:21 says, *"Then Peter came to Jesus and asked, 'Lord, how many times shall I forgive my brother or sister who sins against me? Up to seven times?"* Peter was probably feeling rather good about himself by saying seven times. But look at verse 22: "Jesus answered, 'I tell you, not seven times, but seventy-seven times.' " Some translations say seventy times seven. Jesus' response probably startled Peter. Who could keep count of that many offenses? But that was exactly the point Jesus was trying to make: Love "keeps no record of wrongs."[1] By the time he had forgiven his brother that many times, he would be in the habit of forgiving. Jesus was promoting a lifestyle of forgiveness.

Jesus told a parable in Matthew 18:23-35 (NIV): *"Therefore, the kingdom of heaven is like a king who wanted to settle accounts with his servants. As he began the settlement, a man who owed him ten thousand bags of gold was brought to him. Since he was not able to pay, the master ordered that he and his wife and his children and all that he had be sold to repay the debt. At this the servant fell on his knees before him. 'Be patient with me,' he begged, 'and I will pay back everything.' The servant's master took pity on him, canceled the debt and let him go. But when that servant went out, he found one of his fellow servants who owed him a hundred silver coins. He grabbed him and began to choke him. 'Pay back what you owe me!' he demanded. His fellow servant fell his knees and begged him, 'Be patient with me, and I will pay it back.' But he refused. Instead, he went off and had the man thrown into prison until he could pay the debt."*

When we read this story, we think, *What a horrible man to do such an evil thing*. But this story was written for our benefit. When we walk in unforgiveness, we are acting just like this unmerciful man. This man owed 10,000 talents. Adam Clarke's commentary said the amount would equal $67,500,000 pounds sterling; a sum equal to the annual revenue of the British Empire.[2] Another commentary wrote that what he owed would be equivalent to 60 million days of wages.[2] That is approximately 164,384 years. Methuselah didn't even live that long. Whatever the correct answer is, we get the point. This man had a debt that he had no possible way of repaying. Yet, the servant fell on his knees before him and said. 'Be patient with me, and I will pay back everything.' This man had no concept of the magnitude of his debt.

Immediately after the King canceled this huge debt, the man went out and choked another man who owed him roughly $15[3] and had him thrown into prison. Ridiculous, right? This is a picture of how God sees us when we walk in unforgiveness. He has forgiven us of a huge debt, one that we could never repay. Yet, we go out and hold bitterness and unforgiveness against our fellowman.

Sometimes forgiveness is hard. We often think we are punishing our offender by holding onto the offense, but look at what really happened in the story. Matthew 18:32-35 (NIV): *"Then the master called the servant in. 'You wicked servant,' he said, 'I canceled all that debt of yours because you begged me to. Shouldn't you have had mercy on your fellow servant just as I had on you?' In anger his master turned him over to the jailers to be tortured, until he should pay back all he owed. "This is how my heavenly Father will treat each of you unless you forgive your brother from your heart."*

This is one of the scariest verses in the entire Bible. God Himself will hand us over to be tortured. Other translations say "to the tormentors," until we forgive from our hearts.

One reason we sometimes have trouble forgiving is that we also have no concept of the magnitude of the debt that we owed because of sin. Ephesians 2:1 says we *were dead in transgressions and sins*. Romans 5:6 calls us *powerless* and *ungodly*. Romans 5:10 calls us *God's enemies*. Romans 8:7-8 calls us *hostile to God, does not submit, cannot please God*. Ephesians 2:2-3 calls us *sons of disobedience* and *children of wrath*. Ephesians 2:12

says, *"...you were separate from Christ, excluded from citizenship in Israel and foreigners to the covenants of the promise, without hope and without God in the world."* We were in debt and there was no hope of ever paying it back.

But look at what God did for us. Colossians 2:13-14 (NAS) says, *"And when you were dead in your transgressions and the uncircumcision of your flesh, He made you alive together with Him, having forgiven us all our transgressions, having canceled out the certificate of debt consisting of decrees against us, which was hostile to us; and He has taken it out of the way, having nailed it to the cross."*

Praise God, all of our sins have been forgiven, and all of our debt has been canceled. Since God did all of that for us, He would like us to forgive others in return.

Why don't we do that right now? The first thing we need to do is to ask Holy Spirit if there is anyone that we need to forgive. Next, ask what debt does he/she/they owe? Then pray to cancel the debt that is owed. Lastly, remind ourselves as often as needed that the debt has been canceled.

If you are not sure how to do that, you could pray something like this:

"Father God, _____ hurt me when _____. I feel like they owe me _____. I am not sure why they did that, but I choose right now to cancel the debt. I ask You to cancel their debt, too. Please don't hold it against them. I release them, and I ask You to bless them, in Jesus name."

---

*If you would like to learn more about forgiveness, I highly recommend the book *Forgiveness* by Rodney Hogue.[4]

CHAPTER 21   FORGIVENESS

Questions - Forgiveness

1. Even the most spiritual people can get caught off guard sometimes and get too busy and forget to take the time to process what happened and forgive.   T or F

2. Matthew 18:21 says, "Lord, how many times shall I forgive my brother or sister who sins against me?"
    a. 0
    b. 3
    c. 7
    d. 77
    e. 70 x 7

3. Jesus encouraged a lifestyle of _____.

4. The man in Matthew 18 owed a debt that he had no way to pay.
   T or F

5. The King canceled his huge debt, and the man goes out and chokes another man who owes him the equivalent of _____.

6. The point of this parable is that this is how God sees us when we walk in unforgiveness.   T or F

7. We are punishing our offender when we hold onto the offense.
   T or F

8. God will hand us over to be tortured, or tormented unless we forgive from our _____.

9. One of the reasons we have trouble forgiving is because we have no concept of the magnitude of the debt that we owed because of sin. T or F

10. Colossians 2:13-14 NAS says, "When you were _____ in your _____ and the uncircumcision of your flesh, He made you _____ together with Him, having forgiven us _____ our transgressions, having canceled out the certificate of _____ consisting of decrees against us, which was hostile to us; and He has taken it out of the way, having nailed it to the Cross."

22
Spirit, Soul, and Body

We read in 1 Thessalonians 5:23-24: *"Now may the God of peace Himself sanctify you completely; and may your whole spirit, soul, and body be preserved blameless at the coming of our Lord Jesus Christ. He who calls you is faithful, who also will do it."* Many people think that our soul and spirit are the same thing. If this were true, why would the apostle Paul, led by Holy Spirit, separate them? Failure to understand the soul and the spirit has kept many people from realizing what God did in us when we were born again.

Hebrews 4:12 says, *"For the Word of God is living and powerful, and sharper than any two-edged sword, piercing even to the division of soul and spirit, and of joints and marrow, and is a discerner of the thoughts and intents of the heart."* Your soul and spirit are so closely connected that only the Word of God can separate them.

Genesis 1:26 states: *"Then God said, 'Let Us make man in Our image, according to Our likeness …'"* Notice it says to let "US" make man in "OUR" image. God is a three-part being. We call His three-part nature the Trinity: Father, Son, and Holy Spirit. We are made in their image. Therefore, we are a three-part being as well. We are a SPIRIT, just like

God, (God is Spirit. See John 4:24). We have a SOUL, which is our mind, will, and emotions. And we live in a BODY.

Our body is the easiest for us to understand because we are in direct contact with it every day. By checking your body, you can instantly tell how you feel. You may feel tired, weak, strong, or sore, etc. You can also tell instantly if the water in the shower is too hot or too cold for your body. It is the physical part of us that we can touch and see in the mirror every day.

Did you know that you have never seen your face without the help of a mirror? Mirrors help us know what we look like. With a mirror, we can check our hair to make sure it looks nice. We can check our teeth to make sure we don't have food stuck in them. We can look at our face to make sure we don't have anything on it like a milk mustache, ketchup or mustard smears from eating a hotdog, or smudged mascara. All these things can be checked with the help of a mirror. Without a mirror, we can never truly know what we look like.

My wife and I have a friend who went to Haiti for missions work. While he was there, his team took pictures of the young children and placed the photographs on a table so they could keep a copy for themselves. Amazingly, the children could not identify their own pictures, as they had never seen their own faces. They had to have their friends help them get their correct photo. In the same way, we need help to know what we look like in our born-again spirits.

James 1:23-24 (NIV) says, *"Anyone who listens to the word but does not do what it says is like a man who looks at his face in a mirror and, after looking at himself, goes away and immediately forgets what he looks like."* The Word of God is our spiritual mirror. In the same way that we need a mirror to tell us what our face looks like, we need the Word of God to tell us what our born-again spirit looks like.

Hebrews 10:14 (KJV) says, *"For by one offering he hath perfected for ever them that are sanctified."* This verse says that by Christ's sacrifice of

Himself, He has (past tense) perfected believers forever. Forever! That is a very long time. We don't usually feel like we are perfect. My wife loves me very much, but she would not say that I am perfect. God spends more time with us than anyone else ever could, and He says we are forever perfect. This is amazing! But how can it be?

Is this talking about our body? Not likely. Jesus' sacrifice did not make us instantly skinny, muscular, or pimple free. Is this talking about our soul—our mind, will, and emotions? No, it can't be. If we lacked intelligence before, we will still lack intelligence after we are born again. If we were an emotional roller coaster before, we will be after, that is until God does a work in our emotions. So, by process of elimination, the only conclusion left is that it's referring to our spirit.

When we were born again, Jesus perfected our spirit forever. Hebrews 12:23 says that the spirits of righteous men were made perfect. Ephesians 4:24 says our born-again spirit was recreated righteous and truly holy. 2 Corinthians 5:17 says, *"Therefore, if anyone is in Christ, he is a new creation; old things have passed away; behold, all things have become new."* All things have become new in our spirit. It is our spirit that is perfected forever. It is our spirit that is recreated righteous and truly holy. Praise God, this is where the change takes place, and the only way for us to know this is by looking in the mirror of God's Word. We won't feel it. We won't understand it or totally comprehend it. We must believe it because God said it.

This revelation of spirit, soul, and body, which I first learned through Andrew Wommack, helped make sense of many Bible verses that I did not understand before. For example, 1 John 4:17, *"Love has been perfected among us in this: that we may have boldness in the day of judgment; because as He is, so are we in this world."* This is saying that in this world, we are exactly like Him now. Not when we die and go to Heaven. Understanding spirit, soul, and body helped me to realize that this promise is referring to my spirit. My spirit looks just like His, perfect forever. As He is, so am I in my born-again spirit.

1 Corinthians 6:17 says: *"But he who is joined to the Lord is one spirit with Him."* I have heard people say that God cannot live in a dirty vessel. I thought, *That doesn't leave Him with many options then.* In order to live in us, He perfected a place in us forever, a place called the *spirit.* This is the place where God lives. This is the place where we have become one spirit with Him. Praise God, because of the sacrifice of Jesus, our spirit is perfected forever, and Christ now lives in us there.

CHAPTER 22　　　　　　　　　　　　　　　　SPIRIT, SOUL, AND BODY

Questions - Spirit, Soul, and Body

1. Our spirit and soul are the same thing.   T or F

2. We are a three-part being.   T or F

3. Which part of us is the easiest for us to understand?

4. The only way to tell what our born-again spirit looks like is by looking at the _____ of God's Word.

5. According to Hebrew 10:14 our bodies are now perfected forever. T or F

6. Our soul is now perfected forever.   T or F

7. Our spirit is now perfected forever.   T or F

8. According to 2 Cor 5:17, the old is _____ _____ and all things have become new.

9. My spirit is what has become new.   T or F

10. Ephesians 4:24 says our born-again spirit is recreated
    a. Righteous and truly Holy
    b. Like a worm
    c. But still has a sinful nature
    d. All of the above

11. As He is, so are we in this world. T or F

23
Identity (Part 1)

Identity theft is a major problem in the world today. Nearly 60 million Americans have been affected by identity theft, according to a 2018 survey. In 2018 alone, California lost more than $214 million through cybercrime. In the 2017 Official Annual Cybercrime Report, it's estimated that global cybercrime will cost $6 trillion annually by 2021. In 2015, that figure was around $3 trillion. Cybercrime is now becoming more profitable than the global trade for illegal drugs![1] Cybercrime affected my life when someone charged over $1,000 to my credit card. Praise God, I did not have to pay for this.

Today, thieves are investing a great amount of time and effort into stealing identities. I believe our enemy, the devil, is doing this, too. He does not want you to know who you are. John 10:10 says that *"The thief does not come except to steal, and to kill, and to destroy ..."* Notice the first tactic mentioned here is to steal. He wants to steal from you. The biggest thing he wants to steal is your spiritual identity, more than he wants to steal your money, your health, or your peace. If we don't know who we are in Christ, if we don't know Whose we are, we will be powerless against his schemes and powerless in the things of God.

This issue of identity theft isn't anything new. In fact, we can see it all the way back in the Garden of Eden. Do you remember when the devil spoke with Eve? What did he say? Genesis 3:4-5 says, *"You will not certainly die," the serpent said to the woman. For God knows that when you eat from it your eyes will be opened, and you will be like God, knowing good and evil."* Notice how the devil tricked her regarding one of her personal desires. She wanted to be like God, but the thing is, she already was. Eve was a perfect creation. She knew no sin. She didn't know anything about sin nature, or sin consciousness. She walked with God in the cool of the day. She was not only a daughter of God but the chosen mother of all who would ever live. She was a perfect creation. Yet the devil made her believe that she wasn't like God and that she needed to do something to make herself more like Him. So she ate the forbidden fruit. The devil went after her identity.

Let's look at what God had previously said about Eve. In Genesis 1:26-27 we read, *"Then God said, 'Let us make mankind in our image, in our likeness, so that they may rule over the fish in the sea and the birds in the sky, over the livestock and all the wild animals, and over all the creatures that move along the ground.' So God created mankind in his own image, in the image of God he created them; male and female he created them."*

The words "image" and "likeness" are very similar in meaning and are even sometimes interchanged.[2] They mean statue, copy, replica, shadow,[3] resemblance, model, shape, similitude.[4] Eve was created in the image of God, a copy, a replica, like His very own shadow, a perfect creation in every way. Yet, the devil made Eve believe that there was something wrong with her and that she wasn't like God, when she was already like her Creator in every possible way.

When Jesus was fasting in the wilderness, the devil came to tempt Him while He was at His weakest. There are three recorded temptations the devil brought to Jesus. Two of them challenged His identity. In Matthew 4:3, *"The tempter came to him and said, 'If you are the Son of God, tell these stones to become bread.' "* Matthew 4:6, *"If you are the Son of God," he said, "throw yourself down. ..."* The devil was trying to tempt Jesus to prove that He was the Son of God.

Just before this fast began, Jesus was baptized in the Jordan by John the Baptist. When He came up out of the water, Jesus heard His Father say, *"This is my beloved Son, in whom I am well pleased."* (See Matthew 3:16-17.)

Right after this amazing experience with His Father, Jesus was led by the Spirit into the wilderness to fast. But notice during these temptations that the devil took out one key word: *"beloved."* He did not say, "If you are the beloved Son of God ..." He said, *"If you are the Son of God ..."* The devil went after His identity.

If the devil challenged Eve and also Jesus in the area of identity, we can be sure he will try this with us, too. The devil has and will continue to try and tempt us to doubt our true identity and to doubt the fact that God loves us. If we have doubt in these two areas, it will stunt our spiritual growth.

Paul said in 2 Corinthians 11:3 (NAS), *"But I am afraid that, as the serpent deceived Eve by his craftiness, your minds will be led astray from the simplicity and purity of devotion to Christ."* An important aspect of the Gospel is knowing who we are in Christ and knowing we are deeply loved and highly favored by Father God. Being certain of this will cause us to grow spiritually, help us to resist Satan's attacks on our identities, and open the way for us to experience true freedom and life in Christ.

Questions - Identity (Part 1)

1. John 10:10 says the thief comes to _____, kill, and destroy.

2. What is the biggest thing the devil wants to steal from you?

3. Identity theft began in the Garden of Eden. T or F

4. According to Genesis 1:26 Adam and Eve were created in the _____ and _____ of God.

5. The devil tempted Eve to believe that she wasn't really like God and that God was holding something back from her. T or F

6. How many times did Satan tempt Jesus to doubt who He was?
    a. 1
    b. 2
    c. 3
    d. 4

7. What word did Satan leave out when he tempted Jesus?

8. Will the devil try and tempt you to doubt the love of God and who you are in Christ? Y or N

24
Identity (Part 2)

When we read through the New Testament, we see the term "in Christ" many times. Kenneth Hagin encouraged people to go through the New Testament and mark every time they saw the words, "in Christ," "in Him," "in Whom," "through Whom," etc. Kenneth said there were approximately 140 such references.[1] Paul and the other writers of the New Testament were trying to help us understand the dramatic change that takes place in our identity when we are born again.

In this lesson, we will look at two things: the changes that take place when we are born again, and our new identity when we are in Christ.

After Adam sinned in the garden, his spirit died, or was spiritually separated from God. The entire human race was identified with his sin as if we had all sinned (Romans 5:12). The consequences of that sin were passed down generation after generation through physical death and spiritual death.

This is what mankind looked like spiritually after the fall:

We were dead in transgressions and sins. (Ephesians 2:1)

We were given over to the power of darkness. (Colossians 1:13)

We were sons of disobedience; our ruler was Satan. (Ephesians 2:2)

We were children of wrath. (Ephesians 2:3)

We were powerless and ungodly. (Romans 5:6)

We were God's enemies. (Romans 5:10)

We were hostile toward God, and unable to submit or please God. (Romans 8:7-8)

We were separated from Christ, excluded from citizenship in Israel, foreigners to the Covenants of the promise, without hope, and without God in the world. (Ephesians 2:12)

Mankind was without hope and without God in this world, and there was nothing man could do about it. But God had a plan. Mankind needed a Savior. God so loved the world that He sent Jesus to die in our place, not only *for* us but *as* us. The sin and the punishment for sin was placed upon Him. 2 Corinthians 5:21 says, *"For He made Him who knew no sin to be sin for us, that we might become the righteousness of God in Him."* All of our sin was upon Jesus so that all of His righteousness could be on us. We could truly live again.

John 20:21-22 says, *"So Jesus said to them again, 'Peace to you! As the Father has sent Me, I also send you.' And when He had said this, He breathed on them, and said to them, 'Receive the Holy Spirit.'"* This is the second time that God breathed on man. The first time was in the garden when God created Adam. Genesis 2:7 says, *"And the LORD God formed man of the dust of the ground, and breathed into his nostrils the breath of life; and man became a living being."* The second time Jesus breathed on the disciples, they were born again. They were made alive spiritually once again. Romans 5:19 says, *"For as by one man's disobedience* (Adam) *many were made sinners, so also by one Man's obedience* (Jesus) *many will be made righteous."* And Romans 5:17 says, *"For if by the one man's offense*

CHAPTER 24 — IDENTITY (PART 2)

(Adam) *death reigned through the one, much more those who receive abundance of grace and of the gift of righteousness will reign in life through the One, Jesus Christ."*

In the same way mankind identified with Adam's sin, as if all sinned (making us sinners), we identify with Jesus' righteousness and become righteous when we place our faith in Jesus.[2] We spiritually inherit righteousness as a gift of grace by faith. When this happens, our nature changes. We are translated out of the kingdom of darkness and into the Kingdom of His Dear Son (see Colossians 1:13). We are now partakers of the divine nature (2 Peter 1:4). Our identity is now in Christ.

2 Corinthians 5:17 says, *"Therefore, if anyone is in Christ, he is a new creation; old things have passed away; behold, all things have become new."* Everything changed! We went from death to life. From darkness to light. Everything about our spirit and how we relate to God has changed. All the blessings and benefits we have in our Christian life are due to the fact that we are now in Him.

I would like to encourage you as Kenneth Hagin did, to go through your Bible and highlight every time you see the words, "in Christ," "in Him," "in Whom," "through Whom" and meditate on them. This is your new identity. This is who you are in Christ.

Questions - Identity (Part 2)

1. Adam's sin spiritually separated him from God. T or F

2. According to Romans 5:12, when Adam sinned, it was as if all men sinned. T or F

3. The consequences of that sin were passed down generation after generation through physical death and _____.

4. What did man's fallen spiritual condition look like after the fall?

5. 2 Corinthians 5:21 says, "He made Him who knew no sin to be sin for us, that we might become the _____ of God in Him."

6. Romans 5:19 says, "For as by one man's (_____) disobedience many were made sinners, so also by one Man's obedience (_____) many will be made righteous."

7. 2 Corinthians 5:17 says, "Therefore, if anyone is in Christ, he is a new creation; old things have passed away; behold, _____ things have become new."

8. Read the verses on the I AM sheet and meditate on your new identity in Christ. Share two that are the easiest for you to believe and two that are the hardest.

CHAPTER 24 — IDENTITY (PART 2)

Below is an identity confession called "I AM." Please read these verses and meditate on your new identity in Christ. As you read these verses aloud, say "I am" before each verse. For example, *"I am ... a child of God,"* and so on.

I AM ...

1. A child of God. (Rom. 8:16)
2. Redeemed from the hand of the enemy. (Ps. 107:2)
3. Forgiven. (Col. 1:13-14)
4. Saved by grace through faith. (Eph. 2:8)
5. Justified. (Rom. 5:1)
6. Sanctified. (1 Cor. 6:11)
7. A new creature. (1 Cor. 5:17)
8. A partaker of His Divine Nature. (2 Peter 1:4)
9. Redeemed from the curse of the Law. (Gal. 3:13)
10. Delivered from the powers of darkness. (Col. 1:13)
11. Led by the Spirit of God. (Rom. 8:14)
12. A son/daughter of God. (Rom. 8:14)
13. Kept in safety wherever I go. (Ps. 91:11)
14. Getting ALL my needs met by Jesus. (Phil. 4:19)
15. Casting ALL my cares upon Jesus. (1 Peter 5:7)
16. Strong in the Lord and in the Power of His Might. (Eph. 6:10)
17. Doing ALL things through Christ Who strengthens me. (Phil. 4:13)
18. An heir of God and a joint heir with Jesus. (Rom. 8:17)
19. An heir to the Blessings of Abraham. (Gal. 3:13-14)

I AM ...

20. Observing and doing the Lord's Commandments. (Deut. 28:12)
21. Blessed coming in and blessed going out. (Deut. 28:6)
22. An heir of Eternal Life. (1 John 5:11-12)
23. Blessed with all spiritual blessings. (Eph. 1:3)
24. Healed by His Stripes. (1 Peter 2:24)
25. Exercising my authority over the enemy. (Luke 10:19)
26. Above only and not beneath. (Deut. 28:13)
27. More than a conqueror. (Rom. 8:37)
28. Establishing God's Word here on Earth. (Matt. 16:19)
29. An overcomer by the Blood of the Lamb and the word of my testimony. (Rev. 12:11)
30. Daily overcoming the devil. (1 John 4:4)
31. Not moved by what I see. (2 Cor. 4:18)
32. Walking by faith and not by sight. (2 Cor. 5:7)
33. Casting down vain imaginations. (2 Cor. 10:4-5)
34. Bringing every thought into captivity. (2 Cor. 10:5)
35. Being transformed by the renewing of my mind. (Rom. 12:1-2)
36. A laborer together with God. (1 Cor. 3:9)
37. The Righteousness of God in Christ. (2 Cor. 5:21)
38. An imitator of Jesus. (Eph. 5:1)
39. The light of the world. (Matt. 5:14)
40. Blessing the Lord at all times and continually praising the Lord with my mouth. (Ps. 34:1)

25
Holy Spirit

In the Scriptures, there are several types and shadows of Holy Spirit, such as fire, wind, oil, water, a cloud, and a dove. In Acts 2, fire was poured out from Heaven. But what kind of fellowship can we have with fire? How about wind or oil? What about water? Yes, we need to drink water to live, but can we have fellowship with water? How about a cloud? Can you hold or easily touch a cloud? What about a dove? Have you ever tried to catch a bird? It is exceedingly difficult. Five of these six types possess no shape or form, or they take the shape of their container. And the other is exceedingly difficult to catch and hold on to. Is this the picture that God is trying to show us about Holy Spirit? That He is an inanimate object or that He is hard to obtain or hold on to and that He is easily scared away? Who is Holy Spirit, and Who is He to us?

Back in Bible College, our choral team used to sing a song titled "Send It On Down" by the Brooklyn Tabernacle Choir. We sang it all the time. But is Holy Spirit an "It"? Let's see what the Bible has to say.

HOLY SPIRIT'S ACTIONS DEMONSTRATE PERSONALITY.

Holy Spirit speaks.
1 Timothy 4:1, *"The Spirit clearly says that in later times some will abandon the faith and follow deceiving spirits and things taught by demons."*

Holy Spirit teaches.
John 14:26, *"But the Counselor, the Holy Spirit, whom the Father will send in my name, will teach you all things and will remind you of everything I have said to you."*

Holy Spirit bears witness.
John 15:26-27, *"But when the Helper comes, whom I shall send to you from the Father, the Spirit of truth who proceeds from the Father, He will testify of Me. And you also will bear witness, because you have been with Me from the beginning."* Just as the apostles (who were "personal beings") would bear witness, so also Holy Spirit bears witness.

Holy Spirit guides, speaks, hears, and tells.
John 16:12-13 *"I have much more to say to you, more than you can now bear. But when he, the Spirit of truth, comes, he will guide you into all truth. He will not speak on his own; he will speak only what he hears, and he will tell you what is yet to come."* From these verses we see that Holy Spirit guides, speaks, hears and tells. Notice how Jesus consistently refers to Holy Spirit as "He." All these descriptive words about Holy Spirit demonstrate personality.

HOLY SPIRIT HAS PERSONAL ATTRIBUTES.

Holy Spirit has a mind and thoughts.
Romans 8:27 says, *"And he who searches our hearts knows the mind of the Spirit, because the Spirit intercedes for the saints in accordance with God's will."*

Holy Spirit possesses knowledge, and He knows the thoughts of God.
1 Corinthians 2:11 says, *"For who among men knows the thoughts of a*

man except the man's spirit within him? In the same way no-one knows the thoughts of God except the Spirit of God."

Holy Spirit has a will.
1 Corinthians 12:11, *"But one and the same Spirit works all these things, distributing to each one individually as He wills."* All of these are characteristics of a being, who possesses intelligence and personality.

HOLY SPIRIT HAS FEELINGS AND EMOTIONS.

Holy Spirit can be grieved.
Ephesians 4:30, *"And do not grieve the Holy Spirit of God, with whom you were sealed for the day of redemption."*

Holy Spirit has love.
Romans 15:30, *"I urge you, brothers, by our Lord Jesus Christ and by the love of the Spirit, to join me in my struggle by praying to God for me."*

Holy Spirit possesses love, joy, peace, patience, etc.
Galatians 5:22-23, *"But the fruit of the Spirit is love, joy, peace, longsuffering, gentleness, goodness, faith, meekness, temperance: against such there is no law."*

We can easily see that Holy Spirit is not an "It." I have lots of "its" in my house, a lot of "things" that I spend time with, like my car, television, computer, cell phone, power tools, lawnmower, etc. I spend a lot of time with these things, but I do not enjoy close fellowship with them like I do with my family and friends. In the same manner, Holy Spirit is not an object to be referred to as an "It." He has a mind and a will. He speaks, He hears, He has emotions and feelings. He is a person, not a human person, but a person, the third person in the Godhead, and He desires to have intimate fellowship with each of us.

Holy Spirit will empower you.
Acts 1:8, *"But you will receive power when the Holy Spirit comes on you; and you will be my witnesses in Jerusalem, and in all Judea and Samaria, and to the ends of the earth."* The word for "power" in the original Greek

language is the word *dunamis,* and it means "strength, ability, power, empowerment, and specifically miraculous power."[1] This word is where we get our English word for dynamite.

When Holy Spirit comes upon us, He empowers us with supernatural, miraculous, explosive power.

We receive the can-do ability of God. Philippians 4:13 says, *"I can do all things through Christ who strengthens me."* "Christ" is not Jesus' last name. "Christ" is a title attributed to Jesus. "Christ" means *anointed* or *anointed One.*[2] The word "anointed" has a root meaning to rub into, a soaking into a fabric, or to marinate, like we would do to a piece of chicken or steak. What was Jesus anointed with? Acts 10:38 says, *"how God anointed Jesus of Nazareth with the Holy Spirit and power, and how he went around doing good and healing all who were under the power of the devil, because God was with him."* Jesus was anointed or marinated with Holy Spirit and power. The anointing that Jesus was anointed with empowered Him to walk in supernatural power. And this is what will happen to you when Holy Spirit comes upon you.

Holy Spirit will never leave you.

John 14:16-17 *"And I will ask the Father, and he will give you another advocate to help you and be with you forever—the Spirit of truth. The world cannot accept him, because it neither sees him nor knows him. But you know him, for he lives with you and will be in you."* The Father gave us Holy Spirit to be with us forever. He does not run away and hide when things get hard or challenging. He is always right there with you and in you to comfort and counsel you. Hebrews 13:5 says, *"… 'I will never leave you nor forsake you.' "* Never means *never*. He does not leave when you fail. He does not hide from you if you sin. He will never leave you nor forsake you. Holy Spirit is faithful to the Word and to you.

Holy Spirit is a friend closer than a brother.

Proverbs 18:24 says, *"… there is a friend who sticks closer than a brother."* That friend is Holy Spirit. He desires to have a close intimate relationship with you. Holy Spirit will talk with you. He will counsel you, comfort you, help you, teach you, convict you, correct you, reveal things to you, fellowship with you, testify to you. He will remind you. He will guide you. He will warn you. He will intercede for you. He anoints you. He baptizes you. He empowers you. He strengthens you. He encourages you. He brings renewal and refreshing. He gives us joy, peace, patience, goodness, kindness, faithfulness, gentleness, and self-control. He is the spirit of truth. He is the gift giver, the fruit grower. He is with you and in you. He will convict the world of guilt, righteousness, and judgment. He will speak what He hears God say. He will tell you what is yet to come. He brings glory to Jesus when He reveals things to you. He bears witness with our spirit, that we are the children of God. He pours out the Love of God into our hearts.

This list can go on and on because Holy Spirit is the Spirit of God; He *is* God. John 4:24 says, *"God is Spirit, and those who worship Him must worship in Spirit and truth."*

I want to encourage you today to draw near to God, and He will draw near to you. Enjoy intimate fellowship with Holy Spirit, knowing that He will never leave you nor forsake you, and that He is closer than a friend or a brother.

Questions – Holy Spirit

1. Which of the following is symbolic of Holy Spirit?
    a. Fire
    b. Water
    c. Oil
    d. Cloud
    e. Wind
    f. Dove
    g. All of the above

2. Holy Spirit is a person.   T or F

3. Holy Spirit is God.   T or F

4. Holy Spirit's actions demonstrate personality.   T or F

5. Holy Spirit has a mind and a will.   T or F

6. And do not _____ the Holy Spirit of God, with whom you were sealed for the day of redemption. (Ephesians 4:30)

7. The word for "power" in the original Greek language is the word *dunamis,* and it means:
    a) Strength
    b) Ability
    c) Power
    d) Empowerment
    e) Miraculous Power
    f) All of the Above

8. How long will Holy Spirit abide with you?

26
Baptism in the Holy Spirit

When I was growing up, my denomination did not teach on the baptism in the Holy Spirit. This was an experience that they did not promote, and I'm not sure why. In my senior year of Bible College, I was involved in prayer meetings with friends. Some of them were Charismatic (walking in spiritual gifts). Over time, in our prayer meetings, I started to notice something different about the Charismatic believers. They stood out to me, and I didn't know why. After some time, I learned that the ones who stood out to me were all baptized in the Holy Spirit. This led me on a journey to learn all I could about this spiritual experience. I studied every verse in the Bible that spoke about the baptism in the Holy Spirit. I didn't think there would be very many, but to my surprise, there were. How could something so important in the Bible and to the early Church be overlooked in the church circles I grew up in?

I learned later that my denominational leaders believed spiritual gifts went away with the early apostles. They quoted 1 Corinthians 13:8-10, *"... But whether there are prophecies, they will fail; whether there are tongues, they will cease; whether there is knowledge, it will vanish away. For we know in part and we prophesy in part. But when that which is perfect has come, then that which is in part will be done away."* These verses say that when perfection comes, these charismatic gifts will cease or stop. They believed that the perfection referred to here, was the canonization of Scripture, or when the Bible was completed (397 AD). But if that is true, according to these same Scriptures, wouldn't that mean that knowledge has vanished away, too? Obviously, knowledge has not passed away. If anything, it has increased. The truth is, these gifts have not ceased, and they will not cease until after the second coming of Christ, when the *real* Perfection comes again.

I discovered some ministers also believed that these gifts were only for certain people, people who were good enough, holy enough, or chosen by God's sovereign will. They made it sound like this was a rare event. But that is not what I saw in the Bible. In Acts 2, on the day of Pentecost, there were 120 people in the upper room. The group consisted of men, women, and most likely children. When Holy Spirit fell on them, all of them were filled with the Holy Spirit, and all began to speak in tongues. This exemplified that it was for everyone. When Paul visited with 12 new disciples in Acts 19, he said, *"Did you receive the Holy Spirit when you believed?"* They were Christians, they were believers, but they had not received the Holy Spirit yet. Acts 19:6-7 says, *"And when Paul had laid hands on them, the Holy Spirit came upon them, and they spoke with tongues and prophesied. Now the men were about twelve in all."* Paul prayed for 12 men, and all 12 received. Again, indicating it is for everyone.

In Acts 10, Peter went to the house of Cornelius (a Gentile). Cornelius had called together his relatives and close friends to hear Peter speak. At the time, it was forbidden for Jews to fellowship with Gentiles. Peter preached the Gospel to them, and while he was still speaking, Holy Spirit fell upon them. Acts 10:44 says, *"While Peter was still speaking these words, the Holy Spirit fell upon all those who heard the word."* Verse 46 tells us that they spoke in tongues and magnified God.

Again, the Holy Spirit fell on all; men, women, and children.

After Holy Spirit fell on the 120 in Acts 2, a crowd of more than 3,000 people gathered around their house where they were praying. Because of the unusual things they were seeing and hearing, the people outside thought the 120 were drunk. Peter told them that they were not drunk since it was only 9:00 am. He told them, *"But this is what was spoken by the prophet Joel."*[1] Joel 2:28 says, *"And it shall come to pass afterward that I will pour out My Spirit on all flesh ..."* Joel prophesied about a day that was coming when the Holy Spirit would be poured out on everyone. Peter testified saying that this was that very day. In Acts 2:38-39 he continues addressing the crowd and says, *"Repent, and let every one of you be baptized in the name of Jesus Christ for the remission of sins; and you shall receive the gift of the Holy Spirit. For the promise is to you and to your children, and to all who are afar off, as many as the Lord our God will call."* Clearly, this shows that the baptism in the Holy Spirit is for everyone—Jews, Gentiles, males, females, and children.

We can see that the baptism in the Holy Spirit is for all who believe, but for what purpose? Acts 1:8 says, *"But you shall receive power when the Holy Spirit has come upon you; and you shall be witnesses to Me in Jerusalem, and in all Judea and Samaria, and to the end of the earth."* While the Holy Spirit comes to live inside of you when you are saved and seals your born-again spirit, He also comes upon you when you are baptized in the Holy Spirit. He comes upon you to empower you to be a witness wherever you go. This promise is for you and for your children, and to all who are afar off, as many as the Lord our God will call.[2]

Therefore, I encourage you to eagerly desire spiritual gifts because they are from God, and they are for you and your empowerment.

Questions - Baptism in the Holy Spirit

1. When will/did gifts of Holy Spirit stop?
   a. When the Bible was finished
   b. When the last apostle died
   c. When Jesus comes again
   d. All of the above

2. The crowd outside the house in Acts 2 thought the 120 were _____.

3. How many of the 120 in the upper room were filled with Holy Spirit in Acts 2?

4. How many of the 12 men in Acts 19 were filled with the Holy Spirit?

5. How many of Cornelius' friends and family were filled in Acts 10?

6. How many did Joel say would be filled in Joel 2?

7. The gift of the Holy Spirit was promised to _____ in Acts 2:38-39.

8. What does this tell you about the will of God?

9. You will receive _____ when Holy Spirit comes upon you. Acts 1:8

27
How to Receive the Baptism in the Holy Spirit

Since I grew up in a denomination that did not believe in the baptism of the Holy Spirit, I struggled to receive this baptism. How could I receive if I wasn't fully convinced that it was God's will? If you remember from one of our previous lessons, faith means to be fully convinced, and the only way we receive from God is through faith. So, I needed to be fully convinced about God's will in this area. The first thing I did was to study and write out every verse in the Bible that talks about the experience of being baptized in the Holy Spirit. I had no idea there would be so many. (I attach my list for you to read and study for yourself.) I came across verses like:

Matthew 3:11: *"I indeed baptize you with water unto repentance, but He who is coming after me is mightier than I, whose sandals I am not worthy to carry. **He will baptize you with the Holy Spirit and fire.**"* [emphasis added]

Acts 1:4-5: *"And being assembled together with them, He commanded them not to depart from Jerusalem, but to wait for the Promise of the Father, "which," He said, "you have heard from Me; for John truly baptized with water, but **you shall be baptized with the Holy Spirit not many days from now.**"* [emphasis added]

Acts 2:1-4: *"When the Day of Pentecost had fully come, they were all with one accord in one place. And suddenly there came a sound from heaven, as of a rushing mighty wind, and it filled the whole house where they were sitting. Then there appeared to them divided tongues, as of fire, and one sat upon each of them. And **they were all filled with the Holy Spirit and began to speak with other tongues, as the Spirit gave them utterance**."* [emphasis added]

Acts 2:32-33: *"This **Jesus God** has raised up, of which we are all witnesses. Therefore being exalted to the right hand of **God**, and having received from the **Father the promise of the Holy Spirit**, He poured out this which you now see and hear."* [emphasis added]

Verse after verse spoke to me. Prior to this, I was under the impression that the baptism of the Holy Spirit was a wrong teaching, otherwise someone would have taught me about it. But in these verses, Jesus was the one who baptized in the Holy Spirit and fire. I saw that God the Father gave Jesus the promised Holy Spirit, and Jesus poured out what they saw and heard. This is the Holy Trinity. Father, Son, and Holy Spirit. How could this be bad? Through studying these verses, my thoughts and beliefs began to change.

Because I perceived the baptism of the Holy Spirit was negative, I always read Scriptures about the gifts of the Spirit from a negative perspective. However, the more I read, the more I saw that this wasn't the perspective of the writers at all. For example, in 1 Corinthians 14:18, Paul said, *"I thank my God I speak with tongues more than you all."* 1 Corinthians 14:5, he said, *"I wish you all spoke with tongues."* And in 1 Corinthians 14:2, it says, *"For he who speaks in a tongue does not speak to men but to God."* These verses caused me to have a lot of questions. How can speaking to God be bad? If speaking in tongues is bad, why would Paul want all of us to do it? And why would he do it more than everyone else? I started thinking, Paul spoke in tongues more than everyone else and he wrote roughly half of the New Testament. He also saw many mighty miracles and witnessed a great number of converts. I wondered whether there was a connection between Paul's

CHAPTER 27   HOW TO RECEIVE THE BAPTISM IN THE HOLY SPIRIT

powerful life and his experience with Holy Spirit. I also started thinking about the other people who wrote the New Testament. After studying, I came to the conclusion that everyone who wrote a book in the New Testament prayed in tongues. They were all baptized in the Holy Spirit. So then, how could this be wrong? It became obvious to me that the way I had been taught was incorrect. The promise of the Holy Spirit and the associated gifts are for today, and they are for all who believe.

I started praying and asking God to baptize me with the Holy Spirit and fire.[1] The first time I prayed this, it was a pretty weak prayer. I prayed, "God, I don't really understand this tongues stuff or why you would want me to pray like that, but I guess if you really want me to, that's okay with me." There was not a lot of faith in this prayer but at least I was being honest with God. The more I studied these verses and prayed, the more I was convinced and the stronger my prayers became.

One night about two weeks later, I had some friends at my house for prayer. The presence of God was so heavy and sweet that I laid on the floor to worship and pray. One of my friends came over and laid his hands on my belly and started praying for me. I felt an increase in God's presence and power come on me. Out of my belly gushed bold words in other tongues. I had no idea what I was saying, but it felt amazing. What I had been praying for had come to pass, I had received the baptism in the Holy Spirit, and I was speaking in tongues! Power and boldness gripped my heart. I soon got up off the floor empowered with boldness and excitement and went to McDonald's to witness to others. This encounter with God changed my entire life.

You might think, "That is a great story, but what about me? How do I receive the baptism in the Holy Spirit?" Well, first, you must believe. You must be fully convinced that this is God's will for you. This will happen by studying the scriptures. Study them, meditate on them, and ask God questions. Once you are fully convinced, ask Jesus to baptize you with the Holy Spirit and fire. You can receive alone or have a believing friend lay hands on you. Tongues may accompany immediately, or it may follow later, but either way, receive it by faith. Then thank God for baptizing you in the Holy Spirit, even if you don't feel anything. Keep thanking Him in the past tense for already filling you. It is a done deal because the promise is for you and all who are afar off (Acts 2:39). All of God's promises are yes and amen (2 Corinthians 1:20). If we know that He hears us, we have what we ask for in prayer (1 John 5:15).

I want to encourage you to study the Scriptures and to receive the gift the Father promised. I know it will change your life, just like it changed mine.

BAPTISM IN THE HOLY SPIRIT SCRIPTURES

Matthew 3:11: "I indeed baptize you with water unto repentance, but He who is coming after me is mightier than I, whose sandals I am not worthy to carry. He will baptize you with the Holy Spirit and fire."

Luke 12:49: "I came to send fire on the earth, and how I wish it were already kindled!"

Acts 1:4-5: "And being assembled together with them, He commanded them not to depart from Jerusalem, but to wait for the Promise of the Father, which, He said, "you have heard from Me; 5 for John truly baptized with water, but you shall be baptized with the Holy Spirit not many days from now."

Acts 1:8: "But you shall receive power when the Holy Spirit has come upon you; and you shall be witnesses to Me in Jerusalem, and in all Judea and Samaria, and to the end of the earth."

Acts 2:1-4: "When the Day of Pentecost had fully come, they were all with one accord in one place. 2 And suddenly there came a sound from heaven, as of a rushing mighty wind, and it filled the whole house where they were sitting. 3 Then there appeared to them

CHAPTER 27   HOW TO RECEIVE THE BAPTISM IN THE HOLY SPIRIT

divided tongues, as of fire, and one sat upon each of them. 4 And they were all filled with the Holy Spirit and began to speak with other tongues, as the Spirit gave them utterance."

Acts 2:32-33: "This Jesus God has raised up, of which we are all witnesses. 33 Therefore being exalted to the right hand of God, and having received from the Father the promise of the Holy Spirit, He poured out this which you now see and hear."

Acts 2:38-39: "Then Peter said to them, "Repent, and let every one of you be baptized in the name of Jesus Christ for the remission of sins; and you shall receive the gift of the Holy Spirit. 39 For the promise is to you and to your children, and to all who are afar off, as many as the Lord our God will call."

Acts 5:32: "And we are His witnesses to these things, and so also is the Holy Spirit whom God has given to those who obey Him."

Acts 8:14-19: "Now when the apostles who were at Jerusalem heard that Samaria had received the word of God, they sent Peter and John to them, 15 who, when they had come down, prayed for them that they might receive the Holy Spirit. 16 For as yet He had fallen upon none of them. They had only been baptized in the name of the Lord Jesus. 17 Then they laid hands on them, and they received the Holy Spirit. 18 And when Simon saw that through the laying on of the apostles' hands the Holy Spirit was given, he offered them money, 19 saying, "Give me this power also, that anyone on whom I lay hands may receive the Holy Spirit."

Acts 9:17-18: "And Ananias went his way and entered the house; and laying his hands on him he said, "Brother Saul, the Lord Jesus, who appeared to you on the road as you came, has sent me that you may receive your sight and be filled with the Holy Spirit." 18 Immediately there fell from his eyes something like scales, and he received his sight at once; and he arose and was baptized."

1 Corinthians 14:18: "I thank my God I speak with tongues more than you all;"

Acts 10:44-46: "While Peter was still speaking these words, the Holy Spirit fell upon all those who heard the word. 45 And those of the circumcision who believed were astonished, as many as came with Peter, because the gift of the Holy Spirit had been poured out on the Gentiles also. 46 For they heard them speak with tongues and magnify God."

Acts 11:15-18: "And as I began to speak, the Holy Spirit fell upon them, as upon us at the beginning. 16 Then I remembered the word of the Lord, how He said, 'John indeed baptized with water, but you shall be baptized with the Holy Spirit.' 17 If therefore God gave them the same gift as He gave us when we believed on the Lord Jesus Christ, who was I that I could withstand God?" 18 When they heard these things they became silent; and they glorified God, saying, "Then God has also granted to the Gentiles repentance to life."

Acts 19:2-7: he said to them, "Did you receive the Holy Spirit when you believed?" So they said to him, "We have not so much as heard whether there is a Holy Spirit." 3 And he said to them, "Into what then were you baptized?" So they said, "Into John's baptism." 4 Then Paul said, "John indeed baptized with a baptism of repentance, saying to the people that they should believe on Him who would come after him, that is, on Christ Jesus." 5 When they heard this, they were baptized in the name of the Lord Jesus. 6 And when Paul had laid hands on them, the Holy Spirit came upon them, and they spoke with tongues and prophesied. 7 Now the men were about twelve in all."

Romans 8:26-27: "Likewise the Spirit also helps in our weaknesses. For we do not know what we should pray for as we ought, but the Spirit Himself makes intercession for us with groanings which cannot be uttered. 27 Now He who searches the hearts knows what the mind of the Spirit is, because He makes intercession for the saints according to the will of God."

CHAPTER 27 HOW TO RECEIVE THE BAPTISM IN THE HOLY SPIRIT

Mark 16:17-18: "And these signs will follow those who believe: In My name they will cast out demons; they will speak with new tongues; 18 they will take up serpents; and if they drink anything deadly, it will by no means hurt them; they will lay hands on the sick, and they will recover."

1 Corinthians 14:2-5: "For he who speaks in a tongue does not speak to men but to God, for no one understands him; however, in the spirit he speaks mysteries. 3 But he who prophesies speaks edification and exhortation and comfort to men. 4 He who speaks in a tongue edifies himself, but he who prophesies edifies the church. 5 I wish you all spoke with tongues, but even more that you prophesied; for he who prophesies is greater than he who speaks with tongues, unless indeed he interprets, that the church may receive edification."

1 Corinthians 14:13-19: "Therefore let him who speaks in a tongue pray that he may interpret. 14 For if I pray in a tongue, my spirit prays, but my understanding is unfruitful. 15 What is the conclusion then? I will pray with the spirit, and I will also pray with the understanding. I will sing with the spirit, and I will also sing with the understanding. 16 Otherwise, if you bless with the spirit, how will he who occupies the place of the uninformed say "Amen" at your giving of thanks, since he does not understand what you say? 17 For you indeed give thanks well, but the other is not edified. 18 I thank my God I speak with tongues more than you all; 19 yet in the church I would rather speak five words with my understanding, that I may teach others also, than ten thousand words in a tongue."

1 Corinthians 14:28: "But if there is no interpreter, let him keep silent in church, and let him speak to himself and to God."

John 7:37-39: "On the last day, that great day of the feast, Jesus stood and cried out, saying, "If anyone thirsts, let him come to Me and drink. 38 He who believes in Me, as the Scripture has said, out of his heart will flow rivers of living water." 39 But this He spoke concerning the Spirit, whom those believing in Him would receive; for the Holy Spirit was not yet given, because Jesus was not yet glorified."

John 14:16: "And I will pray the Father, and He will give you another Helper, that He may abide with you forever—"

John 20:20-22: "When He had said this, He showed them His hands and His side. Then the disciples were glad when they saw the Lord. 21 So Jesus said to them again, "Peace to you! As the Father has sent Me, I also send you." 22 And when He had said this, He breathed on them, and said to them, "Receive the Holy Spirit."

Jude 20: "But you, beloved, building yourselves up on your most holy faith, praying in the Holy Spirit."

CHAPTER 27   HOW TO RECEIVE THE BAPTISM IN THE HOLY SPIRIT

Questions - How to Receive the Baptism in the Holy Spirit

1. Who will baptize you in the Holy Spirit and fire?

2. Tongues are often associated with the baptism of the Holy Spirit. T or F

3. According to Acts 2:32-33, Jesus received from the Father the promised gift of the Holy Spirit and _____ out what they saw and heard in the upper room.

4. In 1 Corinthians 14:18, Paul said, "I thank my God, I speak with _____ more than you all."

5. In 1 Corinthians 14:5 Paul said, "I wish you _____ spoke with tongues."

6. 1 Corinthians 14:2 says, "For he who speaks in a tongue does not speak to men but to _____."

7. The Father, the Son, and Holy Spirit are equally in favor of the baptism in the Holy Spirit. T or F

8. The promise is for _____ and all who are far off (Acts 2:39).

9. After reading the previous list of "Baptism in The Holy Spirit Scriptures," what stood out to you the most? Why do you think this impacted you?

28
Benefits of Praying in Tongues

The gift of tongues might be the most feared and controversial of all the other spiritual gifts combined. This gift has been misused and wrongly taught, causing some Christians to feel bad about themselves and even doubt their salvation. I want you to know that you do not have to pray in tongues to go to Heaven. God loves you the same whether you do or do not pray in tongues. On the opposite side of the spectrum, others have ignored, neglected, and misrepresented the gift of tongues. This has caused many to believe that the gift has passed away and is not available to us today. This is simply not true.

I believe the reason there is so much controversy and confusion surrounding the gift of tongues is that the devil doesn't want us to pray in tongues. He knows this is a powerful gift, with many benefits, and he wants us to be ignorant of these things. Hosea 4:6 says, *"My people are destroyed for lack of knowledge ..."* Not understanding what God has freely given us in the gift of tongues has left many people wounded and defeated. It is time to know the truth that sets us free.

1 Corinthians 12:4-7 says, *"There are diversities of gifts, but the same Spirit. There are differences of ministries, but the same Lord. And there are di-*

versities of activities, but it is the same God who works all in all. But the manifestation of the Spirit is given to each one for the profit of all."

There are diversities of gifts, ministries, and activities involved in these giftings, but it is the same Spirit, Lord, and God who is working in them all. There is also a variety of manifestations given by the Spirit, but the same Lord is working them for the benefit of all. How the Holy Spirit works in me and how the Holy Spirit works in you might not look exactly the same. There are diversities in these gifts.

The gift of tongues, which is included in the list at the end of verse 10, also comes in various forms and includes many benefits. For example, the gift of tongues for our personal prayer language is usually done in private. This is the type of tongues Paul was referring to when he said he wished we all spoke in tongues.[1]

There is also another manifestation of tongues for a public setting. I call this "speaking in tongues." Speaking in tongues is a message spoken out in a public setting (like a church service) in a language not known by the speaker. In this setting, the message in tongues should be interpreted by either the one giving the tongue or another person with the gift of interpretation.[2] Not every believer will speak in tongues during a church service and/or interpret a message in tongues, but every believer can pray in tongues. You see, there are different kinds of tongues and different manifestations of those tongues.

Another manifestation of the gift of tongues sometimes happens on the mission field. By the Spirit, an individual understands and speaks a native dialect foreign to him without receiving training in the language. St. Francis Xavier, in his mission to the far east, is said to have spoken Japanese as if he had lived in Japan all his life. It is recorded that he "spoke to the various tribes with ease in their languages."[3]

The fact is, there are many benefits to praying in tongues. I can remember the first time I read my Bible after I was baptized in the Holy Spirit. It was like I was reading an entirely new book. Things that

CHAPTER 28 — BENEFITS OF PRAYING IN TONGUES

I had read many times before were now jumping off the pages to me with revelation knowledge being released. I was a senior in Bible College that read the Bible a lot, but now it seemed like I was reading the Bible for the first time. It was amazing. Praying in tongues was helping me receive fresh revelation of God's word.

Another benefit is that praying in tongues builds you up. It strengthens you from the inside out. 1 Corinthians 14:4 says, *"He who speaks in a tongue edifies himself ..."* The word *edifies* in the original Greek language means "to be a house builder."[4] When we pray in tongues, we are building ourselves up. Jude 1:20 says, *"But you, beloved, building yourselves up on your most holy faith, praying in the Holy Spirit."* Notice it says we are building ourselves up in the most holy faith when we pray in tongues (praying in the Holy Spirit).

Powerful intercession is another benefit of praying in the spirit. Years ago, my wife and I were working in a children's home as house parents. One day, as the shift opposite us left to go home, I felt a heaviness in my spirit like something was wrong. I asked my wife and she felt it, too. We didn't know how to pray as we ought to, so we prayed in tongues. We had no idea who or what we were praying for. After around ten minutes, peace came into our hearts, and we knew we could stop praying. We both wondered what it was all about. Although we had no idea, it felt like a life or death situation.

About two weeks later, some of the teens we worked with were traveling to an NBA basketball game. On the way to the game, they were in a horrible accident. One student was ejected through the windshield. Another went through the front passenger window. Miraculously, no one was injured. The driver, a friend of mine, somehow unbuckled during the crash and moved out of the way before a huge piece of metal sliced through his seat. Both students who were thrown from the car only had minor bumps and scratches. When the police officers arrived on the scene, they could not believe that someone didn't die in the crash. When my wife and I heard about the accident and the amazing supernatural protection that took place, we knew that this was the heaviness we had prayed in tongues about.

Another time, God awoke my wife and me around 2:00 a.m. Again, we felt a strong need to intercede for someone. We started to pray in tongues, and shortly after, I felt like I knew who we were praying for. I didn't know what the situation was, but it felt like life or death. We prayed for ten to fifteen minutes until we felt a peace and then quickly fell back asleep. A few days later this same teenage boy, the one I felt we were praying for, was in a serious car accident. He was driving down a steep, winding road and went off an embankment. His car flipped multiple times, and he wasn't wearing his seatbelt. His airbag did not work properly. It deployed, hitting him in the face after the car had totally stopped. Amazingly, he was not hurt at all. He only had a few marks on his face from the airbag. When he came home, we hugged him and were very thankful for God's protection. He went upstairs to get a shower and, when he took off his shirt, there was a huge hand-shaped mark on his chest at an angle that would have been impossible to make himself. This hand mark was much larger than a human hand. We asked God, and He confirmed to us that this was what we had been praying about at 2:00 a.m. a few nights before. Praise God for spiritual gifts and groanings of intercession! Powerful intercession is just one of the many benefits of praying in tongues. Romans 8:26, *"Likewise the Spirit also helps in our weaknesses. For we do not know what we should pray for as we ought, but the Spirit Himself makes intercession for us with groanings which cannot be uttered."*

Praying in tongues is a gift from God given to you because He loves you, and He knows it is good for you. It is a free gift available for all believers today.

CHAPTER 28　　　　　　　　BENEFITS OF PRAYING IN TONGUES

Questions - Benefits of Praying in Tongues

1. You are not born again unless you can pray in tongues. T or F

2. The gift of tongues passed away with the last apostle or the canonization of Scripture. T or F

3. God loves you more if you can pray in tongues. T or F

4. Praying in tongues is a _____ from God.

5. All believers can speak in tongues in a church setting, for interpretation. T or F

6. All believers can pray in tongues. T or F

7. There are benefits to praying in tongues. T or F

8. Jude 1:20 says, "But you, beloved, building yourselves up on your most holy faith, _____ in the Holy Spirit."

9. Praying in tongues _____ you up. 1 Corinthians 14:4.

10. Have you received the Holy Spirit since you believed? Have you prayed in tongues yet? Share your experience on the next page:

MY EXPERIENCE

29
Authority of The Believer

We know that God has all authority, all dominion, and all power. He is totally sovereign. He has power in Himself that doesn't come from any other source. He is the King of Kings, and Lord of Lords. When God created man, He created them in His image and likeness. Genesis 1:26 says, "Then God said, *'Let Us make man in Our image, according to Our likeness; let them have dominion over the fish of the sea, over the birds of the air, and over the cattle, over all the earth and over every creeping thing that creeps on the earth.'*" We were created to rule and have dominion on the earth. Other verses confirm this, like Psalm 115:16, *"The heaven, even the heavens, are the Lord's; But the earth He has given to the children of men."*

When the devil came into the garden to tempt Adam and Eve he did not come as a woolly mammoth or an elephant. He did not come and push them down telling them to submit to him, or else he would kill them. No, he did not do that because he did not have the authority or power to do so. He came as a snake. The most subtle animal of all. The word "subtle" means sly, shrewd, or crafty.[1] The reason Satan came as a snake was because he didn't have the ability to force Adam and Eve to do anything. They had been given power and authority. He could only try to deceive them. When Adam chose to believe the devil instead of believing God, Adam lost his authority, and that authority was transferred over to the devil.

I will show you a few verses to back up this statement. 1 John 5:19 (NIV) says, *"We know that we are children of God, and that the whole world is under the control of the evil one."* 2 Corinthians 4:4 (NKJV) says, *"whose minds the god of this age has blinded, who do not believe, lest the light of the gospel of the glory of Christ, who is the image of God, should shine on them."* Then in Luke 4:5-6 (NIV) says, *"The devil led him up to a high place and showed him in an instant all the kingdoms of the world. And he said to him, 'I will give you all their authority and splendor; it has been given to me, and I can give it to anyone I want to.'"* From this, you can see that the devil has been given authority over the kingdoms of this world. He was not given this authority by God; Adam and Eve gave him their authority through disobedience.

When Jesus came on the scene, He came to destroy the works of the devil (1 John 3:8). He came to set us free from the devil's tyranny, He came to reconcile us back to the Father (2 Cor. 5:18) and give us back the authority that the devil had stolen (John 10:10).

Jesus is fully God and fully man at the same time. He already had authority as God but came to take back authority as a man. After His death, burial, and resurrection, Jesus said, *"... All authority in heaven and on earth has been given to me"* (Matthew 28:18). Jesus now holds all authority in Heaven and on Earth. And since Jesus knew no sin and never will sin, His authority is secure forever. Think about this: If all authority has been given to Jesus, how much authority does the devil now have?

In the same way that Adam gave his authority to the devil, and the devil told Jesus that he could give that authority to anyone that he wants to, Jesus delegated His authority to believers (Matthew 18:19).

The devil now has no authority over you at all. Colossians 2:15 says, *"And having disarmed the powers and authorities, he made a public spectacle of them, triumphing over them by the cross."* You do not need to be afraid of the devil. He is afraid of you. James 4:7 (NIV) says, *"Submit yourselves, then, to God. Resist the devil, and he will flee from you."* Praise God, Jesus' victory is our victory!

A police officer has the authority to stop cars that are breaking the law, but he really doesn't have the physical power to do so. If the driver wanted to keep driving, the officer could not physically stop him. But because of the power and authority behind his badge and the uniform, the car will stop. They know that the entire police force is behind the officer if he needs help. In the same way, the power that is in us is greater than any power that is in the world. The power that backs our authority is far beyond that which backs our enemies.

1 John 4:4 (KJV) says, *"Ye are of God, little children, and have overcome them: because greater is he that is in you, than he that is in the world."* Praise God, the greater One lives in believers, and we now have delegated authority over all the schemes of the enemy. That is the authority of the believers.

Questions - Authority of the Believer

1. We were created to rule and have dominion on the earth.   T or F

2. Psalm 115:16 says, "… But the _____ He has given to the children of men."

3. The reason Satan came as a snake was because he didn't have the ability to force Adam and Eve to do anything.   T or F

4. 1 John 5:19 (NIV) says, "We know that we are children of God, and that the whole world is under the control of the _____ _____."

5. The devil was given authority over the kingdoms of this world. He wasn't given this authority by God, he _____ it from man.

6. Jesus is fully God and fully man. He already had authority as God, but He came to get _____ back as a man.

7. If all authority has been given to Jesus, how much authority does the devil have?

8. Colossians 2:15 (NIV): "And having _____ the powers and authorities, he made a public spectacle of them, triumphing over them by the Cross."

9. James 4:7 (NIV): "Submit yourselves, then, to God. Resist the devil, and he will flee from _____."

10. 1 John 4:4 (KJV) says: "Ye are of God, little children, and have overcome them: because _____ is he that is in you, than he that is in the world."

30
Biblical Basis for Healing

It is the will of God for you to be healed. You may not hear that at every church you go to because some people are basing God's will on their experiences. However, you don't learn the will of God from looking at the lives of others. We learn the will of God from looking at His Word. Faith comes by hearing the Word of Christ. In this lesson, I am going to show you types and shadows of Christ from Old Testament scriptures that reveal the will of God in the area of healing. It is my prayer that as you read through this lesson, you will be convinced that it is God's will for you to be healed.

Healing in Communion

Communion was foreshadowed in Passover. Exodus 12:13 (NIV) says, *"The blood will be a sign for you on the houses where you are, and when I see the blood, I will pass over you. No destructive plague will touch you when I strike Egypt."* Verse 22 (NKJV) says, *"And you shall take a bunch of hyssop, dip it in the blood that is in the basin, and strike the lintel and the two doorposts with the blood that is in the basin. And none of you shall go out of the door of his house until morning."* In this verse, we see a type and shadow of Jesus Christ. The Israelites were to strike the doorposts with a branch dipped in the blood of a lamb. The blood was the only thing that was protecting their families from death and destruction. If it were me applying the blood on the door frame, I would probably have applied it very heavily, and I would have made sure that door frame was completely covered. There would not be one section of wood that wasn't covered in blood!

The word "strike" in this verse carries the meaning *to punish or to beat*.[1] This is a foreshadowing of Jesus being whipped with a cat-o'-nine tails and His blood being spilled out for us.

Verse 13 makes it clear that the blood was applied for the Israelites' protection. It seems logical to believe that the death of the firstborn sons in each Egyptian home would be enough to cause Pharaoh to finally release the Israelites from slavery, so why bother to eat the lamb? Why eat the whole lamb? Why eat the head, legs, and inner parts? Why eat unleavened bread? (See Exodus 12:8-9.) If the removal of leaven from the Israelites' houses represented removing sin from their homes, what did the eating of lamb and the eating of unleavened bread represent? Well, the meat and the bread represented our sinless, spotless Lamb that was slain for us. He is the Bread of Heaven. These symbols represented Jesus' body that was broken, crushed, pierced, bruised, and beaten for us. And He wanted them to eat it. He wanted them to take these representations of His body and put them into their bodies.

The result of eating this first Passover meal was amazing! Psalm 105:37 says *"He brought them out with silver and gold, and there was none feeble among His tribes."* Imagine, more people than the city of Chicago, and there was not one feeble, weak, frail, lame, or sick person among them. Every person in all twelve tribes, more than 3 million people, if they had need of strengthening, of healing, or of a creative miracle, they ate the lamb and the bread, and they received it. If anyone was weak, sick, or lame, they were all supernaturally healed! After they partook of the Passover Lamb and the unleavened bread, a supernatural strengthening took place for every single one of them.

Joseph Prince said, "Now we know that the lamb was a mere shadow of the real substance. So, if the body of a 'shadow lamb' could bring such supernatural results, how much more the body of the true 'substance lamb,' our Lord Jesus Christ."[2] Healing is in Communion!

Healing in the Redemptive Names of Jehovah

Jehovah is the redemptive name of God and means "the self-existing one who reveals himself."[3] As you probably know, there are seven of these names scattered throughout the Old Testament.

1. Jehovah-Jireh—the Lord will provide a sacrifice. (Genesis 22:14)
2. Jehovah-Rapha—the Lord our healer. (Exodus 15:26)
3. Jehovah-Nissi—the Lord our banner. (Exodus 17:15)
4. Jehovah-Shalom—the Lord our peace. (Judges 6:24)
5. Jehovah-Raah—the Lord my shepherd. (Psalm 23:1)
6. Jehovah- Tsidkenu—the Lord our righteousness. (Jeremiah 23:6)
7. Jehovah-Shammah—the Lord is present. (Ezekiel 48:35)

Think about this for a minute. The redemptive name *Jehovah*, was it applied to Jesus? If the name Jehovah-Jireh applies to Jesus, and every Christian would agree that it does, then the name Jehovah-Rapha must also apply. If Jesus is God's provided sacrifice for our sins, then Jesus also must be our healer. Healing is in the redemptive name of Jesus!

Healing in the Covenant

Exodus 15:26 (NIV) says, *"If you listen carefully to the voice of the LORD your God and do what is right in his eyes, if you pay attention to his commands and keep all his decrees, I will not bring on you any of the diseases*

I brought on the Egyptians, for I am the LORD, who heals you." (Or, I am Jehovah-Rapha.) In this Covenant between the Israelites and the Lord, there was healing, or better yet, there was divine health. If they obeyed, they were healthy. If they disobeyed there was sickness. Health is called a blessing, while sickness is called a curse. If healing was in the Old Covenant, then healing must be in the New Covenant because Hebrews 8:6 (NIV) says, *"But in fact the ministry Jesus has received is as superior to theirs as the covenant of which he is mediator is superior to the old one, since the new covenant is established on better promises."* Healing is in the Covenant.

Healing in the Atonement

Isaiah 53:3-4 says, *"He is despised and rejected by men, a Man of sorrows and acquainted with grief. And we hid, as it were, our faces from Him; He was despised, and we did not esteem Him. Surely He has borne our griefs and carried our sorrows; yet we esteemed Him stricken, smitten by God, and afflicted."* The word "griefs" here is usually translated *sicknesses*,[4] and the word "sorrows" is almost always translated *pains*.[5] This is shown in the **Young's Literal Translation** of verse 4 which says, *"Surely our sicknesses he hath borne, And our pains -- he hath carried them, And we -- we have esteemed him plagued, Smitten of God, and afflicted."*

Verses 5 and 6 continue, *"But he was pierced for our transgressions, he was crushed for our iniquities; the punishment that brought us peace was on him, and by his wounds we are healed. 6 We all, like sheep, have gone astray, each of us has turned to ours own way; and the LORD has laid on him the iniquity of us all."* Matthew 8:17 says, *"that it might be fulfilled that was spoken through Isaiah the prophet, saying, 'Himself took our infirmities, and the sicknesses he did bear.'"* This is a direct reference to Isaiah 53:4 properly translated. Then 1 Peter 2:24 says, *"who Himself bore our sins in His own body on the tree, that we, having died to sins, might live for righteousness—by whose stripes you were healed."* Peter is quoting Isaiah 53:5 here, but he changes the tense of the verse. Isaiah said, *"by his wounds,* **we are** *healed,"* Peter said, *"by whose stripes **you were healed**."* Peter wrote this in the past tense form because he was writing after the Cross. Isaiah wrote his Scripture before the Cross. On the Cross, Jesus said, "It is finished." Healing is in the Atonement!

Healing in the Cross

Numbers 21:4-9 (NIV): *They traveled from Mount Hor along the route to the Red Sea, to go round Edom. But the people grew impatient on the way; they spoke against God and against Moses, and said, "Why have you brought us up out of Egypt to die in the wilderness? There is no bread! There is no water! And we detest this miserable food!" Then the LORD sent venomous snakes among them; they bit the people and many Israelites died. The people came to Moses and said, "We sinned when we spoke against the LORD and against you. Pray that the LORD will take the snakes away from us." So Moses prayed for the people. The LORD said to Moses, "Make a snake and put it up on a pole; anyone who is bitten can look at it and live." So Moses made a bronze snake and put it up on a pole. Then when anyone was bitten by a snake and looked at the bronze snake, they lived.*

These Israelites were poisoned by venomous snakes. They were extremely sick and close to dying. In fact, verse 6 says that many of them had died. Some probably even died while waiting for Moses to finish crafting the bronze snake. But once the snake was lifted up on the pole and the people turned and looked at it, they were healed, they were restored, and they lived. This is a type and shadow of Christ. In John 3:14, Jesus said, *"Just as Moses lifted up the snake in the wilderness, so the Son of Man must be lifted up."* Why was the snake in the desert lifted up? It was lifted up for their physical healing. If any of them chose not to look at the snake on the pole, they died because they were physically sick. Clearly, this is a foreshadowing of Jesus being lifted up for our healing. But why did God pick a snake to be a type of Christ? When Jesus was lifted up on the Cross, He became sin so that we could become righteous. Just as all who looked at the bronze snake were healed, when Jesus, our sin-bearer, was lifted up, all who look to Him for their health and healing can be healed as well. Healing was in the Old Testament cross.

If healing was in the Passover, if healing is in the redemptive names of God, if healing was in the Old Covenant, if healing was in the Atonement, and if healing was in the Old Testament cross where the pole was lifted up, then healing must be for us today in the New Covenant. How could the New Covenant be better if it did not include healing? But it does. Healing is for us today. It is in our Covenant. Healing is in the Atonement, and healing is in the Cross of Christ. By His stripes, we were healed.

CHAPTER 30   BIBLICAL BASIS FOR HEALING

Questions - Biblical Basis for Healing

1. Communion was foreshadowed in _____.

2. The Israelites were to _____ the doorposts with a branch dipped in the blood of a _____. This is a clear foreshadowing of Jesus being _____ with a cat-o-nine tail and His _____ being poured out for us.

3. The blood on their doorposts was for their protection. T or F

4. The meat and the bread were for their healing. T or F

5. If the name Jehovah-Jireh applies to Jesus, then the name Jehovah-Rapha must also apply to Jesus. T or F

6. Jehovah-Rapha, the Lord our _____. Exodus 15:26.

7. Isaiah 53:4: Surely our _____ he hath borne, And our _____ he hath carried them, And we, we have esteemed him plagued, Smitten of God, and afflicted. (Young's Literal Translation)

8. Matthew 8:17 says, that it might be fulfilled which was spoken by Isaiah the prophet, saying: "He Himself took our infirmities and bore our sicknesses." T or F

9. By whose stripes were you healed? 1 Peter 2:24.

10. Isaiah wrote, "by his wounds we are healed" before the Cross. Peter wrote, "by whose stripes you were healed" in the past tense because he was writing after the Cross.   T   or   F

11. Once the snake was lifted up on the pole, the people turned and looked at it, and were healed.   T   or   F

12. Who said, "Just as Moses lifted up the snake in the desert, so the Son of Man must be lifted up" (John 3:14)?

13. Jesus was lifted up so that all who look to Him may be healed.
    T   or   F

31
Hindrances to Healing

One time I was ministering to a man who was struggling with a great deal of back pain. I asked him if he needed prayer for anything and he said, "Pray that I won't lose the joy of my salvation. God sent this pain my way, and I am going to try and learn all I can from this test." I asked, "Can I pray for you?" He said, "Yes." I asked more specifically, "Do you mind if I pray for the pain to leave?" He said, "Well, duh," obviously meaning yes. Notice the contradiction here. He believed God sent him this pain to teach him a lesson. But when I asked if he wanted me to pray for the pain to leave, he said yes. This man, like a lot of Christians, did not know what he really believed about healing. They don't know the will of God because they are trying to figure it out by observing what is happening around them. They pray a prayer, and they don't see the desired results immediately, so they assume that the answer is no. Then they assume that must be the will of God. But the only way to know the will of God is through His Word.

Let's look at some Scriptures to show you His will. Jesus said in Mark 11:24, *"Therefore I say to you, whatever things you ask when you pray, believe that you receive them, and you will have them."* And in John 16:23-24, He said, *"And in that day you will ask Me nothing. Most assuredly, I say to you, whatever you ask the Father in My name He will give you. Until now you have asked nothing in My name. Ask, and you will receive, that your joy may be full."* Then in John 15:7 Jesus said, *"If you abide in Me, and My words abide in you, you will ask what you desire, and it shall be done for you."*

1 Peter 3:12: *"For the eyes of the LORD are on the righteous, and His ears are open to their prayers; but the face of the LORD is against those who do evil."* James 5:16: *"... The effective, fervent prayer of a righteous man avails much."* You can see through these verses that the heart of God is for us to experience answered prayer. And the potential is there for us to have our prayers answered every time. So, if it is the will of God for something to happen when we pray, why isn't it happening? One reason is that God won't violate one part of His Word to honor another.

1 Timothy 6:12 says, *"Fight the good fight of faith ..."* We don't fight God. We don't fight humans. We battle not against flesh and blood. So, we can look at these verses and realize that there is a fight to our faith. In the healing ministry, there will be challenges. There is going to be a battle. Some are won very easily, and some are particularly challenging and drawn out. It is not the sovereign will of God that picks some to be healed and some to die. There is a spiritual battle involved and potentially other factors as well.

Even in the Old Testament in Exodus 15:26, God said, *"If you diligently heed the voice of the Lord your God and do what is right in His sight, give ear to His commandments and keep all His statutes, I will put none of the diseases on you which I have brought on the Egyptians. For I am the Lord who heals you."* So, who did God say was responsible here? Was it God, or was it the people?

Just as there were factors involved in the Old Testament, there are factors involved in the New Testament as well. In 1 Peter 3:7 we read: *"Husbands, likewise, dwell with them with understanding, giving honor to the wife, as to the weaker vessel, and as being heirs together of the grace of life, that your prayers may not be hindered."* How we treat our spouse will hinder our prayers.

Matthew 5:23-24: *"Therefore if you bring your gift to the altar, and there remember that your brother has something against you, leave your gift there before the altar, and go your way. First, be reconciled to your brother, and then come and offer your gift."* Bitterness and unforgiveness hinder our prayers.

Matthew 6:5: *"And when you pray, you shall not be like the hypocrites. For they love to pray standing in the synagogues and on the corners of the streets, that they may be seen by men. Assuredly, I say to you, they have their reward."* Their reward was looking good to men, not the reward of answered prayer. The love of man will hinder our prayers.

James 1:6-7: *"But let him ask in faith, with no doubting, for he who doubts is like a wave of the sea driven and tossed by the wind. For let not that man suppose that he will receive anything from the Lord."* Doubt and unbelief will hinder our prayers.

James 4:2-3 (NIV) *"You desire but do not have, so you kill. You covet but you cannot get what you want, so you quarrel and fight. You do not have because you do not ask God. When you ask, you do not receive, because you ask with wrong motives, that you may spend what you get on your pleasures."* Coveting, quarreling, fighting, wrong motives, and greed will hinder our prayers.

Galatians 5:6 (KJV) *"For in Jesus Christ neither circumcision availeth anything, nor uncircumcision; but faith which worketh by love."* Faith works by love. When you are not walking in love, your prayers will be hindered. This one can really sum up all the previous ones. Disrespect towards our spouse, bitterness, and unforgiveness, fear of man, pride, doubt, unbelief, coveting, quarreling, fighting, and greed, these things are not of love, and these things will all hinder our prayers. When you are praying about something, make sure you are sensitive to these hindrances to your faith and remember to walk in love because faith works by love.

Questions - Hindrances to Healing

1. We know the will of God by observing what is happening around us. T or F

2. The only way to know the will of God is through His _____.

3. Mark 11:24, "Therefore I say to you, whatever things you ask when you pray, believe that you receive them, and you _____ have them."

4. John 15:7, "If you abide in Me, and My words abide in you, you will ask what you desire, and it shall be _____ for you."

5. God won't violate one part of His Word to honor another. T or F

6. It is the sovereign will of God that picks some to be healed and some to die. T or F

7. In the Old Testament, their obedience was a factor in their _____.

8. How we treat our spouse can hinder our prayers. T or F

9. Bitterness and unforgiveness will hinder our prayers. T or F

10. Doubt and unbelief will hinder our prayers.   T   or   F

11. Which of these will hinder our prayers?
    a. Coveting
    b. Quarreling
    c. Fighting
    d. Wrong motives
    e. Greed
    f. All of the above

32

Deliverance

When I first started praying for the sick to be healed, I witnessed some demonic manifestations that made me feel quite uncomfortable. I remember praying to the Lord one day and saying, "I am okay with praying for the sick to be healed, but I don't want any part of this deliverance stuff." The Lord quickly answered, "You can't have one without the other because they overlap." God was giving me a choice, quit praying for the sick or continue and deal with manifestations as they come. I reluctantly agreed to continue praying for people, and I asked the Lord to give me some more training in deliverance. Years have passed since that day, and I have had many other uncomfortable experiences, including my own deliverance. I have since received some very empowering training and have witnessed the freedom and healing that deliverance brings.

In this process, I realized that I needed to establish my own understanding about demons. I didn't know what I believed. For example, could a Christian have a demon? I quickly found out that the answer is yes. You see, when we are born again, God does a work in our spirits. Our spirit is recreated righteous and truly holy (see Ephesians 4:24).

But our soul—our mind, will, and emotions—are not recreated. They are not made new at the new birth. Our souls need to be transformed. Our soul realm is where demons live. They intend to influence our mind, will, and emotions in a negative way. So even though our spirits are perfected forever, our souls have some work that needs to be done. Deliverance is part of our sanctification process.

Think about this: Jesus said in Matthew 12:43-45, *"When an unclean spirit goes out of a man, he goes through dry places, seeking rest, and finds none. Then he says, 'I will return to my house from which I came.' And when he comes, he finds it empty, swept, and put in order. Then he goes and takes with him seven other spirits more wicked than himself, and they enter and dwell there, and the last state of that man is worse than the first. So shall it also be with this wicked generation."* If we were to do deliverance on unsaved people, what authority would they have to keep the unclean spirits from returning? For one, their continuance in sin would open the doors for them to return. This doesn't seem to be a wise thing to do since Jesus said the last state of that man is worse than the first. Would this be an act of love? Clearly the answer is no. So, the only group of people remaining that would not be practicing sin, that would have authority over the spirits from returning, are Christians. The only logical persons for deliverance would be believers.

Carlos Annacondia, an anointed minister from Argentina, developed a 10-step model for dealing with demons that has worked well for him for many years. I would like to share that with you.

TEN-STEP DELIVERANCE MODEL[1]

1. Make the person the priority. Keep a loving attitude. Be encouraging, raise hope that Jesus is our deliver.

2. If a spirit manifests, bring it under submission, in the name of Jesus. Take authority over the spirit. Ex: "Be quiet, in Jesus' name," or, "Submit, in the name of Jesus." You may have to do this a few times.

3. Establish and maintain communication with them. If necessary, bring the person to consciousness. It is important to have their cooperation.

4. Ask the person what they want to be free from, and make sure they really want to be free. We must respect their decision either way. Going forward without their consent will do more harm than good. If the person wants to leave after partial ministry, allow them to go.

5. **Receive** – The person must receive Christ for deliverance to be effective and long-lasting.

6. **Reveal** – Interview the person to discover the events, the conduct, or the relationship situations that have led to his or her bondages. Here, God reveals areas where the enemy has legal ground, where forgiveness is required, where healing, repentance, and breaking of bondages are needed. Reveal open doors. If no obvious place, start with parents. Also, consider possible curses.

7. **Renounce** – Lead the person in "closing" the "doors" that were open. Forgive whoever caused the pain or led them into wrong conduct. Repent and ask forgiveness for specific sins. It is important to be specific, such as, "Father, forgive me for … (hate, bitterness, sharing my body with _____, reading horoscopes, etc.)."

Then renounce all sins or spirits involved, in Jesus' name. Renounce soul ties, spirits received by the sins of others, spirits received from each sexual partner (use person's first name), pacts with Satan, and inner vows made. They must be renounced and the curses broken.

Possible Prayers – "In the name of Jesus, I renounce the spirits of _____ and _____," or "In the name of Jesus; I renounce the vow I made to never/always _____."

"In the name of Jesus, I break the power of the spirit(s) of _____ over (the person) so that when they are cast out, they can never return."

"In the name of Jesus, I break the power of every curse over (the person) from _____ (ex. father's careless critical words, mother's rejection, etc.)."

8. **Rebuke** – When all doors are closed, cast out the unclean spirits. If the demon doesn't respond, go back to steps 6-7 to get more revelation of past issues.

9. **Rejoice** – Praise God for His mighty deliverance and the freedom that now is ours.

10. **Rebuild** – Fill the house. Pray for them to be filled with the Holy Spirit and fire.

After reading this, you will probably have some questions. That is a *good* thing. I want to encourage you to study the Word of God. See how Jesus dealt with demons. Ask Holy Spirit to teach you, and He will do so.

CHAPTER 32   DELIVERANCE

Questions - Deliverance

1. Your soul was recreated righteous and truly holy (Eph 4:24).
   T or F

2. Your soul consists of your _____, _____, and _____.

3. Demons try to influence your soul. T or F

4. After demons leave, the house is cleaned, but it is empty. T or F

5. The house needs to be filled with the _____.

6. When demons leave people, they try to _____.

7. Matthew 12:45 says, "Then he goes and takes with him seven other spirits more wicked than himself, and they enter and dwell there; and the last state of that man is _____ than the first.

8. Is it wise to do deliverance on an unsaved person?

9. Christians can have demons. T or F

10. After reading the **10-Step Model for Deliverance**, which of the steps seem the easiest, which steps seem the hardest, and why? *(Answer below.)*

33
The Old Covenant

Our God is the God of Covenants. He is the Covenant-making and Covenant-keeping God. He made a Covenant with Adam and Eve. He made a Covenant with Noah. He made a Covenant with Abraham. He made a Covenant with Moses. And He made a Covenant with David. Each of these Covenants that God made did not just affect the individual person that He made it with. The person of the Covenant was a representative of a group of people. The representative was called a *mediator*.

In each of these Covenants, there were terms, a mediator, and signs. In Adam's Covenant, he was the mediator, and the sign was the Sabbath. In Noah's Covenant, he was the mediator, and the sign was the rainbow. In Abraham's Covenant, he was the mediator, and the sign was circumcision. In Moses' Covenant, he was the mediator, and the sign was the Ten Commandments. In David's Covenant, he was the mediator, and the sign was Solomon's Temple. God relates to man through Covenants.

As I mentioned before, in the Covenant with Moses, he was the mediator, and the sign was the Ten Commandments. The Ten Commandments were the terms of their Covenant, or the terms in which they related to God. In Deuteronomy 27, Moses was in his final days on earth and God spoke to him to add 12 more laws to the 10 commandments. Deuteronomy 28 lists 53 verses describing the curses that would happen if they disobeyed the Laws. There were curses against their land, their families, their finances, and their personal health. Deuteronomy 28 also shares 14 verses describing the blessings that would happen if they obeyed the Law. The blessings were on their land, their families, their finances, and their health. God said in Deuteronomy 30:19, *"I call heaven and earth as witnesses today against you, that I have set before you life and death, blessing and cursing; therefore choose life, that both you and your descendants may live."*

The Laws of the Old Covenant were how the people connected or related to God. If they performed well, they were blessed. If they did not perform well, they were cursed, cut off, or killed. The Old Covenant was totally based on their performance.

The word "covenant" means *to cut*. Every time a Covenant was made, it involved cutting and blood. Why was there so much blood? Leviticus 17:11 (NIV) says, *"For the life of a creature is in the blood, and I have given it to you to make atonement for yourselves on the altar; it is the blood that makes atonement for one's life."* The Bible also says that *"... without the shedding of blood there is no forgiveness"* (Hebrews 9:22 NIV). So blood is special, in that it is the only thing that God will accept to atone for sins and provide forgiveness for the guilty.

In the Covenant that God made with Moses and the children of Israel, there was bloodshed every day. For example, on the Day of Atonement, they would sacrifice one bull for the priests and his family's sins and two goats for the people's sins. One goat was sacrificed to the Lord as a sin offering for the people. And the other goat would become the scapegoat. These sacrifices covered the people's sins for an entire year. Even though their sins were covered for an entire year, they still offered other sacrifices. They daily offered two lambs as burnt offerings, one in the morning, and one in the evening (Exodus 29:38-39) for unintentional sins that the people may have committed without realizing it. There were also five other offerings (Burnt, Grain, Peace, Sin, Trespass); three of these were volunteer offerings, and two of them were mandatory. So, we can see that there was bloodshed all around. There would be blood on the priests, blood on the ground, blood around the altar, blood on the utensils, blood everywhere. Hebrews 9:22, *"In fact, the law requires that nearly everything be cleansed with blood ..."*

These animal sacrifices continued for approximately 1,500 years.[1] Just imagine how many animals were sacrificed. In one year, 114 bulls, 37 rams, 175 lambs, and 32 goats were killed. Totaling 358 animals. Plus, 804 lambs a year for daily sacrifices.[2] That equals 1,246 animals a year. Plus, the daily volunteer offerings of some three million Israelites. Just for numbers' sake, let's say that 10% of the people offered sacrifices every year. That's 300,000 sacrifices. Totaling 301,246 animals a year. Multiply that times 1,500 years, and that equals 451,869,000 animals. And these numbers are very conservative.

2 Chronicles 7:5 says when Solomon dedicated the temple that 22,000 head of cattle and 120,000 sheep and goats were sacrificed. According to the *Talmud*, a Jewish religious text, priests waded up to their knees in blood, and other texts describe 1.2 million animals being slaughtered in one day.[3] I am not sure how that would be possible unless they had a very large number of priests, but that is what history says. So, the exact number of sacrifices is impossible to figure out. We do know it was a lot. And technically, these sacrifices go all the way back to the Garden of Eden. Even so, after all this blood, it was impossible for the blood of bulls and goats to take away sins. They could only atone for them or cover them. And they were a constant reminder of their sins.

Apart from the Covenant and the sacrifices made on the altar, there was no way to approach God. A man once picked up sticks on the Sabbath, and he was stoned to death. If a priest went into the Holy of Holies in an improper way or at the wrong time, he would die. Uzziah touched the Ark of the Covenant when it was falling from the cart, and he died. When the 70 men from Beth Shemesh looked inside the Ark of the Covenant, they died. When Aaron's two sons, Nadab and Abihu, who were priests, offered unauthorized fire to the Lord, they died. Just imagine how Aaron felt. He was the High Priest. This was tough. This was harsh. But there was no way to approach God except through the way that He had already ordained.

In the same way that we can't say to a police officer that we didn't know the law or the speed limit, they couldn't say to Moses or to God that they didn't know the Law. Just like it is our responsibility to know the law, it was their responsibility to know the Law. If they did not know it and they broke it, there were consequences, sometimes serious consequences. But this was part of their Covenant. They had to know the Law, and they had to obey the Law, or else. But God found fault with this Covenant and set out to establish another (Hebrews 8:7-8).

CHAPTER 33 — THE OLD COVENANT

Questions - The Old Covenant

1. The person of the Covenant was a representative of a group of people, and that representative is called a _____.

2. In Abraham's Covenant, he was the mediator, and the sign was _____.

3. In Moses' Covenant he was the mediator, and the sign was the ____ _____.

4. God relates to man through Covenants. T or F

5. Deuteronomy 30:19, "I call heaven and earth as witnesses today against you, that I have set before you _____ and _____, _____ and _____; therefore choose _____, that both you and your descendants may _____.

6. If they performed well, they were _____. If they didn't perform well, they were cursed, cut off, or killed.

7. The Old Covenant was totally based on their performance. T or F

8. Now the word "Covenant" means to _____.

9. Without the shedding of _____ there is no forgiveness of sins. (Heb 9:22)

10. On the Day of Atonement, the sacrifices offered covered the people's sins for an entire year. T or F

11. Hundreds of thousands of animals were sacrificed every year to atone for sin, but it was impossible for the blood of bulls and goats to take away sins. T or F

12. Apart from the Covenant and the sacrifices, there was no way to approach God. T or F

34
The New Covenant

From the days of Moses, until the days of Jesus, priests were put in place to be mediators between God and man. On the day of atonement, the High Priest would go into the Holy of Holies with the blood of a lamb and place it on the mercy seat or the lid of the Ark of the Covenant. Once this was completed, the sins of all of Israel were covered for an entire year. This went on year after year for centuries. When priests would die, they would install new priests from the tribe of Levi, in the order of the first High Priest Aaron (Moses' brother) to take their place. We see this in Hebrews 7:23, *"Also there were many priests, because they were prevented by death from continuing."* But God found fault with this covenant and set out to establish another (see Hebrews 8:7-8).

Jeremiah 31:31-34 says, *"Behold, the days are coming, says the Lord, when I will make a new covenant with the house of Israel and with the house of Judah—not according to the covenant that I made with their fathers in the day that I took them by the hand to lead them out of the land of Egypt, My covenant which they broke, though I was a husband to them, says the Lord. But this is the covenant that I will make with the house of Israel after those days, says the Lord: I will put My law in their minds, and write it on their hearts, and I will be their God, and they shall be My people. No more shall every man teach his neighbor, and every man his brother, saying, 'Know the LORD,' for they all shall know Me, from the least of them to the greatest of them, says the LORD. For I will forgive their iniquity, and their sin I will remember no more."* Here Jeremiah prophesied about a New Covenant, and in this New Covenant, our sins and our lawless deeds God would remember no more.

In this New Covenant, we had a new High Priest installed, Jesus Christ Himself. Hebrews 7:21 says, "... *The Lord has sworn and will not relent, 'You are a priest forever according to the order of Melchizedek.*" This was Jesus' swearing-in ceremony as our new High Priest forever. The strange thing was that Jesus did not come from the tribe of Levi. He was from the tribe of Judah. No one from the tribe of Judah had ever served as a priest before. And Jesus did not serve in the order of Levi or Judah, but in the order of Melchizedek. We see this in Hebrews 7:11-13, *"Therefore, if perfection were through the Levitical priesthood (for under it the people received the law), what further need was there that another priest should rise according to the order of Melchizedek, and not be called according to the order of Aaron? For the priesthood being changed, of necessity there is also a change of the law. For He of whom these things are spoken belongs to another tribe, from which no man has officiated at the altar."* Verse 12 tells us that when the priesthood changed from the order of Aaron to the order of Melchizedek, it was necessary for the Law to change. The new law is the law of love found in John 13:34, *"A new commandment I give to you, that you love one another; as I have loved you, that you also love one another."*

After Jesus was resurrected from the dead, after He spoke with Mary Magdalene at the Garden tomb, He ascended into Heaven, and He entered the Most Holy Place, and He placed His own blood on the Mercy Seat of God. Hebrews 9:11-12, *"But Christ came as High Priest of the good things to come, with the greater and more perfect tabernacle not made with hands, that is, not of this creation. Not with the blood of goats and calves, but with His own blood He entered the Most Holy Place once for all, having obtained eternal redemption (for us)."* By this act He sealed the New Covenant forever.

Jesus was not only installed as our new High Priest, but He is also the mediator of the New Covenant. Hebrews 8:6 says, *"But now He has obtained a more excellent ministry, inasmuch as He is also Mediator of a better covenant, which was established on better promises."* The New Covenant is a more excellent ministry than the old, and it has a better High Priest, a better Mediator, a better Covenant, founded on better blood, with better promises, and Jesus is the Mediator of this New Covenant. When Moses was the mediator of the Old Covenant, he represented all of Israel to God. He was the mediator between God and man. In the New Covenant Jesus is our Mediator and He represents all of us. He is our Mediator between God and man. The amazing thing is that Jesus is both. He is fully God and fully man at the same time. In the past when God made Covenants with men, they would fail and break the Covenant. But that is not the case with our new Mediator. He will never fail. He will never sin or break the Covenant, so our Covenant is secure. It is unchangeable. It is eternal (Hebrews 13:20 NASB).

When this New Covenant was established, the old one was made obsolete. We no longer relate to God through our performance. We relate to God through the performance of our Mediator, Jesus. We relate to God through the Covenant that Father God made with Jesus on our behalf. You see, this Covenant was not made with us individually. This happened long before we were even born. It was made with Jesus as our mediator, our representative, and we are now the benefactors of this Covenant. And since He lives forever, since He will never sin, He is the surety of our New Covenant. Hebrews 7:22-25, … *"by so much more Jesus has become a surety of a better covenant. Also, there were many priests, because they were prevented by death from continuing. But He, because He continues (to live) forever, has an unchangeable priesthood. Therefore He is also able to save to the uttermost those who come to God through Him, since He always lives to make intercession for them."*

Jesus is the High Priest of our New Covenant. He is the Mediator of our New Covenant. He is our surety of the New Covenant. And since He will never sin, or die again, our Covenant is eternal, it is guaranteed, it is forever. We are not just saved a little bit. Praise God, verse 25 says we are saved to the uttermost. This is not based on our performance but was established through His. This is our New Covenant with God.

Now if God honored the blood of bulls and goats, how much more will He honor the blood of His Son? If God honored the Old Covenant that He made with Moses, how much more will He honor the Covenant that He made with His Son? You see, knowing these things changes everything. We are not righteous based on our behavior. We inherited righteousness as a gift. We are righteous through the Covenant. Jesus became sin, and when we place our faith in Him and what He did for us, when we place our faith in this Covenant that He made with God, we receive the gift of His righteousness or the gift of right standing with God. This is the New Covenant, and we as believers are the benefactors. This is good news. Praise God for the New Covenant.

CHAPTER 34 — THE NEW COVENANT

Questions - The New Covenant

1. God found fault with the Old Covenant, so He establish another (Heb 8:7-8). T or F

2. Jeremiah prophesied about a New Covenant, where our sins and our lawless deeds would be remembered _____ _____.

3. In the New Covenant, we had a new High Priest installed, _____ _____ Himself.

4. Jesus did not serve in the order of Levi or _____, but in the order of Melchizedek.

5. When the priesthood changed from the order of Aaron to the order of Melchizedek it was necessary for the Law to change (Heb 7:12). T or F

6. After Jesus was resurrected from the dead, He ascended into Heaven, and He entered the Most Holy Place, and He placed His own blood on the _____ _____ of God.

7. In the New Covenant Jesus is our _____ and He represents all of us to God.

8. In the past when God made Covenants with men they would fail and break the Covenant. That is not the case with our new Mediator. He will never fail. He will never sin or break the Covenant. So, our Covenant is secure. It is unchangeable. It is _____ (Heb 13:20 NASB).

9. When the New Covenant was established, the old one was made obsolete. We no longer relate to God through our _____ performance.

10. The New Covenant was not made with us individually. This happened long before we were even born. It was made with Jesus as our Mediator, our Representative, and we are now the _____ of this Covenant.

11. Jesus is the High Priest of our New Covenant. He is the Mediator of our New Covenant. He is the Surety of our New Covenant. And since He will never sin, or die again, our Covenant is eternal, it is guaranteed, it is forever.   T or F

12. We are not righteous based on our behavior. We inherited righteousness as a gift. We are righteous through the Covenant. When we place our faith in Him, when we place our faith in the Covenant that He made with God on our behalf, we receive the gift of His righteousness, or the gift of right standing with God.   T or F

35
The Church

It is easy to understand why people can be confused about the meaning of the word "church." The word is often used in many different ways. It can mean a particular building, like the church on Main Street. It can refer to a denomination like the Baptist or Methodist Church. It can even mean a particular Sunday morning service. For example, someone might ask, did you go to church today? None of these meanings are actually biblical. So, what does the word "church" really mean?

The word "church" in the original Greek language is the word *ekklesia,* and it literally means, "a gathering of citizens called out from their homes into some public place." For example, "an assembly of Christians gathered for worship."[1] The church is not the building. The church is the people of God assembling together to worship. I am not, and you are not the church individually. We are the church collectively when we join together to praise His name. Years ago, we attended a church in Roanoke, VA. On their sign, it read, "Grace Covenant Church meets here." What a fantastic statement of truth! The building is not the church. We are the church, and we gather together in certain buildings.

Paul started many local churches (Romans 16:3-5, 1 Corinthians 16:19, Galatians 1:2, 1 Thessalonians 1:1) and he checked in on them as often as he could. He set up leadership in these churches and he asked Titus (1:5) to help him do the same. This shows us that church government was God's idea.

Acts 2:46-47 says, *"So continuing daily with one accord in the temple, and breaking bread from house to house, they ate their food with gladness and simplicity of heart, praising God and having favor with all the people. And the Lord added to the church daily those who were being saved."* This local church in Jerusalem met frequently to hear the teachings of the apostles and to pray, but they also ate together and had meaningful fellowship among themselves in their homes. They would meet both in the temple (large meetings), and in their homes (small meetings). This is a good model for us to follow. Public gatherings are a great place for worship and hearing the Word, but there often isn't enough time for socializing. One effective way for us to have close fellowship with one another is through life groups. In the time of Paul, a group of believers met in the house of Aquila and Priscilla (1 Corinthians 16:19). This was a common practice in those days, as shown in Acts 5:42, Acts 20:20, Colossians 4:15, and Philemon 2.

The Expository Dictionary of Bible Words says, "Ecclesia in the New Testament can encompass any number of believers. It can be used of small groups that met in homes (Romans 16:5). It encompassed all believers living in a large city (Acts 11:22), or a large geographical district, such as Asia or Galatia." It goes on to say, "The typical meeting of the church was in a home. When such a congregation met 'everyone had a hymn, a word of instruction, a revelation, a tongue or an interpretation' (1 Corinthians 14:26). Individuals shared and others 'weighed carefully what was said' (1 Corinthians 14:29), such sharing remains essential to the very existence of the church as a community of faith. Each person was expected to contribute and to serve others with his or her spiritual gift(s)."[2] It should be the same today.

Jesus, our ultimate example, was in the habit of going to the synagogue to meet with believers. Luke 4:16 says, *"So He came to Nazareth, where He had been brought up. And as His custom was, He went into the synagogue on the Sabbath day, and stood up to read."* Attending church on the Sabbath was His custom, but I think Jesus was probably there every chance He had. Jesus referred to the church as His Father's house (Luke 2:49), as a house of prayer (Matthew 21:13), and He said He would build His church, and the gates of Hell would not prevail against it (Matthew 16:18). It is known as the body of Christ (1 Corinthians 12:27), the bride of Christ (Romans 7:4), the house of God, the church of the living God, and the pillar and ground of the truth (1 Timothy 3:15).

Hebrews 10:25 says, *"Not forsaking the assembling of ourselves together, as is the manner of some, but exhorting one another, and so much the more as you see the Day approaching."* I have heard people say that they don't have to go to church to be saved. That is true. You do not have to go to church to be saved. But the Bible clearly shows that we should go to church because we are saved. We should assemble together so that we can be encouraged, and we can encourage someone else. When I hear someone say something like this, I wonder why they would not want to go? Why would they not want to gather with other believers? Usually, those who say things like that have been hurt by someone in the church. This is sad, but it does happen, unfortunately, more often than we might think. But we still should not neglect the assembling of ourselves together as the church. If we don't go to church, where do we pay our tithes? Who do we submit to? Who is going to watch over our souls? Hebrews 13:17 says, *"Obey those who rule over you and be submissive, for they watch out for your souls, as those who must give account. Let them do so with joy and not with grief, for that would be unprofitable for you."*

One of the tactics of the enemy is isolation. Do you remember in Mark 5 the man from the country of the Gadarenes who was demonized?

Where did he live? He lived among the tombs. This is not what I would call prime real estate. But he lived there all by himself, tormented without anyone to help him. When we get hurt, it is a natural temptation to draw back and try to be alone. But this is not healthy. We do better together. We grow better in community. God designed us to be together. Don't let the enemy discourage you into isolation from the body of Christ. It isn't always easy to find a place where you belong. But your tribe is out there somewhere, you just need to find it. Psalm 133:1-3 says, *"Behold, how good and how pleasant it is for brethren to dwell together in unity! It is like the precious oil upon the head, running down on the beard, the beard of Aaron, running down on the edge of his garments. It is like the dew of Hermon, descending upon the mountains of Zion; for there the Lord commanded the blessing—Life forevermore."*

Questions - The Church

1. The Church is the building that people meet in. T or F

2. The Church is the assemblying of people together for the purpose of worship, prayer, praise, or just looking unto God. T or F

3. Paul established many local churches. T or F

4. Church government is God's idea. T or F

5. Acts 2:46-47 says, "So continuing daily with one accord in the _____, and breaking bread from _____ to house, they ate their food with gladness and simplicity of heart, praising God and having _____ with all the people. And the Lord _____ to the church daily those who were being saved."

6. Which of the following is an example of ecclesia in the New Testament?
   a. Small groups that met in homes
   b. The church in Jerusalem
   c. The church in Asia
   d. The church is Galatia
   e. All of the above

7. When a congregation meets together, everyone has a _____, a _____ of instruction, a _____, a _____ or an _____ (1 Corinthians 14:26).

8. Jesus was in the habit of going to church. T or F

9. You have to go to church to be saved. T or F

10. The Bible clearly shows that we should go to church because we are saved. T or F

11. We go to church to:
    a. Worship
    b. Praise
    c. Pray
    d. Hear the Word of God
    e. Use our spiritual gifts
    f. Encourage others and be encouraged
    g. Fellowship
    h. All of the above

12. We are to submit and obey those in spiritual authority over us (Hebrews 13:7). T or F

13. The enemy wants to isolate us and keep us from meeting together. T or F

14. When brethren dwell together in unity, there God commands the blessing. T or F

36
The Sovereignty of God

The Lord God is absolutely sovereign. This means He has all power and authority that emanates from Himself and not from any outside source. He is the top of the food chain, so to speak.

But what does His sovereignty mean to us? Does this mean that everything that happens in this life comes from God? This is a big question that a lot of people wonder about. Many saved and unsaved people believe that everything comes from God. For example, insurance companies declare storms and floods as acts of God. But is this what the Bible teaches?

Many have also heard pastors and leaders preach that God puts sickness on us to teach us a lesson. But these same people are very quick to go to the hospital for assistance. If they really believe it is the will of God, why don't they embrace sickness? If they really believe this teaching, shouldn't they pray for others to receive sickness to learn a lesson from God as well?

These ideas imply that God sovereignly does both good and evil. In this extreme sovereignty-of-God belief system, there isn't any room for an enemy. Since God sovereignly does everything, there isn't any place for the devil. The Bible clearly says that our battle is not against flesh and blood but against rulers, principalities, and spiritual forces of wickedness.[1] It also says that we are to resist the devil, and he will flee from us.[2] If everything comes from the hand of God, what are we supposed to battle and resist?

God is absolutely sovereign, and in His sovereignty, He has chosen to co-labor with people who believe. You might be thinking, *"But, doesn't it say that God causes the rain to fall on the just and the unjust?"* (Matthew 5:45). It does! But the Word of God also says that it is impossible to please God without faith (see Hebrews 11:6). And that the man without faith ought not to expect to receive anything from the Lord (James 1:7).

So the next natural question is, what is faith? Hebrews 11:1 (NASB1995) says, *"Now faith is the assurance* [substance] *of things hoped for* [expected], *the conviction* [evidence] *of things not seen."* [Bracketed words are from Footnotes.] Other translations and commentaries say that faith is being sure, certain, convinced, confident, having a firm trust, an assurance, a conviction, and the proof that you have the unseen thing that you hoped for. This is not based on your senses but on your beliefs and convictions.

People also blame the will of God and God's sovereignty when things don't happen the way they hoped, but often they haven't been practicing Bible-believing faith. For example, they say, "I'll believe it when I see it." This is not faith; it is the opposite of faith. Faith is being confident that we already have what we cannot see based on God's Word. Once we see it, we don't need faith for it.

These types of people are running in the same camp as doubting Thomas. He said the same thing speaking about the resurrection of Jesus; *"… Unless I see in His hands the print of the nails, and put my finger into the print of the nails, and put my hand into His side, I will not believe."*

Eight days later, Jesus visited with the disciples again. *"Then He said to Thomas, 'Reach your finger here, and look at My hands; and reach your hand here, and put it into My side. Do not be unbelieving, but believing." And Thomas answered and said to Him, "My Lord and my God!" Jesus said to him, "Thomas, because you have seen Me, you have believed. Blessed are those who have not seen and yet have believed"* (John 20:25-29).

On Jesus' previous visit, Thomas was not there. The other disciples saw Jesus, but Thomas would not believe their report. You might think, *Well sure, it is easy for the other disciples to believe, they saw Jesus.* But their report wasn't the word that Thomas was expected to believe. Thomas was expected to believe the report that Jesus gave many times before, that in three days He would rise from the dead. Jesus wanted the disciples to take Him at His Word.

I want to show you a stark contrast to Thomas' attitude. In John 4:50-52 (NIV), a nobleman's son was sick and close to death, so he asked Jesus to come and pray for his son. *"Go," Jesus replied, "your son will live." The man took Jesus at his word and departed. While he was still on the way, his servants met him with the news that his boy was living. When he inquired as to the time when his son got better, they said to him, "Yesterday, at one in the afternoon, the fever left him."*

To this father's credit, he took Jesus at His word and received what he asked for—healing for his son. But what an amazing contrast between the nobleman and Thomas; one took Jesus at His Word and the other wouldn't believe unless he saw it with his own eyes. The nobleman received a miracle, and his whole household became believers as a result. Sadly, Thomas is known as "Doubting Thomas" even to this day.

When some people receive a bad doctor's report, they say, "Well, all we can do now is pray." Is there any faith in this statement? Negative faith, yes; positive faith, no. Others say, "If it be your will." I do realize that sometimes the will of God is not known from the Bible. For example, who we are going to marry, where we are going to college, what job to take, if we should buy a certain house or not. However, if the will of God is shown in the Bible, it is our responsibility to know it, believe it, and take Him at His Word. We have no need to pray "if it be Your will" when the will of God is known. If you don't know the will of God, ask Him. The sons of God are led by the Spirit of God.

We are blessed when we believe God's Word without relying on what we see with our eyes. This is the faith that pleases God. This is the faith that receives from God. This is the faith that Jesus said was blessed.

Misunderstanding the sovereignty of God causes some to question the will of God when something bad happens. Jesus answers this very question in John 10:10. He says, *"The thief does not come except to steal, and to kill, and to destroy. I have come that they may have life, and that they may have it more abundantly."*

Anything in our lives that is stealing, killing, or destroying comes from the devil. It is the devil's autograph. Jesus came that we would have abundant life in Him. Let this truth rest in your heart and mind.

CHAPTER 36 THE SOVEREIGNTY OF GOD

Questions - The Sovereignty of God

1. Everything that happens is the will of God for my life. T or F

2. God is absolutely sovereign, but in His sovereignty, He has chosen to co-labor with people who believe. T or F

3. It is impossible to please God without _____. (Hebrew 11:6)

4. It is impossible to _____ from God without faith. (James 1:7)

5. True Bible-believing faith is:
   a. Having assurance of things hoped for
   b. Having a strong conviction for things you can't see
   c. Being sure, certain, convinced and confident
   d. Having a firm trust
   e. All of the Above

6. Thomas was known for only believing what he could see. T or F

7. The Centurion took Jesus at His _____.

8. According to Ephesians 6:12, our battle isn't with flesh and blood but against rulers, principalities, and powers. T or F

9. Who is asked to resist the devil so that he will flee?

10. The thief comes to _____, _____, _____ (John 10:10). Jesus came that we might have _____, and have it more abundantly.

37
Under Law or Under Grace?

A few years ago, I was in Israel, and I heard a man say, "If someone tells you that we are not under the Law anymore, that person doesn't know what they are talking about." These kinds of statements have been debated for centuries. In the community where I live, if I were to go door to door asking different churches if we are still under the Law, I think many of them would say yes, and a few might say no. I believe a big part of the confusion comes from not understanding what it really means to be under the Law.

So, what *does* it mean to be under the Law? In the Old Covenant, they had many laws. Some say up to 613 laws.[1] They had to keep all the moral laws, sacrificial laws, and ceremonial laws. Being under the Law in the Old Covenant was how the people connected and related to God. If they performed well, they were blessed. If they didn't, they were cursed, cut off, or killed (see Deuteronomy 28). So, being under the Law was totally based on their performance. For example, in Numbers 15:32-36 a man was found gathering wood on the Sabbath day. The entire assembly took the man outside the camp and stoned him to death, as the Lord commanded Moses.

For some reason, this is the way some people want to relate to God—based on their performance because they believe they obey all the laws and they are good enough. But obviously, from the story on the previous page where the man was gathering wood on the Sabbath, this is not the case. James 2:10 (NIV) says, *"For whoever keeps the whole law and yet stumbles at just one point is guilty of breaking all of it."* It is like shooting a big picture window with a BB-gun. You may have only put a small hole or crack in the window, but you have ruined or broken the whole thing. If you break one Law, you are guilty of breaking all of it.

Galatians 3:10 (NIV) says, *"For all who rely on the works of the law are under a curse, as it is written: 'Cursed is everyone who does not continue to do everything written in the Book of the Law.'"* Galatians 2:21 (KJV) says, *"I do not frustrate the grace of God: for if righteousness come by the law, then Christ is dead in vain."* And Galatians 5:4 (NIV) says, *"You who are trying to be justified by the law have been alienated from Christ; you have fallen away from grace."* Other translations say, *"Christ has become of no effect to you"* (KJV), *"you are separated from Christ"* (AMP), *"severed from Christ"* (NAS), *"Christ has become nothing to you"* (WEY). The *Strong's Concordance* says, *"To render entirely idle or useless."* [2] From these three verses, we can see that if we rely on ourselves and not on Christ, we are under a curse, we are frustrating the grace of God, we are separated from Christ, and we have rendered His coming and His work entirely idle and useless. You see, you can't have both at the same time. Either you are under grace, or you have fallen from grace and are separated from Christ. You can't have a mixture of both.

The funny thing is that Gentiles were never intended to be under the Law in the first place. Theologians have created this idea, but this was not God's intent. Acts 21:25 (NIV) says, *"As for the Gentile believers, we have written to them our decision that they should abstain from food sacrificed to idols, from blood, from the meat of strangled animals and from sexual immorality."* The Gentiles were under four laws, and three of the four laws had to do with eating. Yet, people have been trying for centuries to put us under the Law.

The Bible clearly teaches in the New Testament that Jew and Gentile believers alike are not under the Law. Romans 6:14 says that, *"... you are not under law, but under grace."* Romans 7:4, says that, *"... you also died to the law through the body of Christ ..."* Romans 7:6 says, *"... we have been released from the law so that we serve in the new way of the Spirit, and not in the old way of the written code."* Romans 10:4 says, *"Christ is the culmination of the law so that there may be righteousness for everyone who believes."* And Hebrews 8:13 says, that *"By calling this covenant "new," he has made the first one obsolete ..."* (NIV).

So, what does it mean to be under grace? Romans 6:14 (NIV) says, *"For sin shall not be your master, because you are not under law, but under grace."* It means that no longer do we relate to God based on our performance. We relate to God based on the performance of Christ. Jesus is our righteousness. Jesus is our right standing with God. When we put our faith in Him and His finished work on the Cross, we receive right standing with God Himself. Philippians 3:9 (NIV) says, *"and be found in him, not having a righteousness of my own that comes from the law, but that which is through faith in Christ—the righteousness that comes from God on the basis of faith."*

I remember years ago telling a friend at work that we are not under the Law but under grace. He went on to say, "Yes, but there are still important things in the Old Testament for us to learn from and prophecies that are not yet fulfilled." I agree. This is totally true. The Old Testament is filled with great stories and testimonies of the heroes of our faith. We should read the Old Testament. Could you imagine not having Psalms, Proverbs, Isaiah, etc.? But for some reason people are connecting the 39 books of the Old Testament and the Old Covenant that God made with Moses as the same things when they are not.

The Old Covenant is written in the Old Testament. But the Old

Testament is not the same as the Old Covenant. A covenant is an agreement, usually formal, between two or more persons to do or not do something specified.[3] A Testament is a will, especially one that relates to the disposition of one's personal property.[4] Hebrews 9:16-17 says, *"In the case of a will, it is necessary to prove the death of the one who made it, because a will is in force only when somebody has died; it never takes effect while the one who made it is living."* In Hebrews 10:9-10, it says, *"Then he said, 'Here I am, I have come to do your will.' He sets aside the first to establish the second. And by that will, we have been made holy through the sacrifice of the body of Jesus Christ once for all."* Before Jesus died on the Cross, He changed the will. So, there is now a new will and a New Covenant in effect today. And since Jesus died, that will, can never be altered again. Today, we no longer relate to God based on the Law or our performance. We relate to God through the performance of the One-Man Jesus Christ. Praise God, we are not under the Law, but we are under God's grace because of Jesus and His finished work on the Cross.

CHAPTER 37 — UNDER LAW OR UNDER GRACE?

Questions - Under Law or Under Grace?

1. Being under the _____ in the Old Covenant was how the people connected and related to God.

2. If they performed well, they were _____. If they didn't, they were cursed, cut off, or killed (Deut. 28).

3. James 2:10 says, "For whoever keeps the whole Law and yet stumbles at just one point is guilty of breaking _____ of it."

4. Galatians 3:10 (KJV) says, "For as many as are of the works of the Law are under the curse; for it is written, Cursed is every one that continueth not in _____ which are written in the book of the Law to do them.

5. Galatians 2:21 (KJV) says "I do not frustrate the grace of God: for if righteousness came by the Law, then Christ died in _____."

6. Galatians 5:4 (NIV) says "You who are trying to be justified by the Law have been alienated from Christ; you have_____ away from grace."

7. Gentiles were never intended to be under the Law. T or F

8. Philippians 3:9 (KJV) says, "And be found in him, not having mine own righteousness, which is of the Law, but that which is through the faith of Christ, the _____ which is of God by faith."

9. The Old Covenant and the Old Testament are the same things. T or F

10. Today, we no longer relate to God based on the Law or our performance. We relate to God through the _____ of the One Man Jesus Christ.

38
The Purpose of the Law

The Ghost Army, or the 23rd, was an elite group made up of artists, designers, sound technicians, press agents, makeup artists, and professional photographers. This unit was part of the US Army in 1944. The 23rd's mission was to deceive the German Army into believing that their enemies possessed more troops and material than they did. Using sound effects and fake infantry, tanks, and artillery they deceived many Germans soldiers into surrendering without a fight.[1] If the Germans had known the truth about these deceptions, we may have lost the war, or at the very least, our victory may have been delayed and more lives lost. In the same way as the US military, the devil uses deception and trickery on us to make us believe that he is more powerful and that he has more weapons than he does. In reality, all that he has is deception. In a conference meeting in Chicago that I attended, I heard Reinhard Bonnke call the devil, "a mouse in the corner with a megaphone."

Colossians 2:13-15 says, *"When you were dead in your sins and in the uncircumcision of your sinful nature, God made you alive with Christ. He forgave us all our sins, having cancelled the written code, with its regulations, that was against us and that stood opposed to us; he took it away, nailing it to the cross. And having disarmed the powers and authorities, he made a public spectacle of them, triumphing over them by the cross."* What was this written code that He canceled, that was against us, and that stood opposed to us? Some think the written code here refers to our sin, as if our sins were all written down and recorded. But 1 Corinthians 13:5 (NIV) says that love *"keeps no records of wrongs."* There is not a written record of our sins. The regulations it is referring to are the regulations of the Law. Jesus blotted out and canceled the Old Covenant Law that was against us. The Lord not only forgave our transgressions of His Laws, but He also took away the Laws. I know this is a bold statement to make, so let me show you this in Scripture. Romans 10:4 says, *"For Christ is the end of the law for righteousness to everyone who believes."* Romans 7:6 (NIV) says, *"But now, by dying to what once bound us, we have been released from the law so that we serve in the new way of the Spirit, and not in the old way of the written code."* There it is. The written code here is referring to the Law. Jesus canceled it and its regulations that were opposed to us and stood against us, and by doing so, He disarmed powers and authorities. We now have a new way to serve God, and it is not through the Law but by His Spirit.

Paul said that the Law was against us, and it stood opposed to us. This is profoundly different from the way that many Christians think. They embrace the Old Covenant Law as if it were something that God gave us to help us achieve right standing with Him. But this is not the case. 2 Corinthians 3:7 calls the Law *the ministry of death, written and engraved on stones.* 2 Corinthians 3:9 calls the Law *the ministry of condemnation.* Romans 5:20 (NIV) says, *"The law was brought in so that the trespass might increase."* 1 Corinthians 15:56 (NIV) says, *"The sting of death is sin, and the power of sin is the law."* So, the Law is the ministry of death and condemnation, the power of sin is the Law and through the Law, sin increased. If all of this is true, why did God give Moses the Law? To understand this, we need to understand the purpose of the Law.

Romans 3:20 says, *"Therefore no one will be declared righteous in God's sight by the works of the law; rather, through the law we become conscious of sin."* We may be assumed righteous in the sight of men by our outward works, but we will never be declared righteous in God's sight by those works. The purpose of the Law was not to save us or make us righteous. The purpose of the Law was to make us conscious of our sin. It was to condemn us and to make us conscious of our sinful condition and our need for a Savior. Romans 7:12 says that the Law is holy, and its commands are holy, righteous, and good. The problem was that we were not. And we didn't know it. Moses didn't know, and the children of Israel didn't know. So, God gave them the Law to reveal their sinful condition. I heard Andrew Wommack say on television that, "The Old Testament Law was given to show us our sin, not our Savior."

Another purpose of the Law is found in Galatians 3:24-25, which says, *"Therefore the law was our tutor to bring us to Christ, that we might be justified by faith. But after faith has come, we are no longer under a tutor."* The word "tutor" here is not the best word to use because our culture today is very different from theirs. Our tutors today teach. But that was not the case in Bible times. The word "tutor" in the Greek, means *a servant whose job it was to take the children to and from school,*[2] similar to our bus drivers in North America. Our bus drivers are in charge for a time until they arrive at school. They are not in charge of teaching the children, but they will correct the children if they are acting out. Once they get to school, the teachers, the principals, and the other adults are then in charge. So, we can see, that these tutors were put in charge for a season, or a specific length of time, until the children have come of age.

Galatians 3:19 says, *"What purpose then does the law serve? It was added because of transgressions, till the Seed should come to whom the promise was made; and it was appointed through angels by the hand of a mediator."* Again, we see here that the Law had a time limit. It says it was added until the Seed should come to whom the promise was made. What was the promise? In Genesis 3:15 God said, *"And I will put enmity between you and the woman, and between your seed and her Seed; He shall bruise your head, and you shall bruise His heel."* This is a prophecy about a future day when the Seed of Eve would crush the devil's head so hard for what he did in the Garden, that it would bruise His own heel. Who was the Seed? Jesus. Well, has He come? Yes. Then the time of the Law is up.

Jamieson, Fausset and Brown Commentary says, "Moses the lawgiver cannot bring us into the heavenly Canaan, though he can bring us to the border. At that point, he is superseded by the true Joshua, who leads the spiritual Israel into their inheritance. The Law leads us to Christ; there its office ceases." [3]

Why is this so important to know? The purpose of the Law was not for us to follow a huge list of rules to make God happy; so that He could accept us. The purpose of the Law was to help us recognize our sinful condition and our need for a Savior. The Law was also added to be a tutor to lead us to Christ.

For those who are in Christ, Jesus disarmed Satan by blotting out the Law and its regulations that were opposed to us and that stood against us. But when we get back under the Law by relying on our own works of righteousness, we give the devil ammunition that he can use against us to condemn us. Don't let the enemy deceive you into believing that he is more powerful than he is or that he has more weapons than he does. One of his main weapons, the Law, was nailed to the Cross. The reality is that all he has left is deception. Romans 8:1 (NASB), *"Therefore there is now no condemnation at all for those who are in Christ Jesus."*

CHAPTER 38 THE PURPOSE OF THE LAW

Questions - The Purpose of the Law

1. What was the written code that was against us and that stood opposed to us that Jesus canceled?

2. Romans 7:6 says, "But now, by dying to what once bound us, we have been released from the Law so that we serve in the new way of the _____, and not in the old way of the written code."

3. We now have a new way to serve God, and it is not through the Law but by His Spirit. T or F

4. The Law is the ministry of death and condemnation, the power of sin is the Law and through the Law sin increased. T or F

5. The purpose of the Law was to save us and make us righteous.
   T or F

6. Romans 3:20 says that through the Law we become _____ of sin.

7. The purpose of the Law was to make us conscious of our need for a savior. T or F

8. The purpose of the Law, like a tutor, was to bring us to Christ.
   T or F

9. According to Galatians 3:19, the Law was put in charge for a certain length of time? How long was that? The Law was put in charge _____ the Seed should come to whom the promise was made.

10. Has that Seed come?   Y or N

11. Who is now in charge?

12. In your own words, what was/is the purpose of the Law?

39
The Right Way To Use the Law

First Timothy 1:8-10 (NIV) says, *"We know that the law is good if one uses it properly. We also know that the law is made not for the righteous but for lawbreakers and rebels, the ungodly and sinful, the unholy and irreligious; for those who kill their fathers or mothers, for murderers, for the sexually immoral, for those practicing homosexuality, for slave traders and liars and perjurers—and for whatever else is contrary to the sound doctrine."*

There are a few things I want to point out here. First, verse 9 says that the Law is for lawbreakers and rebels and not for the righteous. So, the Law is not intended for those who are in Christ. Do you see that? Secondly, the Law is good IF one uses it properly. 2 Timothy 2:15 says, *"Be diligent to present yourself approved to God, a worker who does not need to be ashamed, rightly dividing the word of truth."* There is a right way and wrong way to use the Law.

So, what is the correct way to use the Law? First, it depends whether you are referring to the right way for righteous, saved people to use the Law or for lawbreakers and rebels. For lawbreakers and rebels, if they are guilty of committing a crime, they should be judged and charged accordingly. That is how God ordained our legal system to work. Romans 13:4 (NIV) says, *"For the one in authority is God's servant for your good. But if you do wrong, be afraid, for rulers do not bear the sword for no reason. They are God's servants, agents of wrath to bring punishment on the wrongdoer."* There is forgiveness and mercy for our sins, but there are also consequences for hurting the people. This is God's Law, and it is also man's law. These servants of God are agents of wrath to bring punishment on the wrongdoer. So, the Law should judge them, it should condemn them, and it should lead them to Christ as we saw in the previous lesson.

For the righteous, saved people, there is a right way to use the Law as well. Acts 28:23-24 says, *"So when they had appointed him a day, many came to him at his lodging, to whom he explained and solemnly testified of the kingdom of God, persuading them concerning Jesus from both the Law of Moses and the Prophets, from morning till evening. And some were persuaded by the things which were spoken, and some disbelieved."* The Law and the Prophets all point to the coming Messiah. Here Paul spoke from morning until evening going over many references with the crowd showing them that Jesus is the one these Scriptures were talking about. The result was that some believed.

This is the same thing that Jesus did with the disciples on the road to Emmaus. Luke 24:25-27 says, *"Then He (Jesus) said to them, 'O foolish ones, and slow of heart to believe in all that the prophets have spoken! Ought not the Christ to have suffered these things and to enter into His glory?' And beginning at Moses and all the Prophets, He expounded to them in all the Scriptures the things concerning Himself."* Jesus spoke from the Law and the Prophets on this walk to Emmaus, and He systematically explained things to them from the Scripture. Wouldn't you love to have been one of the people walking with Jesus and hearing all that He taught? Jesus shared with these two disciples for approximately seven to eight miles,[1] which could have taken anywhere from an hour and a half to three hours to walk,[2] and *"He expounded to them in all the Scriptures the things concerning Himself."* He used the Law and Prophets to show that He was the Messiah.

This was not the only time Jesus revealed that the Old Testament Scriptures were talking about Him. In John 5:39 Jesus said, *"You search the Scriptures, for in them you think you have eternal life; and these are they which testify of Me."* In John 5:46, Jesus said, *"For if you believed Moses, you would believe me, for he wrote about me."* The right way to use the Law and the Prophets is to show people that these Scriptures are all referring to Jesus.

In Acts 2, on the Day of Pentecost, the Holy Spirit fell on 120 people in the upper room. Guests were in town from all over the surrounding regions to celebrate the Feast of Pentecost. When people heard the sounds coming from the upper room, they were confused, and they thought the people were drunk. Peter stood up and addressed the crowd and quoted Acts 2:17 (NIV), *"In the last days, God says, I will pour out my Spirit on all people. Your sons and daughters will prophesy ..."* Peter gives other Old Testament Scriptures pointing to Christ, and he goes on to testify about the resurrection of Jesus. Acts 2:41 says that *"three thousand were added to their number that day."*

In Acts chapter 3, Peter addresses another crowd that had gathered due to the healing of the lame man at the gate called Beautiful. Verses 22-24 say: *"For Moses truly said to the fathers, 'The Lord your God will raise up for you a Prophet like me from your brethren. Him you shall hear in all things, whatever He says to you. And it shall be that every soul who will not hear that Prophet shall be utterly destroyed from among the people. Yes, and all the prophets, from Samuel and those who follow, as many as have spoken, have also foretold these days."* In verse 26, Peter made it clear to the people that the Prophet was Jesus. Peter used the Law and the Prophets to show the people how these Scriptures were all referring to Jesus. In Acts 4:4 it says, *"However, many of those who heard the word believed; and the number of the men came to be about five thousand."*

You see the gospel was preached in the Old Testament. The gospel was preached to Abraham. Galatians 3:8 (NIV) says, *"Scripture foresaw that God would justify the Gentiles by faith, and announced the gospel in advance to Abraham: 'All nations will be blessed through you.'"* All nations were blessed by Abraham because Jesus came through Abraham's lineage. The gospel was also preached to Moses and all of the Israelites in the desert. Hebrews 4:2 says, *"For indeed the gospel was preached to us as well as to them; but the word which they heard did not profit them, not being mixed with faith in those who heard it."* The gospel, the good news of salvation, was preached to the Israelites in the desert but it only benefited those who believed.

When we use the Law and the Prophets the right way, the way Peter did, the way Paul did, and the way Jesus did, people are going to believe. When Peter shared, three thousand believed, and on another occasion, two thousand more believed. When Paul shared all night, it said some believed. And when Jesus shared on the road to Emmaus, the two disciples believed. This is the right way to use the Law and the Prophets. We use the Scriptures to point people to Jesus so that people may believe He is the Messiah, the Christ.

CHAPTER 39   THE RIGHT WAY TO USE THE LAW

Questions - The Right Way to Use the Law

1. The Law is good if one uses it properly (1 Timothy 1:8). T or F

2. The Law is for lawbreakers and rebels and not for the _____.

3. There is a right way and wrong way to use the Law. T or F

4. Romans 13:4 (NIV) says, "For the one in authority is God's servant for your good. But if you do wrong, be afraid, for rulers do not bear the sword for no reason. They are God's servants, agents of wrath to bring punishment on the _____."

5. The Law and the Prophets all point to the coming _____.

6. Luke 24:27 "And beginning at Moses and all the Prophets, He expounded to them in all the Scriptures the things concerning _____."

7. When Peter used the Law correctly in Acts 2, three thousand people believed. T or F

8. When Peter used the Law correctly in Acts 3-4, _____ more believed.

9. When Paul used the Law correctly in Acts 28:23-24, _____ believed.

10. When Jesus used the Law correctly, _____ disciples believed.

11. The right way to use the Law and the Prophets is to show people that the Scriptures are referring to Jesus, the One and only Messiah. T or F

40
How Jesus Fulfilled The Law

Jesus said in Matthew 5:17, *"Do not think that I have come to abolish the Law or the Prophets; I have not come to abolish them but to fulfill them."* When I hear people debating whether we are under the Law or not, they usually quote this verse and say, "See, Jesus didn't come to abolish the Law." And that is true. Jesus did not abolish the Law. The Law is good if one uses it properly (1 Timothy 1:8), as we saw in the last lesson. But Jesus did say that He came to fulfill the Law, or complete it. So, what does that mean? How did Jesus fulfill the Law?

First, Jesus fulfilled the Law by making it even harder; clearly revealing the purpose of the Law. The *Strong's Concordance* says the word "fulfill" means – (literally) to cram (a net), to level up (a hollow), to satisfy.[1] *Thayer's Greek Lexicon* says to make full, to fill, to fill up, to complete, properly, to fill up to the top, to perfect, consummate, to make complete in every particular.[2]

Part of Jesus fulfilling the Law was to make it even harder than it was before, to fill up the net that wasn't filled before, so to speak. Remember the sermon on the mount? I believe this was part of Jesus fulfilling the Law. But before I show you that, I must remind you of the purpose of the Law. Romans 5:20 (NIV) says, *"The law was brought in so that the trespass might increase. But where sin increased, grace increased all the more."* The Law was added to reveal what sin was. But also (and I believe it was an even bigger purpose), it was added to reveal to the individual how utterly sinful they were. God wanted them to know that they had a sin nature and that they were spiritually dead. Romans 8:3 says the Law was weakened by our sinful nature. However, the Law in itself was not weak. We were weak, and we did not know it. God was trying to show mankind how desperately they needed a Savior.

1 Corinthians 15:56 says, *"The sting of death is sin, and the power of sin is the law."* Do you think God wanted people to sin more? No, they were already sinning. Then why add the Law when it says that the power of sin is the Law? Where Law increased, sin increased. The purpose was to reveal to us our nature and to show us how desperately we needed a Savior.

Back to the sermon on the mount, Matthew 5:27-28 says, *"You have heard that it was said, 'You shall not commit adultery.' But I tell you that anyone who looks at a woman lustfully has already committed adultery with her in his heart."* You see, Jesus made the Law tougher. This sin was already in the world since the fall of man, but it was not taken into account where there was no Law. The Law was added, sin increased, the knowledge of sin increased, and the revelation of how utterly sinful we were increased.

Matthew 5:29-30 says, *"If your right eye causes you to stumble, gouge it out and throw it away. It is better for you to lose one part of your body than for your whole body to be thrown into hell. And if your right hand causes you to stumble, cut it off and throw it away. It is better for you to lose one part of your body than for your whole body to go into hell."* Do you think Jesus really wants us to gouge out our eyes and to cut off our hands, or did He have something else in mind? Jesus was making the Law even harder so that people would come to the end of themselves and realize that they do not have the power to fulfill all of the requirements of the Law. The Law is good, the Law is strong, but we are weak, and we need a Savior.

Secondly, Jesus showed people where they were breaking the Law and thereby fulfilled the purpose of the Law. The Pharisees were self-righteous, pompous, arrogant men. They looked down on others and considered themselves better than everyone else. They believed that they were holy and righteous. But Jesus knew better. In John 8:44 Jesus said, *"You belong to your father, the devil, and you want to carry out your father's desires. He was a murderer from the beginning, not holding to the truth, for there is no truth in him. When he lies, he speaks his native language, for he is a liar and the father of lies."*

The Pharisees were the experts of the Law in their day. They were the ones who would interpret, translate, and enforce the Law. They sometimes added to the Law and sometimes took away from the Law to make it more manageable. By that, they could feel like they were fulfilling it. Mark 7:8-13 (NIV) says, *" 'You have let go of the commands of God and are holding on to human traditions.' And he continued, 'You have a fine way of setting aside the commands of God in order to observe your own traditions! For Moses said, 'Honor your father and mother,' and, 'Anyone who curses their father or mother is to be put to death.' But you say that if anyone declares that what might have been used to help their father or mother is Corban (that is, devoted to God)—then you no longer let them do anything for their father or mother. Thus you nullify the word of God by your tradition that you have handed down. And you do many things like that."*

The Pharisees believed they were innocent, when in fact, because they studied the Law and considered themselves to be experts of the Law, they were even more guilty. In John 9:40-41, some Pharisees asked Jesus, *"... 'What? Are we blind too?' Jesus said, 'If you were blind, you would not be guilty of sin; but now that you claim you can see, your guilt remains.' "*

Believe it or not, Jesus did not hate the Pharisees. He was trying to show them that they were guilty of sin, that they were spiritually dead, and that no one could be considered righteous in God's sight by observing the Law. Romans 3:20 (NIV) says, *"Therefore no one will be declared righteous in God's sight by the works of the law; rather, through the law we become conscious of our sin."* He was trying to show them their need for a Savior.

And finally, Jesus fulfilled the Law by obeying every part of it. For example, remember the story of the lady who was caught in the act of adultery? The Pharisees brought her to Jesus and wanted Him to stone her in accordance with the Law, when in fact, the Law required that both adulterers be put to death (see Leviticus 20:10). You know the story in John 8:7. Jesus writes in the sand and then says, *"He who is without sin among you, let him throw a stone at her first."* It would seem here that Jesus did not obey the Law and, in a sense, encouraged the Pharisees not to obey the Law as well. But in reality, Jesus did obey and fulfill the Law by becoming her substitute and taking her punishment in His own body, even unto death. You see, Jesus fulfilled the Law and the consequences of breaking the Law in His own body, for her and for us. Romans 8:3-4 (NIV) says, *"For what the law was powerless to do because it was weakened by the flesh, God did by sending his own Son in the likeness of sinful flesh to be a sin offering. And so he condemned sin in the flesh, in order that the righteous requirement of the law might be fully met in us, who do not live according to the flesh but according to the Spirit."* Jesus fulfilled the Law by obeying all of it and by taking the punishment of mankind for breaking it.

Jesus also fulfilled the Prophets by fulfilling every prophetic word about the Messiah given in the Old Testament; there were approximately 332 distinct predictions (prophecies) that were literally fulfilled by Christ.[3]

* More information and the probability of Jesus fulfilling all these prophecies are given in Chapter 9.

CHAPTER 40 — HOW JESUS FULFILLED THE LAW

Questions - How Jesus Fulfilled The Law

1. Matthew 5:17 states, "Do not think that I have come to abolish the Law or the Prophets; I have not come to abolish them but to _____ them."

2. The word *fulfills* in the Greek language means: "to make full, to fill up to the top, to cram (a net), to level up (a hollow), to satisfy, to complete and to perfect."   T or F

3. Part of Jesus fulfilling the Law was to make it even _____ than it was before.

4. Romans 8:3 shows that the Law was _____ by our sinful nature. The Law was not weak. We were weak, and we didn't know it.

5. Jesus showed people where they were _____ the Law and thereby fulfilled the purpose of the Law.

6. Jesus hated the Pharisees.   T or F

7. What was Jesus trying to show the Pharisees?
   a. That they were guilty of sin
   b. That they were spiritually dead
   c. That no one could be considered righteous in God's sight by observing the Law
   d. That, by the Law, we become conscious of sin
   e. That they have need for a Savior
   f. All of the above

8. Jesus fulfilled the Law by obeying all of it and by taking the _____ of mankind for breaking it.

9. Jesus fulfilled the prophets by fulfilling every prophetic word about the Messiah given in the Old Testament.   T   or   F

41

No More Consciousness of Sin

My wife taught at a Christian school for five years. Chapel services were held every Wednesday. It was not long before she noticed a pattern. Each week, the speakers would focus on sin, going over a list of what not to do in life. There often seemed to be a condemning atmosphere that accompanied the messages. The alters were always filled with students repenting, and the same ones getting "saved" repeatedly over and over again, as they doubted their own salvation. One day, she mentioned this to some of her co-workers. They had never noticed this sin-focused pattern before. One co-worker she spoke to also pastored a local church. Highlighting the sin-conscious sermons hit him hard. He shared with my wife that he began changing his own sermons, shifting from preaching on what not to do, to empowering the people with messages of what to do for a victorious Christian life.

Hebrews 10:1-2 says, *"For the law, having a shadow of the good things to come, and not the very image of the things, can never with these same sacrifices, which they offer continually year by year, make those who approach perfect. For then would they not have ceased to be offered? For the worshipers, once purified, would have had no more consciousness of sins."* What does this mean to have no more consciousness of sins? Does this mean I can now freely sin as much as I want to and not feel bad about it anymore? No, that is not what this means. This is not talking about sin the behavior but sin the nature. Romans 3:20 says, *"Therefore no one will be declared righteous in God's sight by the works of the law; rather, through the law we become conscious of sin."* We might say for the last part of this verse: "… rather, through the Law we become conscious of *our sinful condition."*

Have you ever been self-conscious about something? Perhaps you were invited to a high school reunion, but because you put on a few pounds, started balding, or did not have a glamorous job, you were overly self-conscious and did not want to attend. Maybe you had a big pimple on your nose, and you were so self-conscious about it that you didn't want to go out in public. By being so self-conscious or focused on the problem or insecurity, it has hindered what you felt comfortable doing. This is like sin-consciousness. You are so focused on the problem, that you haven't taken the time to focus on the solution. You are so focused on the problem of sin and your sinful condition that you haven't consciously realized all that Christ did for you.

Hebrews 10:22 (KJV) says, *"Let us draw near with a true heart in full assurance of faith, having our hearts sprinkled from an evil conscience and our bodies washed with pure water."* The word "evil" comes from the root meaning *poor, needy, or a beggar.*[1] You see, our hearts have been sprinkled to wash our conscience free from a place of poverty, free from the place of debt, free from the place of need, free from the place of lack, free from the place of being a beggar and into a place of inheritance and sonship.

Imagine that someone loaned you $10,000. You set up a schedule of repayment. At first, you made all your payments on time and even early. But after a while, you fell on hard times, and you did not have the money to make the payments. One payment was missed, and now the next month's payment is due. Then you see the person who lent you the money at a store, but you hide from them because you don't want them to ask about the loan. Later, they try to call you, but you let it go to voicemail. Being so conscious of the debt, you try and avoid the lender at all costs. This same thing can happen in our spiritual lives. When we are so conscious of our debt, we do not want to speak to the One that we owe. We had a debt that we could not pay, but Jesus paid our debt. We may feel like we owe God something, but even on a payment plan, there is no way we can ever repay God.

The truth is that our debt has been fully paid, even overpaid, and that is why we can now draw near to God with a true heart in full assurance of faith, having our hearts sprinkled from an evil conscience and our bodies washed with pure water. The meaning of the word "conscience" is union, with, together,[2] and to see.[3] So now we need to see our union, we need to see ourselves with God, we need to see ourselves together with Him. If we are still seeing the union with the old sinful nature, we are still going to be conscious of sin, and God does not want that for us. Romans 7:1-4 (NIV) says, *"Do you not know, brothers and sisters—for I am speaking to those who know the law—that the law has authority over someone only as long as that person lives? For example, by law, a married woman is bound to her husband as long as he is alive, but if her husband dies, she is released from the law that binds her to him. So then, if she has sexual relations with another man while her husband is still alive, she is called an adulteress. But if her husband dies, she is released from that law and is not an adulteress if she marries another man. So, my brothers and sisters, you also died to the law through the body of Christ, that you might belong to another, to him who was raised from the dead, in order that we might bear fruit for God."*

The Law makes us conscious of our sinful condition. That is the purpose of the Law. But we are not married to the Law anymore. When we were born again, we died, so that we can be married to another. We are now married to Christ, and because of this new union, He wants us to be conscious of Him. He wants us to be conscious of our righteousness through that union. No more consciousness of sin means that we are now conscious of Him. We are aware of our right standing with God, as one with Him.

When people get married, the Bible says that the two become one flesh. When we enter into the Covenant relationship with Jesus, the Bible says the two become one spirit. We need to see this union.

1 Corinthians 6:17 (NIV) says, *"But whoever is united with the Lord is one with him in spirit."* What are you conscious of, your union with the old sinful nature, or your new union with Christ? Your answer to this question will determine a lot about where you are spiritually.

CHAPTER 41 — NO MORE CONSCIOUSNESS OF SIN

Questions - No More Consciousness of Sin

1. The worshipers, once purified, would have had no more consciousness of sins. T or F

2. This means that we can sin as much as we want to, and our conscience will not feel bad about it anymore. T or F

3. No more consciousness of sins is not referring to sin the behavior, but the sinful nature. T or F

4. According to Hebrews 10:22, "we can now _____ near to God with a true _____ in full assurance of _____, because our hearts have been sprinkled _____ from an evil conscience and our _____ have been _____ with pure water."

5. The word evil comes from the meaning poor, needy, starving, or a beggar. T or F

6. If we are still seeing the union with the old sinful nature, we are still going to be conscious of sin. T or F

7. Romans 7:4 "So, my brothers, you also _____ to the Law through the body of _____, that you might belong to _____, to him who was raised from the _____, in order that we might bear _____ to God."

8. 1 Corinthians 6:17 says, "But he who unites himself with the Lord is _____ with him in spirit."

42
Christology

Christology is the study of the person and work of Jesus Christ.[1] Who is Jesus? Was Jesus just a man, the Son of God, or God Himself? As I read through the Bible growing up, I was sometimes confused as to the correct answer. Many verses show that Jesus is God, but other verses imply that He is not. What is right? Is He or isn't He God? In this lesson, we will address these essential questions.

First, was Jesus a man? B.B. Warfield surveyed the gospels for the emotional make-up of Jesus in his study *"The Emotional Life of Christ."* He noted that Jesus felt compassion and love for the people of Jerusalem and for Lazarus and his family; moral indignation at the money-changers; the affliction of the Man of Sorrows, distress at the thought of the Cross, sorrow unto death; amazement at the faith of the centurion; joy in God's work; anticipation of the Last Supper with the disciples. His emotions displayed themselves in physical reactions. He hungered (Matthew 4:2), thirsted (John 19:20), and was weary (John 4:6). Jesus wept (John 11:35), wailed (Luke 19:41), and sighed (Mark 7:34). A loud cry was wrung from him at the moment of His death. Nothing was missing to make us disbelieve that Jesus was a human being just like us.²

Secondly, is Jesus the Son of God? Well, the centurion believed it. Mark 15:39 (NIV) says, *"And when the centurion, who stood there in front of Jesus, saw how he died, he said, 'Surely this man was the Son of God!'"* Simon Peter believed it. In Matthew 16:16, *"Simon Peter answered and said, 'You are the Christ, the Son of the living God.'"* Evil spirits believed it. Mark 3:11, *"And the unclean spirits, whenever they saw Him, fell down before Him and cried out, saying, 'You are the Son of God.'"* Jesus believed it. In Luke 22:70: *"Then they all said, 'Are You then the Son of God?' So He (Jesus) said to them, 'You rightly say that I am.'"* And God the Father believed it. Matthew 3:17 says, *"And suddenly a voice came from heaven, saying, 'This is My beloved Son, in whom I am well pleased.'"* This one was easy for me. I never doubted that Jesus is God's Son, but is He God Himself?

Several verses made me question this. For example, Mark 10:17-18 (NIV) says, *"As Jesus started on his way, a man ran up to him and fell on his knees before him. 'Good teacher,' he asked, 'what must I do to inherit eternal life?' 'Why do you call me good?' Jesus answered. 'No one is good—except God alone.'"* If Jesus is God, why did He say this?

Matthew 24:36 (NIV) says, *"But about that day or hour no one knows, not even the angels in heaven, nor the Son, but only the Father."* Does God know something that Jesus does not know? How does that work if Jesus is God? Philippians 2:6 (NASB) says, *"...who, as He already existed in the form of God, did not consider equality with God something to be grasped..."* Does this mean that Jesus did not consider equality with God something to be achieved, or that it was out of His reach? James 1:13 says, *"When tempted, no-one should say, 'God is tempting me.' For God cannot be tempted by evil, nor does he tempt anyone."* But Hebrews 4:15 says, *"For we do not have a High Priest who cannot sympathize with our weaknesses, but was in all points tempted as we are, yet without sin."* If God cannot be tempted and Jesus is God, how was He tempted in every way, yet without sin? Questions like these challenged what I thought I believed, and I was not sure what was correct.

Years later, I discovered the answer to these questions when I found the true meaning of Philippians 2:6-7 (NIV). It reads, "Who, being in very nature God, did not consider equality with God something to be grasped, but made himself nothing, taking the very nature of a servant, being made in human likeness." As I mentioned before, I always read this verse to mean that Jesus did not consider equality with God something to be achieved. But the word "grasped" here in the Greek language means, *held on to*.³ So Jesus did not consider equality with God something to be held on to. If He did not hold on to it, that means He let it go. Then in verse 7, it says that He made himself nothing. The words "made Himself nothing," is one word in Greek, the word "kenoo," which means *to empty*.⁴ So Jesus let go of His equality with God and emptied Himself of His divinity. Jesus became extremely limited in the form of a man. Suddenly, he was not everywhere at the same time. He was limited by time and space. He was under the law of gravity. He became tired after a long day of walking and ministry. He had to learn languages and Scripture. He had to grow in wisdom and favor with God and man (Luke 2:52). *He was man*, just like we are.

This is so important to understand. This is how Jesus was tempted. Jesus was tempted *as a man*. God cannot be tempted, but Jesus *as a man* could be. Jesus *as a man* did not know the day or the hour of His second coming. He emptied Himself of all sovereign knowledge. However, *now being glorified*, He knows! And when Jesus asked, *"Why do you call me good, there is no one good except God alone,"* I believe Jesus wanted to test the man to see if he knew who He really was. The man could have answered, "You are the Christ," as Peter did, or "You are the Son of God," like the centurion did, or "You are God." All of these would have been correct. I am sure Jesus would have praised the man for his revelation. These verses seemed to imply, with lack of understanding, that Jesus was not God. He truly was God, Who laid His divinity aside to embrace the fullness of a man while on earth. Now glorified, He carries divinity as He rules and reigns in the Godhead.

John 1:1-4, says, *"In the beginning was the Word, and the Word was with God, and the Word was God. He was with God in the beginning. Through him all things were made; without him nothing was made that has been made. In him was life, and that life was the light of all mankind."* Then verse 14 says, *"The Word became flesh and made his dwelling among us. We have seen his glory, the glory of the one and only Son, who came from the Father, full of grace and truth."*

CHAPTER 42   CHRISTOLOGY

Questions - Christology

1. Christology is the study of the person and work of _____ _____.

2. From the gospels, there was nothing missing to make us disbelieve that Jesus was a human being. T or F

3. Is Jesus the Son of God? Y or N

4. God cannot be tempted by evil (James 1:13). T or F

5. Philippians 2:6 says, "Who, being in very nature God, did not consider equality with God something to be grasped." The word "grasped" here means:
   a. Achieved
   b. Out of reach
   c. Held on to
   d. Accomplished

6. Jesus let go of His equality with God and emptied Himself of His divinity. T or F

7. Jesus was tempted as a man. T or F

8. Jesus as a man did not know the day or the hour of His second coming. T or F

9. John 1:1-4, says, "In the beginning was the _____, and the _____ was with God, and the _____ was God. 2 He was with God in the beginning. 3 Through him all things were made; without him nothing was made that has been made. 4 In him was life, and that life was the light of men." Verse 14, "The _____ became flesh and made his dwelling among us. We have seen his glory, the glory of the one and only Son, who came from the Father, full of grace and truth."

43

The Lord's Supper

Growing up, the preacher would often get us to confess all of our sins before we took the Lord's Supper (Holy Communion) and warned us that if we partook unworthily, we would be eating and drinking damnation on ourselves. That really scared me. How would I know if I was doing it right? As I grew older, the fear subsided somewhat, but I would often feel like I was missing something. Why was I doing this? Was God asking me to do this? In this lesson, we are going to break down Paul's instructions on how to partake of the Lord's Supper properly.

First Corinthians 11:20-22 (KJV) says, *"When ye come together therefore into one place, this is not to eat the Lord's supper. For in eating every one taketh before other his own supper: and one is hungry, and another is drunken. What? have ye not houses to eat and to drink in? or despise ye the church of God, and shame them that have not? what shall I say to you? shall I praise you in this? I praise you not."*

The Corinthian church did not understand what they were doing. They were partaking of the Lord's Supper as if it were a Super Bowl party. Some that came early got full and drunk, and others who came later had nothing. This is the context of Paul's correction.

1 Corinthians 11:23-26: *"For I have received of the Lord that which also I delivered unto you, that the Lord Jesus the same night in which he was betrayed took bread: And when he had given thanks, he brake it, and said, Take, eat: this is my body, which is broken for you: this do in remembrance of me. After the same manner also he took the cup, when he had supped, saying, this cup is the new yestament in my blood: this do ye, as oft as ye drink it, in remembrance of me. For as often as ye eat this bread, and drink this cup, ye do shew the Lord's death till he come."*

Verse 26 uses the word "shew," This is not a word we use every day. It means, to announce, to declare, to make known, to proclaim publicly and to publish.[1] Every time we partake of Holy Communion, we are proclaiming to principalities and powers that Jesus Christ reigns to the glory of God the Father. It is like we are preaching a sermon declaring all that Jesus accomplished through His death, burial, and resurrection for us. This is to be a joyful celebration, not a wild party.

1 Corinthians 11:27: *"Wherefore whosoever shall eat this bread, and drink this cup of the Lord, unworthily, shall be guilty of the body and blood of the Lord."* According to *Vine's Expository Dictionary*, unworthily means, "to treat as a common meal, to treat the bread and cup as common things, not apprehending their solemn symbolic import."[2] So, *unworthily* means "in an unworthy manner." This is what the Corinthian church was doing here. They were stuffing their faces and passing around the elements like it was one of the Jewish feasts. This is an unworthy manner. The problem is, we have taken the word "unworthily" to mean we are unworthy because of sin in our lives. The word "unworthily" is an adverb, which means it modifies the verb. In this case, "unworthily" describes the action of eating and drinking. It is not describing the person who is eating and drinking.[3] So the unworthy manner in context is treating the meal as a common thing.

CHAPTER 43   THE LORD'S SUPPER

1 Corinthians 11:28: *"But let a man examine himself, and so let him eat of that bread, and drink of that cup."* This is the only time this word is translated "examine," from the Greek. Other times it is translated "to try, prove, allow, and approve."[4] This, again, is referring to the manner in which we partake. We are to approve or examine the way we are partaking, not to approve and examine ourselves. Communion is not supposed to be a long introspective process where if we confess enough sins, then we become worthy enough to partake. This is not correct. Colossians 1:12 (ESV) says, *"Giving thanks unto the Father, who has qualified you to share in the inheritance of the saints in light."* Isaiah 43:25 says, *"I, even I, am he who blots out your transgressions for My own sake; And I will not remembers your sins."* Praise God, the Father has qualified us to partake of this Covenant meal. And Jesus has blotted out our sins for His own sake and remembers our sins no more. So, what are we doing remembering our sins? Jesus said that He wanted us to take communion in remembrance of HIM, not in remembrance of our sins.

1 Corinthians 11:29 (KJV): *"For he that eateth and drinketh unworthily, eateth and drinketh damnation to himself, not discerning the Lord's body."* I want you to notice that it says, "not discerning the Lord's body." The blood is not mentioned here. We freely acknowledge and discern the symbol of the blood for forgiveness of sins. But we often overlook the discerning of the Lord's body for our healing. His body was broken for our healing, and His blood was poured out for the forgiveness of sins. When people partake of communion in an unworthy manner, they are eating and drinking damnation on themselves by not discerning the meal correctly and not discerning the Lord's body. The word *discerning* means "to separate, to make a distinction, and to discriminate."[5]

What does it mean to discriminate? When we treat one person one way, and for whatever reason, we treat another person a different way, that is discrimination. God does not want us to treat His Holy Communion the same way you would a regular meal. If you do so, you are not discerning the Lord's body properly, and you are partaking in an unworthy manner. We are to separate it thoroughly, make a distinction that this is not a regular meal. This is the body and blood of our Lord Jesus Christ. When we partake and discern the Lord's body in faith, there is a supernatural infusion of His incorruptible life into our body.[6] When we don't take it correctly, there are negative results, which we will see in the next verse.

1 Corinthians 11:30 (KJV): *"For this cause many are weak and sickly among you, and many sleep."* This is the only place in Scripture where it says why believers get sick. This verse goes on to say that some even die prematurely. The reason is that they have not discerned the Lord's body properly. But if we do discern His body correctly, His divine health is released when we take it by faith. So, we partake of communion in a worthy manner when we properly discern the Lord's body and the sacredness of this Covenant meal, not by confessing our sins.

Verse 26 (NKJV) says, *"For as often as you eat this bread and drink this cup, you proclaim the Lord's death till He comes."* It does not say that we have to take Communion in a church led by a pastor. It can be done this way, but it doesn't have to be. We can partake of Communion at home in a sacred Holy manner by showing proper honor and respect for this Covenant meal. I believe this is an invitation to proclaim everything that the Lord has accomplished for us through His death and resurrection. Maybe you would like to do that now.

If you do not have grape juice or wine, use the best that you have. If that is water, that is okay. Just set it aside for Holy use. Once you are ready, let's continue. Remember, this is not a ritual. You are about to experience His love for you personally.

Take the bread and see the Lord carrying all of your sins and diseases. For He took your sins in His body on the Cross. See Him taking on His body your physical conditions, too. If you have a tumor, see the tumor on His body. Whatever disease you may have, see it on

His body. It is no longer on you. See His health come to you. Isaiah 53:4 YLT, *"Surely our sicknesses he hath borne ..."* We need to see it is surely, and not maybe, He bore our sicknesses and pains. Matthew 8:17 (NASB1995): *"This was to fulfill what was spoken through Isaiah the prophet: 'HE HIMSELF TOOK OUR INFIRMITIES AND CARRIED AWAY OUR DISEASES.'"* His body was broken so that ours can be made whole. Hear Him say to you, *"Take, eat. This is My body, which is broken for you."* With this in mind, eat the bread.

Now take the cup and thank God that all your sins and lawless deeds are remembered no more. Though your sins were like scarlet, they have been made white as snow. As far as the east is from the west, that's how far He has removed your sins from you. See His eyes burning with love for you as He says to you, *"This cup is the new covenant in My blood. This do, as often as you drink it, in remembrance of Me."* Drink the cup.

Now spend some time with the Lord, thanking Him for all He has done for you. If you were healed today through the taking of the Lord's Supper, please let me know. I would love to hear your testimony. You can email me at:

disciplingnations1@gmail.com

Questions - The Lord's Supper

1. For as often as ye eat this bread, and drink this cup, ye do shew the Lord's death till he come. What does the word shew mean?
   a. To announce
   b. To declare
   c. To make known
   d. To preach
   e. To proclaim publicly
   f. All of the above

2. Every time we partake of Holy communion, we are proclaiming all that Jesus accomplished through His death, burial, and resurrection for us. T or F

3. Unworthily does not refer to:
   a. Treating the meal as a common meal
   b. Treating the bread and cup as common things
   c. Not apprehending their solemn symbolic importance
   d. An unworthy manner
   e. Being unworthy because of sin in our lives

4. The word examine is referring to the way we partake. We are to approve or examine the way we are partaking, not approve and examine ourselves. T or F

5. When taking communion, if we confess enough sins then we become worthy enough to partake. T or F

CHAPTER 43   THE LORD'S SUPPER

6. According to Colossians 1:12, who qualified you to share in the inheritance of the saints in the kingdom of light?

7. Jesus said that He wanted us to take communion in remembrance of HIM, not in remembrance of our sins.   T   or   F

8. When people partake of communion in an unworthy manner, they are eating and drinking damnation on themselves because they are not discerning the meal correctly.   T   or   F

9. For this cause, many are weak and sickly among you, and many have died prematurely. And the reason is, that they haven't _____ the Lord's body properly.

10. We partake of communion in a worthy manner when we properly discern the Lord's body and the sacredness of the Covenant meal, not by confessing our sins.   T   or   F

11. Surely our _____ he hath borne. Isaiah 53:4 YLT

12. Matthew 8:17 (NASB1995): This was to fulfill what was spoken through Isaiah the prophet: "HE HIMSELF TOOK OUR INFIRMITIES AND CARRIED AWAY OUR _____."

44
Paul's Thorn

Second Corinthians 12:7-10 (KJV): *"And lest I should be exalted above measure through the abundance of the revelations, there was given to me a thorn in the flesh, the messenger of Satan to buffet me, lest I should be exalted above measure. For this thing I besought the Lord thrice, that it might depart from me. And he said unto me, My grace is sufficient for thee: for my strength is made perfect in weakness. Most gladly therefore will I rather glory in my infirmities, that the power of Christ may rest upon me. Therefore I take pleasure in infirmities, in reproaches, in necessities, in persecutions, in distresses for Christ's sake: for when I am weak, then am I strong."*

So, what was Paul's thorn? When it comes to Paul's thorn there are many opinions. Theologians all over the world differ from an earache; headache; grievous bodily torments.[1] One supposes that the view which he had of the glories of heavenly things so affected his nerves as to produce a paralytic disorder, and particularly stammering in his speech, and perhaps also a distortion of the face or countenance.[2] Many Latin fathers said it was lust, another supposes that it was gout on his head,[3] another non-stop temptations, still another chronic maladies (such as ophthalmia, an inflammation of the eyes, malaria, migraine headaches, and epilepsy).[4] One person told me that Paul had an eye disease, and they believe that it happened when Paul was knocked to the ground on the road to Damascus. The problem with this, and all these ideas is that they are not backed by Scripture. The Bible says that God sent Ananias to pray for Paul's eyes and God healed him (Acts 9:10-19) which means he no longer had eye problems.

When we are answering questions like these, we should let Scripture interpret Scripture instead of making up random ideas. The term "thorn" was obviously not talking about a thorn from a thorn bush. If it was, Paul could have easily removed it himself, and without prayer. Therefore, the term "thorn" was clearly symbolic. In the Old Testament, every time the word "thorn" was used symbolically, it referred to a group of people. For example, in Numbers 33:66, the inhabitants of the land were called thorns in their sides. In Joshua 23:13, God said these nations will become thorns in their eyes. And in Judges 2:3, God says that the people of Bochim shall be thorns in their side. Paul, who was an expert in the Law would know these Scriptures and how the term was used. If Paul used it consistently, then he was also referring to a group of people.

Now let's break down 2 Corinthians 12:7-10. Many of the Bible translators took liberty in translating verse 7, *"And lest I should be exalted above measure through the abundance of the revelations, there was given to me a thorn in the flesh, the messenger of Satan to buffet me, lest I should be exalted above measure."* The phrase "exalted above measure" means *to raise over or above*. The NIV says *"to keep me from becoming conceited."* The NAS says *"to keep me from exalting myself."* The AMP says *"to keep me from being puffed up."* All of these are translated from the perspective that, the surpassing great revelations that Paul was receiving from God were causing him to be puffed up and prideful, that Paul was thinking of himself more highly than he ought to, so God had to send him a thorn in his flesh to help him stay humble. Was this the case? Did Paul struggle with pride? Or is there another way to understand these verses that is more consistent with Paul's life and ministry? Proverbs 16:18 says, *"Pride goes before destruction, and a haughty spirit before a fall."* Proverbs 3:34 (NIV) says, *"He mocks proud mockers but shows favor to the humble and oppressed."* James 4:6 says, *"But he gives us more grace. That is why Scripture says: 'God opposes the proud but shows favor to the humble.'"* So, we can see here that pride goes before destruction, God mocks the proud, and He opposes the proud. Do we see that in Paul's life? Do we see God mocking Paul? Do we see God opposing him? I don't think so.

This leads me to my next question. Is all exaltation a result of pride? Is all exaltation self-exaltation? Luke 14:11 says, *"For whoever exalts himself will be humbled, and he who humbles himself will be exalted."* James 4:10 (NASB) says, *"Humble yourselves in the presence of the Lord, and He will exalt you."* 1 Peter 5:6 says, *"Therefore humble yourselves under the mighty hand of God, that He may exalt you in due time."* There is more than one way to be exalted. One way is to exalt yourself, and God will humble you. The other way is to humble yourself, and God will exalt you. Which one of these do you suppose applies to Paul?

We must know and understand where the exalting came from and where the thorn came from. These revelations were not causing Paul to exalt himself, but they were causing exaltation in the eyes of the people just like they did with Moses and Joshua (Joshua 4:14). In fact, people tried to worship Paul and Barnabas in Acts 14. Paul prayed for a crippled man, and he was healed. The people were so excited they said, "the gods have come down in human form" and they wanted to offer sacrifices to Paul and Barnabas. They refused their worship, tore their clothes, and corrected them. So, the exalting came from the people, not from Paul himself.

Where did the thorn come from? It amazes me how people can say that the thorn came from God when it clearly states it was a messenger of Satan. A messenger of Satan means one sent from Satan himself. The wording doesn't say "a messenger from God." The verse clearly outlines that it was a messenger from Satan, and people still interpret that "a messenger from God."

The gospel was becoming so attractive through the life and ministry of Paul that Satan had to do something about it. So, he sent a messenger to buffet him. The word "buffet" means to strike with clenched hands, or to buffet with the fist.[6] Doesn't this sound like the life of Paul? In 2 Timothy 4:14-15 (NIV), Paul warns Timothy saying, *"Alexander the metalworker did me a great deal of harm. The Lord will repay him for what he has done. You too should be on your guard against him, because he strongly opposed our message."*

2 Corinthians 12:9 (KJV) says, *"And he said unto me, My grace is sufficient for thee: for my strength is made perfect in weakness. Most gladly therefore will I rather glory in my infirmities, that the power of Christ may rest upon me."* The words "weakness" and "infirmities" are the same words in Greek.[7] So, this verse could easily be translated *I will glory in my weakness, that the power of Christ may rest upon me.*

What were Paul's weaknesses that he is referring to? Verse 10 of 2 Corinthians 12 says, *"That is why, for Christ's sake, I delight in weaknesses* [same word], *in insults, in hardships, in persecutions, in difficulties. For when I am weak, then I am strong."* Nowhere does it mention sickness. Nowhere does it say eye problems, or any other physical conditions. He had trouble with insults, hardships, persecutions, and difficulties.

Paul expands on this list in 2 Corinthians 11:23-30 (NASB), *"Are they servants of Christ?—I am speaking as if insane—I more so; in far more labors, in far more imprisonments, beaten times without number, often in danger of death. Five times I received from the Jews thirty-nine lashes. Three times I was beaten with rods, once I was stoned, three times I was shipwrecked, a night and a day I have spent adrift at sea. I have been on frequent journeys, in dangers from rivers, dangers from robbers, dangers from my countrymen, dangers from the Gentiles, dangers in the city, dangers in the wilderness, dangers at sea, dangers among false brothers;I have been in labor and hardship, through many sleepless nights, in hunger and thirst, often without food, in cold and exposure. Apart from such external things, there is the daily pressure on me of concern for all the churches. Who is weak without my being weak? Who is led into sin without my intense concern? If I have to boast, I will boast of what pertains to my weakness.*

Again, nowhere does he mention sickness.

The truth is that Paul's ministry was going so well, and he was becoming so exalted in the eyes of the people that Satan took notice and realized he needed to do something to slow down Paul's ministry. Satan sent a demon spirit from himself, under his command, to beat Paul with blow after blow after blow. Satan did not do this all on his own. He influenced other humans, like Alexander, to do his bidding. Satan thought that by persecuting Paul, he would slow down the growth of the Church. Paul prayed three times for this persecution to be removed from him, but God said, "My grace is sufficient for you." We are redeemed from many things, but we are not redeemed from persecution. 2 Timothy 3:12 says that *"everyone who wants to live a godly life in Christ Jesus will be persecuted."* God's answer was, *"My grace is sufficient* [or enough] *for you"* [bracketed words added], meaning that God was giving Paul more grace to deal with the struggle that he was going through. If the reason for Paul's thorn was pride, why was God giving him more grace? The Word says in James 4:6 (NIV), *"God opposes the proud but shows favor to the humble."*

Why am I sharing this? If we believe that God gave Paul an infirmity/sickness to help him remain humble, how could we ever understand the will of God regarding our health? How could we ever pray the prayer of faith that saves the sick? We would think, "Well, I prayed three times as Paul did, and I'm not healed so I guess this disease must be coming from God. It must be my thorn. It must be God's will. It must be God's way of humbling me." That belief completely discredits the integrity of God's nature, character, His Word, and His Will.

Another note, Galatians 4:13 says, *"You know that because of physical infirmity I preached the gospel to you at the first."* When Paul preached the gospel to the Galatians the first time, he did have a physical infirmity or weakness, but it wasn't from God. Look at what happened to Paul on that first missionary trip to Galatia. Acts 14:19 says, *"Then some Jews came from Antioch and Iconium and won the crowd over. They stoned Paul and dragged him outside the city, thinking he was dead."* This was Paul's weakness or infirmity on his first trip. He had been stoned to the point of death. With severe wounds to his head and his body, he still preached the gospel to them, even in this weakened condition. Paul's thorn was persecution from people who opposed his message, people who were sent from Satan to slow down the spreading of the gospel.

CHAPTER 44 PAUL'S THORN

Questions - Paul's Thorn

1. 2 Corinthians 12:7, "And lest I should be _____ above measure through the abundance of the revelations, there was given to me a _____ in the flesh, the messenger of _____ to _____ me, lest I should be exalted above measure.

2. Paul suffered from an eye disease that began when Paul was knocked to the ground on the road to Damascus. T or F

3. In the Old Testament, every time the word "thorn" was used, symbolically it referred to a group of people. T or F

4. If Paul used the term "thorn" consistently then he was also referring to a group of people. T or F

5. There is more than one way to be exalted. One way is to exalt yourself and then God will humble you. The other way is to humble yourself and God will exalt you. Which one of these do you think applies to Paul?
   a. Exalted himself and was humbled
   b. Humbled himself and was exalted

6. The exalting came from the people, not from Paul himself.
   T or F

7. Where did the thorn come from?

8. What were Paul's weaknesses that he gloried in?
   a. Insults
   b. Hardships
   c. Persecutions
   d. Difficulties
   e. Sickness
   f. All of the Above

9. Paul prayed three times for this thorn to be removed from him, but God said, "My grace is sufficient for you" showing that it was God's will for Paul to remain sick.   T or F

10. Paul's thorn was persecution from people who opposed his message, sent from Satan to slow down the spreading of the gospel.
    T or F

45
Blessed or Cursed

Have you ever met someone, and it seemed like they just didn't have a chance to make it in life, that they were destined to fail, that no matter what they did or what good intentions they had, it was somehow going to turn out bad? Did you ever wonder if maybe they were cursed? Have you ever felt like you were cursed? Perhaps with your job, your marriage, your relationships, or maybe life in general. In this lesson, we are going to look at curses.

What is a curse? *Merriam-Webster's Dictionary* says, "a curse is a prayer for harm or injury to come upon someone."[1] We know that people can be cursed, families can be cursed, houses can be cursed, and land can be cursed. But can these curses belong to the children of God? Deuteronomy 30:19 says, *"This day I call heaven and earth as witnesses against you that I have set before you life and death, blessings and curses. Now choose life, so that you and your children may live."* So, when it comes to curses, God says it's our choice.

In the first 14 verses of Deuteronomy 28, God lists the blessings for obedience. Then God shares 53 verses of curses for disobeying the

Law (15-68). These curses did not just affect the one person or the offender. They could impact three to four generations in a family. Exodus 20:3-5 says, *"You shall have no other gods before Me. You shall not make for yourself a carved image—any likeness of anything that is in heaven above, or that is in the earth beneath, or that is in the water under the earth; you shall not bow down to them nor serve them. For I, the Lord your God, am a jealous God, visiting the iniquity of the fathers upon the children to the third and fourth generations of those who hate Me."* This same warning is repeated in Deuteronomy 5:6-10. Idolatry, idol worship, is the entry place for generational curses.

So, who can be cursed? Proverbs 3:33 (NIV) says, *"The Lord's curse is on the house of the wicked, but he blesses the home of the righteous."* 1 Corinthians 16:22 (NIV) says, *"If anyone does not love the Lord, let that person be cursed!"* So, unbelievers are under a curse. And it's possible for a believer who doesn't really love the Lord to be cursed as well. Galatians 1:8 (KJV) says, *"But though we, or an angel from heaven, preach any other gospel unto you than that which we have preached unto you, let him be accursed."* This can include someone who teaches false doctrines or someone who practices the occult and witchcraft. But in context, this is referring to someone who preaches that you have to obey the Law and get circumcised in order to be saved. Galatians 3:10 says, *"For all who rely on the works of the law are under a curse, as it is written: "Cursed is everyone who does not continue to do everything written in the Book of the Law."* Anyone who relies on their own obedience to the Law for their salvation is under a curse.

What is the cause of curses coming on Christians? Like we just saw, they may not love the Lord. They may be preaching another gospel (like the Law). They may be relying on their own obedience to save themselves. They could even be cursing themselves with their own words. Proverbs 18:21, *"Death and life are in the power of the tongue, and those who love it will eat its fruit."*

Ignorance might be the biggest reason for curses plaguing Christians.

The Bible says in Hosea 4:6, *"My people are destroyed for lack of knowledge."* And Psalm 107:2 (KJV) says, *"Let the redeemed of the LORD say so, whom he hath redeemed from the hand of the enemy."* I believe that many Christians do not know what they have been redeemed from. Therefore, they can't say it. They can't declare it or proclaim it because they do not know. God says here; we should say we are redeemed from the hand of the enemy. But what are we redeemed from?

First, we are redeemed from the curse of the Law. Galatians 3:13-14 says, *"Christ has redeemed us from the curse of the law, having become a curse for us (for it is written, "Cursed is everyone who hangs on a tree"), that the blessing of Abraham might come upon the Gentiles in Christ Jesus, that we might receive the promise of the Spirit through faith."* If we are in Christ, we are not under the curse anymore; we are under His blessing! We are redeemed from all of the 53 curses listed in Deuteronomy 28 because Jesus became cursed in our place. We need to declare it and say so!

Second, we are redeemed from generational curses. Years ago, a member of my church called me on the phone and was extremely excited to share a new revelation with me. She started talking to me about sour grapes and generational curses. I had no idea what she was talking about, but it sounded good. She had been watching Joseph Prince on TV, and it really blessed her. Sometime later, I was alone, walking through my house, praying in the Spirit. While I was in my son's room, I heard the Lord say to me, "sour grapes." I thought this was odd. I didn't know what God was trying to tell me, but I did remember that phone conversation. I went to my computer and opened my Bible program and did a search on sour grapes. I found Scriptures in Ezekiel and Jeremiah prophesying about a day coming when we would no longer be judged for the sins of our fathers.

Ezekiel 18:2-4 says, *"What do you people mean by quoting this proverb about the land of Israel: 'The fathers eat sour grapes, and the children's teeth are set on edge'? As surely as I live, declares the Sovereign LORD, you will no longer quote this proverb in Israel. For everyone belongs to me, the parent as well as the child—both alike belong to me. The one who sins is the one who will die."* And Jeremiah 31:29-30 says, *"In those days people will no longer say, 'The parents have eaten sour grapes, and the children's teeth are set on edge.' Instead, everyone will die for their own sin; whoever eats sour grapes— their own teeth will be set on edge."* These Scriptures declare that a day is coming when we will reap what we sow and not reap what our father, our grandfather, mother, etc. sowed. Each person will be judged according to what he has done. These verses excited me because I sometimes wondered if I would be judged due to generational sins, or if my children would be judged by mine. I had read the verses in the Old Testament that said our sins would be punished to the third and fourth generation (Exodus 34:7, Numbers 14:18). So, I was not sure if we were redeemed from them or not.

Has that day come? John 19:28-30 says, *"After this, Jesus, knowing that all things were now accomplished, that the Scripture might be fulfilled, said, 'I thirst!' Now a vessel full of sour wine was sitting there; and they filled a sponge with sour wine, put it on hyssop, and put it to His mouth. So when Jesus had received the sour wine, He said, 'It is finished!' And bowing His head, He gave up His spirit."* It says here, *"that the Scripture might be fulfilled."* What Scripture(s) do you think this is referring to? I believe this is talking about Ezekiel's prophecy and Jeremiah's prophecy about a day coming when generational curses would be no more. A day when each man would be judged according to his own sin and not the sins of his ancestors. Jesus drank sour grapes so that we could be redeemed from generational curses. He became cursed so that we can be blessed. You see, in the Old Covenant, we were blessed or cursed based on what we did or what our families did. In the New Covenant, we are blessed based on what Jesus has done on our behalf. Praise God, we are redeemed from all curses, and we need to say so.

Questions - Blessed or Cursed

1. When it comes to blessings and curses, God said we can choose. T or F

2. Idol worship is the entry place for generational curses. T or F

3. Who can be cursed?
   a. Those who worship idols (to the 3rd-4th generation)
   b. Those who do not love the Lord
   c. Those who preach another gospel (like the Law)
   d. Those who rely on their obedience to save them
   e. Those who curse themselves with their words
   f. All of the above

4. Proverbs 18:21, "Death and life are in the power of the _____, And those who love it will eat its fruit.

5. Hosea 4:6: That my people are destroyed from or because of lack of _____.

6. Psalm 107:2 (KJV) says, Let the redeemed of the LORD say _____, whom he hath redeemed from the hand of the enemy.

7. Many Christians do not know what they have been redeemed from. Therefore, they can't say it. T or F

8. Christ redeemed us from the curse of the Law by becoming a _____ for us (Gal 3:13).

9. All of the curses listed in Deuteronomy 28:15-68, we are _____ from, because Jesus became cursed in our place.

10. We need to confess with our mouth what we are redeemed from. T or F

11. Jesus fulfilled Scripture(s) when He asked for a drink on the Cross. T or F

12. Jesus drank sour _____ not so much because He was thirsty, but because He wanted to fulfill Scripture(s), and He wanted to redeem humanity from generational curses.

46

God Wants You Blessed

Jesus talked a lot about money. Sixteen of the thirty-eight parables addressed how to handle money and possessions. In the Gospels alone, an amazing one out of every ten verses (288 in all) deals directly with the subject of money. Jesus talked more about money than he did Heaven and Hell combined. The Bible offers 500 verses on prayer, less than 500 verses on faith, but more than 2,000 verses on money and possessions.[1] So we can see that this is important to God, and therefore it is essential to talk about it.

The first thing I want to show you is that God wants you blessed financially, and in every other way as well. Proverbs 10:22 says, *"The blessing of the Lord makes one rich, and He adds no sorrow with it."* 3 John 2 (KJV) says, *"Beloved, I wish above all things that thou mayest prosper and be in health, even as thy soul prospereth."* Psalm 35:27 says, *"… And let them say continually, 'Let the LORD be magnified, Who has pleasure in the prosperity of His servant."* In Deuteronomy 28:1-14, God gives a list of blessings for obedience. These blessings are for our families, our finances, and our health. So, we can see that God wants us blessed financially and in every other way as well. But we also have our part to play in this. Just because something is God's will, does not mean it automatically happens no matter what we do or how we live. In the first verse, the blessing of the Lord had something to do with our prosperity. In the second verse, our soul prosperity had something to do with our prosperity. In the third, our confession had something to do with it. In Deuteronomy 28, our obedience had something to do with our prosperity. And there are other factors as well.

Proverbs 6:9-11, *"How long will you slumber, O sluggard? When will you rise from your sleep? A little sleep, a little slumber, A little folding of the hands to sleep—So shall your poverty come on you like a prowler, And your need like an armed man."* Proverbs 14:23 says, *"Prosperity comes from hard work, but talking too much leads to great scarcity."* 2 Thessalonians 3:10 says, *"… If anyone will not work, neither shall he eat."* You can't ignore these verses and expect the first set of scriptural truths we looked at to put you over the top. They are all equally true! You can't be lazy and not work and expect God to bless you with a boatload of money. God has laws of prosperity set in place. There are things we need to do in order to cooperate with this blessing. I am not talking about works. We can't earn the blessings of the Lord. But there are things that we can do to position ourselves to receive His blessings. The same God that wants us to prosper, wants us to work hard, wants us not to be lazy also wants us to tithe.

Tithing is another factor in our prosperity. Malachi 3:7-10, *"Yet from the days of your fathers you have gone away from My ordinances and have not kept them. Return to Me, and I will return to you," says the Lord of hosts. "But you said, 'In what way shall we return?' "Will a man rob God? Yet you have robbed Me! But you say, 'In what way have we robbed You?' In tithes and offerings. You are cursed with a curse, for you have robbed Me, even this whole nation."* Verse 7 says that the people have gone away from His ordinances. What ordinances had they gone away from? Tithes and offerings. An "ordinance" is an authoritative decree or direction, an order, a law set forth by a governmental authority, something ordained or decreed by fate or a deity.[2] So tithing is an order, it's a Law, it's an ordained decree by God. God wants us to give a tithe (tenth) of our increase to our home church or local storehouse.

Every time we give our tithe, our heart will be tested. Do we really trust God? Is His word true? Is God really going to provide for our family? Will our 90% left over be enough? The unique and beautiful thing about tithing is that it is a two-way test. This is the only place in Scripture where God says we can test Him. Verse 10 says, *"Bring all the tithes into the storehouse, that there may be food in My house, and try Me now in this,"* says the Lord of hosts, *"If I will not open for you the windows of heaven and pour out for you such blessing that there will not be room enough to receive it."* Tithing is a test of our hearts, and through our tithes and offerings, we are invited to put God to the test to see what He will do in our lives.

The number one excuse I hear people use for not tithing is that it's an Old Testament commandment. Or that it was part of the Law, and since we are not under the Law, we do not have to tithe. Let's see what the Bible says.

The first time we see the word "tithe" is in Genesis 14:18-20. This is right after Abram returned from rescuing Lot and some other family members from captivity. Abram meets Melchizedek (who is either a type and shadow of Christ or is Christ himself), Melchizedek blesses Abram, and then Abram gave him a tenth of everything they recovered in the battle. In this text, we see Jesus, we see the tithe, and we see something else. Genesis 14:18 (ESV), *"And Melchizedek king of Salem brought out bread and wine. (He was priest of God Most High.)"* Bread and wine are a type of our communion. Communion is a holy sign and seal of our Covenant of grace. So, in these verses, we see them all connect. We see Jesus, we see tithing, and we see Covenant. Now an important thing to understand is that this happened 500 years before the Law was given. So, tithing predated the Law, and Jesus is now our High Priest in the order of Melchizedek. Melchizedek received tithes from Abram, and Jesus now receives tithes from us. Hebrews 7:8 says, *"Here mortal men receive tithes, but there he receives them, of whom it is witnessed that he lives."* Jesus Christ receives our tithes.

Another excuse I often hear is that there is not a verse in the New Testament that tells us to tithe. That is not true. There is, for sure, no verse telling us not to tithe. Matthew 23:23 (NIV) says, *"Woe to you, teachers of the law and Pharisees, you hypocrites! You give a tenth of your spices—mint, dill, and cumin. But you have neglected the more important matters of the law—justice, mercy, and faithfulness. You should have practiced the latter, without neglecting the former."* What did Jesus say to practice and not neglect? Justice, mercy, faithfulness, and tithing. This verse is in the New Testament. Jesus wants us to tithe.

Another excuse I often hear from people about not tithing is that they can't afford it. My reply is, "I can't afford **not** to tithe." Malachi 3:8-9 says, *"Will a man rob God? Yet you have robbed Me! But you say, 'In what way have we robbed You?' In tithes and offerings. You are cursed with a curse, for you have robbed Me, even this whole nation."* If we do not tithe, we fall under a curse. When we do tithe, we stay under the umbrella of His blessings. Which one do we want to be under? Notice what God said He would do if we tithe, *"I will open for you the windows of heaven and pour out for you such blessing that there will not be room enough to receive it."* When we tithe, we position ourselves to receive His blessing. God said to bring all of the tithes into the storehouse—that is the local church—that there may be food in my house. God is saying here that if we take care of His house, He will take care of our house. God did not create tithing for His sake; He created it for our sake.

So, does God want us blessed? Yes! Is it God's will for us to be blessed? Absolutely! But there are things we need to do to cooperate with the blessing. There are factors involved like soul prosperity, our confession, our obedience, hard work vs. laziness, and tithing. When we do things God's way, we will be blessed and see increase from the Lord in our lives.

CHAPTER 46   GOD WANTS YOU BLESSED

Questions - God Wants You Blessed

1. Jesus talked a lot about _____ .

2. Who has pleasure in the prosperity of His servants?

3. There are factors involved in our prosperity like, soul prosperity, our confession, our obedience, hard work vs. laziness, and _____ .

4. What ordinances in Malachi 3:7-10 had they gone away from?

5. An ordinance is:
   a. An authoritative decree or direction
   b. An order
   c. A law set forth by a governmental authority
   d. Something ordained or decreed by fate or a deity
   e. All of the above

6. Tithing is an order, it's a Law, it's an ordained decree by God.
   T   or   F

7. God wants us to give a tithe (tenth) of our increase to our home church or local storehouse.   T   or   F

8. Tithing is a test of our _____ .

9. We are invited to put God to the test with our tithes and offerings and see what He will do in our lives. T or F

10. Tithing is just an Old Testament commandment. T or F

11. Tithing predated the Law. T or F

12. Melchizedek received tithes from Abram and now _____ receives tithes from us.

13. There is not a verse in the New Testament that tells us to tithe.
    T or F

14. If we tithe, God promised that He would open the windows of heaven and pour out such blessing that there will not be room enough to receive it. T or F

15. When we do things God's way we will be blessed. T or F

47

When Prayers Seem Unanswered

A significant component of faith is knowing that God hears us when we pray. 1 John 5:14-15 says, *"Now this is the confidence that we have in Him, that if we ask anything according to His will, He hears us. 15 And if we know that He hears us, whatever we ask, we know that we have the petitions that we have asked of Him."* These verses promise that if we pray anything according to His will, He hears us, and if we know that He hears us, the answer is always yes. 2 Corinthians 1:20 (NIV) says, *"For no matter how many promises God has made, they are 'Yes' in Christ. And so through Him, the 'Amen' is spoken by us to the glory of God."* If the answer is always yes, why do our prayer requests sometimes seem unanswered? Have you ever felt that way? I know I have.

Daniel 9:21-23 (NIV) says, ... *"while I was still in prayer, Gabriel, the man I had seen in the earlier vision, came to me in swift flight about the time of the evening sacrifice [3 pm[1]]. He instructed me and said to me, 'Daniel, I have now come to give you insight and understanding. As soon as you began to pray, a word went out, which I have come to tell you, for you are highly esteemed. Therefore, consider the message and understand the vision ..."*

Then in Daniel 10:10-13 (NIV), *"A hand touched me and set me trembling on my hands and knees. He said, 'Daniel, you who are highly esteemed, consider carefully the words I am about to speak to you, and stand up, for I have now been sent to you.' And when he said this to me, I stood up trembling. Then he continued, 'Do not be afraid, Daniel. Since the first day that you set your mind to gain understanding and to humble yourself before your God, your words were heard, and I have come in response to them. But the prince of the Persian kingdom resisted me twenty-one days. Then Michael, one of the chief princes, came to help me, because I was detained there with the king of Persia.'"*

The first time, as soon as Daniel began to pray, the answer immediately came while he was still praying. It took only a few minutes or seconds. The second time, his words were heard the first day, but the answer was delayed 21 days. Both times the angel called him "highly esteemed," which is translated, *greatly beloved* in the KJV. But the first time, the delay was noticeably short, and the second time his prayer request took 21 days. The same person prayed. God heard and responded both times as soon as He heard. Gabriel was sent with the answer both times. What was the difference? We know that a spiritual battle took place in the heavenlies in the second story, but why was there no apparent spiritual battle the first time? The answer to that question is unclear. However, we do know that both times, God heard and responded immediately. Both times God called Daniel *highly esteemed*, and *greatly beloved*. The delay does not mean a lack of love or care toward us on God's part. It might just mean that there is a war in the heavenlies over the answer.

Galatians 6:9 says, *"And let us not grow weary while doing good, for in due season we shall reap if we do not lose heart."* This means if we don't lose heart or quit, we will reap a harvest. This is why we must pray and believe and not give up. Matthew 7:7-8 also says, *"Ask, and it will be given to you; seek, and you will find; knock, and it will be opened to you. For everyone who asks receives, and he who seeks finds, and to him who knocks it will be opened."* Sometimes we need to keep knocking until that door is open for us. Just like the story in Luke 11:5-8, *"And He said to them, 'Which of you shall have a friend, and go to him at midnight and say to him, "Friend, lend me three loaves; for a friend of mine has come to me on his journey, and I have nothing to set before him"; and he will answer from within and say, "Do not trouble me; the door is now shut, and my children are with me in bed; I cannot rise and give to you"? I say to you, though he will not rise and give to him because he is his friend, yet because of his persistence he will rise and give him as many as he needs.'"*

Perseverance is essential in prayer when we experience delays in our answers. But know this, just because we don't see the desired result in prayer right away does not mean that the answer is no, and it does not mean we should quit, for we shall reap a harvest if we do not lose heart or give up.

In 2005, we were living in Roanoke, Virginia. We had one vehicle, and every time I went to work, my wife and kids were left at home without transportation. I started noticing a variety of cars for sale and was comtemplating getting a small loan. One morning, as soon as I woke up, God said to me, "Won't you let me give you a car?" I was stunned. I said, "God, You want to give me a car?" And He responded, "Of course." He then told me to write down the type of car that I wanted and to be specific. I immediately thought about the car my parents had when I grew up, a tan Honda Accord. I learned to drive in that car and had lots of fun memories of it. So I wrote that down; a tan Honda Accord, with power windows, AC, and a stereo. Then I said to the Lord, "What do I do now?" and He said, "Thank me for your car." Thanking God for a car that I did not have and that I could not see felt very strange. At first, it felt empty or shallow, but I continued to thank God multiple times a day. After about a week of thanking God for my car, it started to feel real. It began to feel like the car belonged to me. It went past obedient lip service and into heart faith.

Ten days later, we went out to eat after church at a local restaurant.

As we entered, just inside the door were some friends from another church in town. The couple asked us if we needed a car. Holly and I both looked at each other, smiled, and answered, "Yes, we do." After lunch, we drove over and picked up the car. It was a tan, 1988 Honda Accord with everything I had asked for. Praise the Lord! The next day, the couple added to the blessing by changing the oil and putting four new tires on it. On top of that, later that evening, they called to check on how the car was working. He also asked me about the stereo and speakers. He said, "If I remember right, the back speakers in that car are blown." Then he added, "I actually bought new speakers for that car, but I didn't have time to install them. Would you like them?" With great excitement, I quickly replied, "Yes!" The next day, I drove to his house to pick up the speakers. They were an expensive brand, still new in the box with the receipt attached. I noticed the receipt showed the speakers were purchased on my birthday almost a year before I had even asked God for the car. What an over-the-top answer to my prayer for a car.

We don't usually know how God is going to do things, but if we stand firm and do not quit, God will honor our faith, and we will reap a harvest. Delays happen when we pray, but that doesn't mean that the answer is no. That is why we are instructed in Hebrews 10:23 to *"... hold fast the confession of our hope* (faith) *without wavering, for He who promised is faithful."* We are not told to confess anything about the delay, but we are to confess the reason for the hope that we have. The reason for our hope is that the One who promised us is faithful, and He will not change His mind. He will watch over His Word to carry it out until completion.

CHAPTER 47 — WHEN PRAYERS SEEM UNANSWERED

Questions - When our Prayers Seem Unanswered

1. 1 John 5:14-15 promises that if we pray anything according to God's will, that He hears us, and if we know that He hears us, the answer is always _____.

2. For no matter how many promises God has made, the answer is "Yes" in Christ. And through Christ, the "Amen" is spoken by _____ to the glory of God (2 Corinthians 1:20).

3. In Daniel chapter 9, how long did it take God to give an answer to Daniel's prayer?

4. In Daniel chapter 10, how long did it take God to give an answer to his prayer?

5. How long did it take Gabriel to get the answer to Daniel each time?

6. Galatians 6:9 says, "And let us not grow weary while doing good, for in due season we shall reap if we do not lose _____."

7. Matthew 7:7-8 says, "_____, and it will be given to you; _____, and you will find; _____, and it will be opened to you. For everyone who asks _____, and he who seeks _____, and to him who knocks it will be _____."

8. _____ is key in prayer when we experience delays in our answers. (Luke 11:5-8)

9. We don't usually know how God is going to answer our prayers but if we don't cave in or quit, God will honor our faith and we will reap a harvest.   T or F

10. Hebrews 10:23 says, to hold fast the confession of our hope (faith) without wavering, for He who promised is _____.

48
Self-Centeredness

While training fighter pilots, the captain said to his men, "Suppose you were to take off from an airport at the equator with the intention of circumnavigating the globe, but your course was off by just one degree. By the time you returned to the same longitude, how far off course would you be?" The men answered, "Just a few miles. A hundred miles." But they were way off. "An error of only one degree would put you almost 500 miles off course, or one hour of flight time for a jet."[1]

Sometimes in life, our focus, our direction, our aim can be off by just a small margin, but the effects can be huge. When I was young, we were living in Nova Scotia, Canada. One night, my dad stayed up late to watch the end of a hockey game. When the game was over, he was trying to get upstairs and into bed without waking anyone up. He turned off the lights and made his way upstairs. As he got closer to his room, he stretched out his arms to feel for the door. To his shock and surprise, the door went right between his arms and smashed him in the nose. He yelled out in pain and woke Mom up. His nose was bleeding. He was heading in the right direction, but he was off by just a little bit, and the result was very painful.

In life, we can get so busy doing good things, doing the right thing, doing things well, that we lose focus on what is going on around us. We can get so caught up in our own lives and our to-do lists that we do not see what is happening right in front of us. If I were to ask you today, what is the biggest problem that you are facing, most of us would not say our focus. We would probably say, my job, my boss, my co-worker, my neighbor, my spouse, my friend, my teacher, my finances, etc. But our focus can be a significant problem in our lives today. Let me show you an example.

Mark 9:33-34 (NIV) says, *"They came to Capernaum. When he was in the house, he asked them, 'What were you arguing about on the road?' But they kept quiet because on the way they had argued about who was the greatest."* Just imagine this argument. Most likely, the brothers would have gone first. I can imagine Peter and Andrew arguing over who is the greatest. James and John were arguing over the same thing. Others might overhear and chime in saying they were the greatest. What do you suppose was the measuring stick that they were using when they were judging who was the greatest? I am guessing that it was not based on their fishing stories. I would guess they were more likely comparing miracle stories. The disciples were doing the right things. They were spending time with Jesus. They were doing the works of the kingdom. But the focus was on themselves.

James 4:1-3 (NIV) says, *"What causes fights and quarrels among you? Don't they come from your desires that battle within you? You desire but do not have, so you kill. You covet but you cannot get what you want, so you quarrel and fight. You do not have because you do not ask God. When you ask, you do not receive, because you ask with wrong motives, that you may spend what you get on your pleasures."* The Word of God says here that fights and quarrels come from our desires that battle within us. When we don't get what we want, we quarrel. People covet and even kill others over not getting what they want. Verse 3 says that we may spend what we

CHAPTER 48 — SELF-CENTEREDNESS

get on ourselves and our pleasures. Therefore, the root of fighting, quarreling, and arguing is self-centeredness.

Proverbs 13:10 (KJV) says, *"Only by pride cometh contention: but with the well-advised is wisdom."* The heart behind the fight the disciples were having over who was the greatest was self-centeredness and pride. Self-centeredness is the source of much of the pain we experience today. Some might think that pride cannot be the only source of contention or strife. But the Scripture says that only by pride comes contention. It's not one of the leading causes of contention; it's the only cause. Some might disagree with this and think, "I've got many problems in my life, but pride isn't one of them." They may agree that they struggle with low self-esteem but think there is no way that they struggle with pride. Well, we may need to redefine what pride really is.

When we think of pride or arrogance, we may think of an athlete or an actor or even somebody else that we know. But pride isn't just thinking you're better than somebody else. Pride is seeing yourself as the center of everything. Self-centeredness is really the root of all pride. I remember in 10th grade, a senior player on the basketball team told me that I was the most insecure person he had ever met. Someone also told me once that I was arrogant. I agree that I was very insecure, but I never considered myself arrogant. Andrew Wommack said, "Pride isn't just thinking you are better than everybody else—it's self-centeredness. It's like having a stick with arrogance on one side and low self-esteem on the other side. Those are opposite expressions of the same thing, but they are both on the same stick. It's self-centeredness. A timid, shy person is very proud and self-centered, thinking only about themselves."[2]

Romans 12:3 says, *"For I say, through the grace given unto me, to every man that is among you, not to think of himself more highly than he ought to think; but to think soberly, according as God hath dealt to every man the measure of faith."* Looking back, I don't feel I thought of myself more highly than others in many circumstances, but I actually saw myself as inferior to others and struggled with low self esteem. The real problem here is not seeing ourselves as more highly or lowly, but more often than we ought to. When we think about ourselves too much, then we are self-centered. It is possible to spend so much time looking at ourselves that we do not take the time to notice others. Our focus is off.

What is the cure for self-centeredness and pride? In Mark 9:35, Jesus said to the disciples, *"If anyone desires to be first, he shall be last of all and servant of all."* Jesus basically said to them, so, you want to be the greatest? You want to be the best? Then become a servant. Deny yourself, take up your cross, and follow my example of being a servant. *"For even the Son of Man did not come to be served, but to serve, and to give his life a ransom for many."* (Mark 10:45). Think about this for a minute, the Creator of the universe, whom the whole world should revolve around did not come to be served, but to serve us. If Jesus, who was God in the flesh, could humble Himself and value the good of others above His own welfare, then we should certainly be able to do the same. It can happen when we die to self and live unto God. I guess this all boils down to the golden rule. Matthew 7:12 (NIV) says, *"So in everything, do to others what you would have them do to you, for this sums up the Law and the Prophets."*

The remedy for self-centeredness and pride is to be God-centered and others-centered, to become a servant and to treat others the way we would like to be treated. For some of us, we may need to get our focus back on track. We may need to make a course correction.

CHAPTER 48 — SELF-CENTEREDNESS

Questions - Self-Centeredness

1. Our focus can be a significant problem in our lives. T or F

2. What were the disciples arguing about on the road?
   a. How to get to Capernaum
   b. Who was the greatest?
   c. Who caught the biggest fish?
   d. Who forgot the food?

3. What causes fights and quarrels among you?

4. According to Proverbs 13:10, what is the only thing that causes contention?

5. Pride isn't just thinking you're _____ than somebody else. Pride is seeing yourself as the _____ of everything. A timid and shy person can be just as _____ as someone who is loud and arrogant because they are totally _____ on themselves.

6. Pride is like a stick with "Arrogance" on one side and "Low Self-Esteem" on the other side. They are opposite expressions of the same thing, but they're both pride. T or F

7. Humility is not thinking less of yourself; it is thinking of yourself less. T or F

8. According to Mark 9:35, if someone wants to be first, they must become what?

9. According to Matthew 7:12, what is the cure for self-centeredness?
   a. To be God-centered
   b. To be others-centered
   c. To treat others the way we want to be treated
   d. All of the Above

49
Marriage

In the beginning, God created the heavens and the earth. Everything He created, He said was very good. The only thing that God said was not good was for man to be alone. Genesis 2:21-24 says, *"And the LORD God caused a deep sleep to fall on Adam, and he slept; and He took one of his ribs and closed up the flesh in its place. Then the rib which the LORD God had taken from man He made into a woman, and He brought her to the man. And Adam said: 'This is now bone of my bones and flesh of my flesh; she shall be called Woman, because she was taken out of Man.' Therefore, a man shall leave his father and mother and be joined to his wife, and they shall become one flesh."*

There are a lot of things we can learn from these Scriptures. First, it was not good for Adam to be alone, so God made a suitable helper just for him. The two became husband and wife, and they became one flesh. Secondly, it was God's original intention that one man should marry one woman. It was not for men to have multiple wives or for women to have multiple husbands. Nor was it God's intention to have same-sex marriages. I know that many characters in the Old Testament had more than one wife. But that does not mean it was

God's idea. In the New Testament, God tells us through the apostle Paul that elders and deacons should be the husband of one wife, revealing the heart of God for marriage.

The Bible says that marriage is a joining together, and it is where two become one flesh. But it is more than that. Malachi 2:14 (ESV) says, *"... the LORD was witness between you and the wife of your youth, to whom you have been faithless, though she is your companion and your wife by covenant."* The Lord witnessed a Covenant oath that the husband and wife made to each other in their youth. A new word is introduced here in connection to marriage, the word "Covenant." The word *covenant* means "alliance, pledge, treaty, constitution, ordinance, and agreement."[4] When a couple is joined together in marriage, they make a solemn oath before God and their wedding guests. They pledge to forsake everyone else and declare that they will be faithful to each other. A Covenant is formed that God does not want broken. Jesus said in Matthew 19:6, *"... Therefore what God has joined together, let not man separate."* This is a commitment for life, till death do they part. It should never be taken lightly, but with a sincere heart. Hebrews 13:4 says, *"Marriage is honorable among all, and the bed undefiled; but fornicators and adulterers God will judge."*

In Ephesians 5, the husband is called to love his wife, even as Christ loved the Church. How did Christ love the Church? He gave Himself for her. He laid down His life for the benefit of His Bride. He did not put His own interests first, but the best interests of His wife. He surrendered everything to serve His Bride. He fully committed Himself to her. The Covenant of marriage is intended to represent the relationship Christ has with His Church, His bride. His Covenant with us is never ending, never failing. He desires the same for marriage. This requires laying down our lives to serve the other, putting their needs ahead of our own. We must love like Christ loves the Church.

If you love and serve your spouse well, your marriage will go well. Take the time to find out what your spouse likes and serve them, honor them, care for them, even when you don't feel like it. It is always good to do what is right, even when your feelings do not align. Feelings are fickle, and they change like the wind. Love is a choice, and love is a Covenant.

God desires healthy marriages and healthy families. However, I do want to highlight that if you find yourself in a marriage relationship that is unhealthy or unsafe for you and/or your children, you may need to separate. God has graciously made provision for divorce in His Word if the partner has broken the marriage Covenant to honor and keep you, which means, to honor and protect you. Sexual immorality and abusive situations are unhealthy and can be biblical grounds for divorce. The desire of God's heart for marriage is that it lasts forever because it represents the Covenant He made with us. But that is not always possible if our partner has broken their vows.

Questions - Marriage

1. It is not good for man to be _____.

2. In a marriage, the two of you become one _____.

3. God's desire for marriage is between one man and one woman. T or F

4. Jesus said in Matthew 19:6, "Therefore, what God has joined together, let not _____ separate."

5. The husband is called to love his wife, even as Christ loved the Church. T or F

6. There is not true love without _____.

7. The Covenant of marriage is intended to represent the relationship _____ has with His _____.

8. The marriage Covenant is to honor and keep, which means, to honor and _____ you.

9. Sexual immorality and abusive situations are unhealthy and can be biblical grounds for divorce. T or F

50
Charismatic Church History

Jesus died and rose again at approximately 30 A.D.; 50 days later, Pentecost happened, and the New Testament Church was born. Around 35 to 37 years following that, Peter and Paul were both martyred. The temple in Jerusalem was destroyed in 70 A.D. Roughly 100 A.D., the Apostle John died.[1] It is believed that John was the only disciple who was not martyred.[2] But what happened after John? Did the gifts of the Holy Spirit end with the passing of the disciples? Did healing and miracles end with them, as many teach today?

This teaching is called "Cessationism." Cessationism is the doctrine teaching that prophetic and miraculous gifts (healing, tongues, prophecy, etc.) passed away with the Apostolic Age. But what actually passed away and when, is debated among various religious circles. This widespread theology of Cessationism has no historical or Biblical evidence. It is a man-made doctrine. In this lesson, we will look at Scriptures and history to see what they have to say about the gifts of the Holy Spirit.

Cessationists have one Scripture for the belief that spiritual gifts ceased when the apostles died and that Scripture has been misapplied.

1 Corinthians 13:8-12 says, *"Love never fails. But whether there are prophecies, they will fail; whether there are tongues, they will cease; whether there is knowledge, it will vanish away. For we know in part and we prophesy in part. 10 But when that which is perfect has come, then that which is in part will be done away. When I was a child, I spoke as a child, I understood as a child, I thought as a child; but when I became a man, I put away childish things. For now we see in a mirror, dimly, but then face to face. Now I know in part, but then I shall know just as I also am known."*

To some Cessationists, the "perfect" that was to come (vs 10) referred to the canonization of scriptures (combining written books into the Bible), which happened in 367 A.D.[3] There is a difference of opinion among the Cessationists. Some say everything ceased when the last Apostle died—John, 100 A.D. Others say it ceased when the last disciple died—believed to be Justin Martyr, who many believe was a disciple of the Apostle John. Justin Martyr was martyred around 165 A.D.[4] Then others believe it ceased in 367 A.D. with the canonization of Scripture. But if you take this logic from the latter group, that means prophecy, tongues, and other gifts ended at 367 A.D., knowledge vanished away in 367 A.D. (vs. 8), full knowledge came in 367 A.D., and now we know fully as we are fully known, since 367 A.D. It would seem more logical that the "perfect" that was to come in verse 10 is referring to Jesus and His second coming and not to the canonization of Scripture.

What about the other Cessationist claims? Did the gifts cease with the last Apostle or disciple? In 1918, B. B. Warfield, a professor of theology at Princeton Seminary in his book, *Counterfeit Miracles*, declared that, "the Lord had not performed a single miracle on earth since the death of the original twelve apostles and those directly associated with them."[5] Let's look together at Church history to see if such a bold claim is valid.

Hermas (150 A.D.) from The Shepherd of Hermas claimed that if a Christian was aware of great mental, physical, or spiritual desperation of a man and did not help, it was a dark sin. Healing was seen as evidence that the Holy Spirit was indwelling and at work in believers. "Since both bodily and mental illness were a sign of domination by some evil entity, the power to heal disease was prime evidence that the opposite spirit—the Spirit of God—was operating in the healer."[6]

Justin Martyr (165 A.D.) wrote to the Roman emperor telling of countless demonized people in the city, and worldwide, that could not be helped by religious incantations or medicine. He shared how many Christians were performing exorcisms in the name of Jesus Christ, seeing those people healed and being set free from demonic oppression.[7]

Tertullian (225 A.D.) was known as the "Father of Latin Theology." In *A Treatise on the Soul*, Tertullian discusses acknowledging and attaining prophetic gifting. He shares about a lady in his church who had revelatory gifts, angelic visitations, and even visitations from the Lord Jesus himself. The lady's prophetic gifting allowed her to know things from people's hearts, allowing her to speak to some of their most hidden needs, which at times included healing.[8] Tertullian also testified to God recalling "men's souls to their bodies," with resurrection life![9]

Origen (254 A.D.) was known as the Church's first systematic theologian. His father was martyred for his faith when Origen was only 16 years of age.[10] Origen continued to live the Christian faith and wrote about believers performing cures and expelling evil spirits. He even attested to some illnesses being cured through baptism. These miraculous events, in turn, caused many to put their faith in Christ and commit to the work of the Church.[11]

Gregory of Nazianzus (396 A.D.) witnessed his sister's healing from a horrible disease that caused her to battle high fevers and comatose-type experiences. Doctors were not able to help her symptoms. She received healing as she partook of the Eucharist bread, the "bread of the Presence" at a church service. She took the bread and rubbed it all over her body. Gregory's father, a bishop, was also healed as he celebrated Mass, and his mother was healed through a spiritual dream.[12]

In the western part of the Roman Empire, four men were recognized as doctors of the Church. These men were Ambrose (397 AD), Jerome (420 AD), Augustine (430 AD), and Gregory the Great (560 AD). All of them wrote about miracles. Four historians in the first 600 years of Christianity also recorded testimonials of miracles. One account states how the king of Persia was plagued with headaches, which he asked the Magi to heal. With no relief from their efforts, the bishop of Mesopotamia, Maruthas, was invited. The king of Persia received healing through his prayers. As a result, the king granted permission for Maruthas to establish churches wherever he wished in Persia.[13]

Gregory the Great (560 A.D.) journaled his knowledge of many accounts of miracles, including people being raised from the dead. Gregory recorded the miraculous testimony of Bishop Boniface, whose garden was invaded by caterpillars. Boniface spoke to the caterpillars, telling them to leave the garden and to stop eating his vegetables. The insects obeyed his prayer of command; every single one disappeared from his garden space. Gregory also recorded the testimony of a young boy who fell into a river as he was drawing water. He was swept away by the strong current. The local monastery leader, Benedict, through a word of knowledge, became aware of the situation. Benedict sent Brother Maurus, the Monk, to rush to the river to rescue the boy. Maurus saw the boy being swept downstream. Running to him, he continued supernaturally, without realization, out on the water until he reached the child. Maurus laid hold of the boy's hair and dragged him safely to the riverbank.[14]

Bernard of Clairvaux (1153 AD) was recognized throughout history for the numerous miracles seen in his ministry. People would bring their sick to him, and even the lame were healed! People were set free from various sicknesses and diseases as a result of Bernard's prayers. A deaf-mute child was able to hear and speak instantly! A Monk reported that a young boy, blind from birth, received sight after receiving prayer from Bernard. As the child's eyes opened, the boy shouted, "I see day, I see everybody, I see people with hair." Clapping his hands in delight, he exclaimed, "My God, now I will no more dash my feet against the stones."[15]

St. Francis of Assisi (1226 A.D.) and his monastery were said to be endowed with incredible spiritual power. It was recorded that it was perhaps the most charismatic group that the Church has ever known.[16]

All these men and women of faith lived after the apostles died, many of them after the Bible was canonized, historically disproving Cessationism. There are numerous historical accounts of spiritual visions and dreams, miracles, spiritual gifts, and healings recorded throughout history, and still being performed today. There are countless other stories from the Quakers, Moravians, John Wesley and the Methodists, First and Second Great Awakenings, Charles Finney, D.L. Moody, Smith Wigglesworth, William Seymour, and the Azusa Street Revival, John G. Lake, William Branham, Oral Roberts, T.L. Osborn, Kenneth Hagin, Reinhard Bonnke, Andrew Wommack, Randy Clark, Bill Johnson, and Plumtree Church documented as well.

Questions - Charismatic Church History

1. It is believed that _____ was the only disciple who wasn't martyred.

2. Have the gifts of the Holy Spirit ceased? Y or N

3. Cessationism is the doctrine that teaches prophetic and miraculous gifts (healing, tongues, prophecy, etc.) passed away with the apostolic age. T or F

4. Cessationists believe that all of the gifts passed away
    a. After the last apostle died
    b. After the last disciple died
    c. After the canonization of Scripture
    d. All of the above

5. The perfect that was to come in 1 Cor. 13:10 is referring to
    a. Jesus and His second coming
    b. The canonization of Scripture

6. The Lord has not performed a single miracle on earth since the death of the original 12 apostles and those directly associated with them. T or F

CHAPTER 50 CHARISMATIC CHURCH HISTORY

7. In Church history, we see people
   a. Healed
   b. Delivered
   c. Prophesy
   d. Walk on water
   e. Raise from the dead
   f. Speak with new tongues they had not learned
   g. Have dreams and visions
   h. All of the above

8. Church history supports the belief in Cessationism. T or F

9. The Bible supports the belief in Cessationism. T or F

10. The belief of Cessationism is false. T or F

51
1 John 1:9

Growing up, I was taught that unless I confessed all my sins, I would not be forgiven. I was even told that if someone died without having confessed all their sins, they would go to Hell. I remember having a whole week of classes in Bible College on this question. A man climbed a fruit tree and stole some fruit because he was hungry. On his way down, he fell out of the tree and died before he had the chance to confess his sin. Would he go to Hell? Some said yes, some said no, but most of us, I think, were unsure.

Fear and doubt in the security of my salvation left me in torment. Would I go to Hell if I sinned and did not have time to confess it? What if I was speeding and died in a car crash before I had time to ask forgiveness? Thoughts like these tormented me. I would lie in bed at night and reflect on my day to remember what sins I had committed so that I could confess them in order to stay saved. Even lullabies were scary and reinforced this. " … If I should die before I wake, I pray the Lord my soul to take." In this lullaby, we are praying for salvation repeatedly every night with no assurance. My friends, this is not freedom, this is torment, and this is not how God desires us to live.

First John 5:13 (NIV) says, *"I write these things to you who believe in the name of the Son of God so that you may know that you have eternal life."* God wants us to know that we *have* eternal life, not just hope.

First John 1:9 says, *"If we confess our sins, He is faithful and just to forgive us our sins and to cleanse us from all unrighteousness."* Does this mean that we lose our righteousness every time we sin? Does God take away our gift of righteousness every time we sin and give it back after we confess? It seems foolish, doesn't it?

Understanding this verse and its proper context is especially important to our Christian walk. If a large portion of the Church is correct, we need to be confessing and confessing. But if they are not correct, what do we do when we sin?

Joseph Prince said, "If you believe that you have to confess your sins to be forgiven, then make sure that you confess everything! Make sure that you don't just confess the 'big sins'. Make sure that you also confess your sins every time you are worried, fearful, or in doubt. The Bible says that 'whatsoever is not of faith is sin.' So, don't just confess what is convenient for you. Make sure you confess everything."[1]

This sure seems like a lot of work. And for me, it was not helping me grow; it was tormenting. So, in this lesson, I want to look at the truth. Do we need to confess our sins in order to stay saved? If we forget to confess a sin or we don't have time before we die to confess our sins, do we go to Hell? Is this what 1 John 1:9 is talking about?

The thought process for confession of sins for believers hinges on one verse in the New Testament. Yet, confession of sins is a significant theology in the Church today. You would think for such a major theology that it would be more prevalent in Scripture. Yet, Paul, who wrote roughly half of the New Testament, never one time instructed us to confess our sins. When Paul was dealing with the sinful issues in Corinth and asked the church to remove the man, he did not ask them to confess their sins. When Corinth was treating communion as a common thing and not partaking of it properly; he did not ask them to confess their sins. So, let's examine the context to see if the practice of confession of sins should have been given such a prevalent place in Christianity.

Let's look at the background of First John. If you remember, John's other two epistles were letters that he addressed to certain people. Second John was written to the elect lady and her children, and Third John was written to Gaius. But First John was not directed to anyone, which has left us with a lot of speculation as to who he was addressing. John stated five purposes for writing his first epistle:

1. That we might have fellowship (1:3).

2. That we might have joy (1:4).

3. That we might not sin (2:1-2).

4. That we might have assurance of our salvation (5:13)

5. That we might overcome error (2:26).[2]

John was dealing with many false teachers in his day. 1 John 2:26 (NIV) says, *"These things I have written to you concerning those who try to deceive you."* 1 John 2:19 (NIV) says, *"They went out from us, but they did not really belong to us. For if they had belonged to us, they would have remained with us; but their going showed that none of them belonged to us."*

You see, John had a church split. The people who left believed differently from John, and they were trying to lead others astray. Commentaries suggest that it could have been one of three groups, or possibly all three.

The first group is Gnosticism, which means "having knowledge." The main emphasis of Gnosticism is "dualism." Dualism is the belief that there is a spirit world, which is good, and a material world that is bad.[3] They also believed that knowledge of truth is more important than living the truth,[4] and that God is unknowable.[5]

The second group is Docetism (branch of Gnosticism), and the word means "to seem, apparition, or phantom." They believed that Jesus' humanity was not real and that He only appeared to have a physical body. It is thought that this sect arose over the contention from John's gospel letter, which said "the Word became flesh."

The third group is called Cerinthus. "According to Church tradition, Cerinthus lived in Roman Asia and was strongly opposed by the Apostle John. Cerinthus was a Gnostic who taught that Jesus was only a man and that the divine Christ descended on Jesus at His baptism and left Him before the Crucifixion."[7] According to early Christian sources, the Apostle John wrote his gospel specifically to refute the teachings of Cerinthus.[8]

These three sects were problems in John's day, not just at the time he wrote First John but all of his books. In the Gospel of John, he wrote: (John 1:1) *"In the beginning was the Word, and the Word was with God, and the Word was God."* (John 1:14) *"And the Word became flesh and dwelt among us, and we beheld His glory, the glory as of the only begotten of the Father, full of grace and truth."* Then in 2 John 1:7, we see this same problem being addressed: *"... many deceivers, who do not acknowledge Jesus Christ as coming in the flesh, have gone out into the world. Any such person is the deceiver and the antichrist."*

With these thoughts in mind, let's read 1 John chapter one and see if we can notice John addressing these severe heretical issues. 1 John 1:1-3 (NIV), *"That which was from the beginning, which we have heard, which we have seen with our eyes, which we have looked at and our hands have touched—this we proclaim concerning the Word of life. The life appeared; we have seen it and testify to it, and we proclaim to you the eternal life, which was with the Father and has appeared to us. We proclaim to you what we have seen and heard, so that you also may have fellowship with us. And our fellowship is with the Father and with his Son, Jesus Christ."*

John was addressing people who did not believe that Jesus came in the flesh. He emphasized that he had heard, seen, and even touched the Lord Jesus. In verse 3, John said that he was proclaiming what he had seen and heard so that the people that did not have fellowship with them could have fellowship with the Father and with His Son, Jesus Christ. John was telling them to repent from these evil beliefs and turn to God and be saved. We see John address this again in chapter 4:1-3, *"Beloved, do not believe every spirit, but test the spirits, whether they are of God; because many false prophets have gone out into the world. By this you know the Spirit of God: Every spirit that confesses that Jesus Christ has come in the flesh is of God, and every spirit that does not confess that Jesus Christ has come in the flesh is not of God. And this is the spirit of the Antichrist, which you have heard was coming, and is now already in the world."* So, for some, the first three verses would be a call to repentance unto salvation, and for those who were already saved, it would be a warning against false doctrine.

1 John 1:4-6 says, *"We write this to make our joy complete. This is the message we have heard from him and declare to you: God is light; in him there is no darkness at all. If we claim to have fellowship with him and yet walk in the darkness, we lie and do not live out the truth."* John is saying that these people claim to be saved, yet they were walking in darkness (living in sin); remember, Gnostics believed knowledge of the truth was more important than living the truth. Verse 7 goes on to say, *"But if we walk in the light, as he is in the light, we have fellowship with one another, and the blood of Jesus, his Son, purifies us from all sin."* John had previously confronted the wrong way of believing and here is showing them the right way to believe and live.

Verses 8-10 say, *"If we claim to be without sin, we deceive ourselves and the truth is not in us. If we confess our sins, he is faithful and just and will forgive us our sins and purify us from all unrighteousness. If we claim we have not sinned, we make him out to be a liar and his word is not in us."* Understanding who this is addressed to is essential. If it were written to Christians, showing them how to deal with sin and how to stay saved, then we had better become excellent at confessing sins, and not just the obvious ones, but everything that is not done in faith (fear, worry, doubt, and unbelief). But if it were written to instruct the Gnostics and others influenced by them how to get saved, it would carry a totally different application. You see, just like in a Sunday morning service where there are lost people and saved people present, John's letter was read in a church service where lost and saved people heard it. If they were lost, it would have one application. If they were saved, it would have another application.

1 John 1:9 was not telling Christians how to stay saved. It was telling the lost how to get saved. It was telling the people that sin is real and that they needed to turn away from their sin and turn to Christ for their salvation.

So, what is the proper place for confession of sins? Our confession blesses our fellowship, not our sonship. Our confession blesses our communion, not our union. James said we should confess our sins one to another. If I was short with my wife, and I did not apologize for a few days, things in my house would start to feel a little cold. We would still be legally married, but we would have fellowship issues. Or, if I was harsh and rude to my children and did not apologize, they would still be my sons and my daughter, but we would have fellowship issues. Our hearts would not be as connected as they should be.

It is the same way with the Lord. Our confession of sins does not save us or keep us saved, but it does affect our fellowship, it does affect our communion. Our hearts will not feel as connected to the Lord as they should be. There is a place for confession of sins, but it is not to be the primary place in our relationship. It should be something we do because we are in a relationship, not something we do to earn it. If my children confessed their sins to me every day, and that was the only thing they talked to me about, after a while, I would say, "Enough! Let's talk about something else. I forgive you." I believe God feels the same way.

If God is not counting our sins against us anymore, why should we focus on them? When we are lying in bed at night, we don't need to reflect back on the day to remember our sins. The Holy Spirit will remind us and convict us if need be. But when we lie in our beds at night, we need to remember that we are the righteousness of God through Christ, that we are saved by grace through faith, that God is for us and not against us, that we are His beloved children in whom He is well pleased.

Questions - 1 John 1:9

1. Unless we confess all of our sins, we will not be forgiven. T or F

2. If we die without confessing all of our sins, we go to Hell. T or F

3. 1 John 5:13 says, I write these things to you who believe in the name of the Son of God so that you may _____ that you have eternal life.

4. Does God take away our gift of righteousness every time we sin and give it back after we confess our sins? T or F

5. Paul, who wrote roughly half of the New Testament, never instructed us to confess our sins? T or F

6. John stated five purposes for writing his first epistle. Which one of these is not a stated reason?
    a. That we might have fellowship (1:3)
    b. That we might have joy (1:4)
    c. That we might learn how to confess our sins (1:9)
    d. That we might not sin (2:1-2)
    e. That we might have assurance of our salvation (5:13)
    f. That we might overcome error (2:26)

7. John experienced a church split. T or F

8. The people who left believed differently than John and were trying to lead others astray. T or F

9. The group(s) troubling John were:
   a. Gnosticism
   b. Docetism
   c. Cerinthus
   d. All of the above

10. In 1 John 1:1-3, John is addressing people who did not believe that Jesus came in the flesh. T or F

11. In verse 3, John said he was addressing people that did not have fellowship with the Father and with His Son, Jesus Christ.
    T or F

12. For some, the first three verses were a call to repentance unto salvation, and for those who were already saved, it was a warning against false doctrine. T or F

13. 1 John 1:7 "But if we walk in the light, as he is in the light, we have _____ with one another, and the blood of Jesus, his Son, purifies us from _____ sin."

14. 1 John 1:9 was addressing:
    a. Christians
    b. The lost
    c. Gnostics
    d. Both "b." and "c."
    e. All of the above

15. Our confession blesses our fellowship, not our sonship. Our confession blesses our communion, not our union. T or F

52
The Fruit of Salvation

My cousin works at a diamond mine in northwestern Canada. This diamond mine is one of the most prosperous in the world. He told me that the average person could walk right past a diamond and not even recognize it because there is a huge process that the stone must undertake before it can be seen as a finished product. After the ore is extracted from the mine, it is crushed three times into smaller, more manageable pieces, washed and placed on a conveyor belt. These pieces look like large pieces of sand.

Rough diamonds have a thick coating of carbon on them, which can be black, gray, or even brown. While on the conveyor belt, the stones pass under an x-ray machine. The rocks with diamonds in them absorb the radiation from the x-ray. The regular ore does not. Then the stones fall off the end of the conveyor belt and pass in front of a radiation sensor. When the sensor detects a radioactive stone, an attached machine shoots a single jet of air and separates the diamonds from the regular ore. The regular ore continues to fall to the ground below, and the radioactive stones are moved into a new storage bin by that jet of air.

At this point, the human eye still could not tell a diamond from the ore. They bathe the stones in grease and wash them off with a type of acid. After all of this, they treat them, size them down, cut them, and polish them. This is a very lengthy process, but it is well worth the investment due to the value of the diamonds.

This process is much like what we experience as a child of God. There usually is an instant transformation in areas of our lives when we are born again, but other areas are transformed over time. That area can be different for each one of us, but there should be transformation. There should be fruit on the outside consistent with the change on the inside.

We see this in one of Jesus' parables. Luke 13:6-9 says, *"A certain man had a fig tree planted in his vineyard, and he came seeking fruit on it and found none. Then he said to the keeper of his vineyard, 'Look, for three years I have come seeking fruit on this fig tree and find none. Cut it down; why does it use up the ground?' But he answered and said to him, 'Sir, let it alone this year also, until I dig around it and fertilize it. And if it bears fruit, well. But if not, after that you can cut it down.'"*

The owner of the vineyard invested money in the land and the fig tree, expecting a harvest. He was very patient, but He still expected a crop. Otherwise, the tree would be cut down and burned. In the same way, God has invested a great deal into us, and He expects a harvest. Jesus said you would recognize believers by their fruit (Matthew 7:20).

It is one thing for us to pray a prayer and say we are born again. It is another thing to actually *be* born again. The proof of our salvation is in our works. For example, 1 John 3:10 says, *"In this the children of God and the children of the devil are manifest: Whoever does not practice righteousness is not of God, nor is he who does not love his brother."*

One indicator that someone may not be saved is unrighteous actions, and another is not loving our brothers and sisters. In Matthew 7:16-20, Jesus said, *"You will know them by their fruits. Do men gather grapes from thornbushes or figs from thistles? Even so, every good tree bears good fruit, but a bad tree bears bad fruit. A good tree cannot bear bad fruit, nor can a bad tree bear good fruit. Every tree that does not bear good fruit is cut down and thrown into the fire. Therefore by their fruits you will know them."*

You may not see fruit immediately with new believers, as fruit is grown over time. Remember the owner of the vineyard is patient. But if one is truly born again, change in behavior and love for others should be evident. Fruit is expected, fruit is required.

Ephesians 2:8-10 say, *"For by grace you have been saved through faith, and that not of yourselves; it is the gift of God, not of works, lest anyone should boast. For we are His workmanship, created in Christ Jesus for good works, which God prepared beforehand that we should walk in them."*

We are not saved through works, but we are saved unto good works. God prepared good works for us to walk in before we were even born. And when we walk in those good works, we are acting like our Father God. We are demonstrating on the outside the work that Jesus has done on the inside.

1 John 2:3-5 tells us how we can know that we are in God's kingdom. It says, *"Now by this we know that we know Him, if we keep His commandments. He who says, "I know Him," and does not keep His commandments, is a liar, and the truth is not in him. But whoever keeps His word, truly the love of God is perfected in him. By this we know that we are in Him."*

It is easy for others to ridicule a child of God. There is a process in our spiritual growth, and we all grow in different ways and different seasons. Struggling with sin in an area does not mean we are not born again. Gifts are given, but fruit is developed. Fruit takes time to grow and mature. If you are practicing sin, however, that is a different story, as we see in 1 John 3:6 (NIV), *"No one who lives in him keeps on sinning. No one who continues to sin has either seen him or known him."*

Let's say you have some knowledge about diamonds, and you find one covered with mud and dirt. Will you allow others to take it away from you by convincing you that it has no value because of its present condition? No way! When our Father looks at you, He knows your real value. He sees the diamond in the rough, and He understands the process. Please don't let other people appraise you, for there is a good chance what you will find are critics who will significantly reduce your value. You have value, and you have worth to the Father. Receive His appraisal and His approval today, living like a true son or daughter, continually growing and maturing in the things of God.

CHAPTER 52   THE FRUIT OF SALVATION

Questions - The Fruit of Salvation

1. There usually is an instant transformation in areas of our lives when we are born again, but other areas change over time.
T or F

2. There should be fruit on the outside consistent with the change on the inside. T or F

3. The owner of the vineyard expected a _____.

4. Jesus said by their _____ you will know them or recognize them (Matthew 7:20).

5. The proof of our salvation is in our _____.

6. Matthew 7:18: "A good tree cannot bear _____ fruit, nor can a bad tree bear _____ fruit."

7. Ephesians 2:10, "For we are His workmanship, created in Christ Jesus for good _____, which God prepared beforehand that we should walk in them."

8. Our good works do not save us, but we are saved unto good works.
T or F

9. 1 John 2:3-5 "We know that we have come to know him if we _____ his commands. The man who says, 'I know him,' but does not do what he _____ is a liar, and the _____ is not in him. But if anyone _____ his word, God's love is truly made _____ in him. This is how we _____ we are in him."

10. We can be born again and still struggle with sin in a particular area. T or F

11. Gifts are given, but fruit is developed. Fruit takes _____.

12. 1 John 3:6 (NIV), "No one who lives in him keeps on _____. No one who continues to sin has either seen him or known him."

13. When our Father looks at you, He knows your real value. He sees the diamond in the rough, and He understands the process. T or F

References

REFERENCES

Chapter 1: Saved by Grace

[1] Rivera, Iona. "The British Royal Family's Most Expensive Weddings." Latin Times, Latin Times LLC, 15 Mar. 2019, www.latintimes.com/british-royal-familys-most-expensive-weddings- 436023.

[2] Holy Bible, New International Version®, NIV® Copyright ©1973, 1978, 1984, 2011 by Biblica, Inc.® Used by permission. All rights reserved worldwide.

[3] "Merit." Merriam-Webster.com Dictionary, *Merriam-Webster*, www.merriam-webster.com/dictionary/merit. Accessed 3 Apr. 2020.

Chapter 3: Water Baptism

[1] PC Study Bible, NT:907, *Biblesoft's New Exhaustive Strong's Numbers and Concordance with Expanded Greek-Hebrew Dictionary*. Copyright 1994, 2003, 2006 Biblesoft Inc. and International Bible Translators Inc.

[2] Exodus 14:14-30

[3] Muller, Lennart. "Crossing of the Red Sea." Flood, The Center for Natural Studies, www.cps.org.rs/Innerpeace/Creation/redsea.html.

Chapter 4: Repentance

[1] PC Study Bible, NT 3341, *Thayer's Greek Lexicon*, Electronic Database Copyright 2000,2003,2006 by Biblesoft, Inc.

[2] PC Study Bible, NT 3339, *Biblesoft's New Exhaustive Strong's Numbers and Concordance with Expanded Greek-Hebrew Dictionary.* Copyright 1994, 2003, 2006 Biblesoft Inc. and International Bible Translators Inc.

[3] Scripture taken from the Holy Scriptures, Tree of Life Version*. Copyright © 2014,2016 by the Tree of Life Bible Society. Used by permission of the Tree of Life Bible Society.

Chapter 5: The Lord our Righteousness

[1] Isaiah 64:6

Chapter 6: Sinners or Saints?

[1] Anderson, Neil T. *Victory over the Darkness*. Christian Art, 2009.

[2] PC Study Bible, NT 264 & 266. *Biblesoft's New Exhaustive Strong's Numbers and Concordance with Expanded Greek-Hebrew Dictionary*. Copyright 1994, 2003, 2006 Biblesoft Inc. and International Bible Translators, Inc.

[3] Anderson, Neil T., *Victory over the Darkness*. Christian Art, 2009.

[4] Romans 3:23

Chapter 7: What Happens When We Sin?

[1] PC Study Bible, NT: 5083, *Thayer's Greek Lexicon,* PC Study Bible formatted Electronic Database. Copyright 2006 by Biblesoft, Inc.

Chapter 8: The True Nature of God

[1] Blog, Washington's. "America Has Been at War 93% of the Time – 222 out of 239 Years – Since 1776." Global Research, 20 Jan. 2019, www.globalresearch.ca/america-has-been-at-war-93-of-the-time-222-out-of-239-years-since-1776/5565946.

[2] Crigger, Megan, and Laura Santhanam. "How Many Americans Have Died in U.S. Wars?" PBS, Public Broadcasting Service, 24 May 2015, www.pbs.org/newshour/nation/many-americans-died-u-s-wars.

[3] John 8:1-11

[4] John 4:4-32

[5] Luke 22:54-62

Chapter 9: The Integrity of God's Word

[1] PC Study Bible, NT: 2503 & 2762, *Vine's Expository Dictionary of Biblical Words*, Copyright 1985, Thomas Nelson Publishers.

[2] Free, Joseph P., and Howard F. Vos. *Archaeology and Bible History*. Zondervan Publ. House, 1997. Page 241.

[3] Stoner, Peter Winebrenner, and Robert C. Newman. *Science Speaks: Scientific Proof of the Accuracy of Prophecy and the Bible*. Moody Press, 1976.

[4] Ibid

Chapter 10: The Power of our Words

[1] Job 38:4

[2] Luke 6:45

Chapter 11: Faith

[1] PC Study Bible, NT: 5287, *Thayer's Greek Lexicon*, PC Study Bible formatted Electronic Database. Copyright 2006 by Biblesoft, Inc.

[2] PC Study Bible, NT: 1650, *Biblesoft's New Exhaustive Strong's Numbers and Concordance with Expanded Greek-Hebrew Dictionary*. Copyright 1994, 2003, 2006 Biblesoft Inc. and International Bible Translators Inc.

[3] PC Study Bible, NT: 2100, *Biblesoft's New Exhaustive Strong's Numbers and Concordance with Expanded Greek-Hebrew Dictionary*. Copyright 1994, 2003, 2006 Biblesoft Inc. and International Bible Translators Inc.

[4] *"Two Important Greek Words in the Bible: Logos and Rhema."* Bibles for America Blog, 25 June 2019, blog.biblesforamerica.org/two-important-greek-words-in-the-bible-emlogosem-and-emrhemaem/

[5] PC Study Bible, NT:2316, *Biblesoft's New Exhaustive Strong's Numbers and Concordance with Expanded Greek-Hebrew Dictionary*. Copyright 1994, 2003, 2006 Biblesoft Inc. and International Bible Translators Inc.

[6] 1 Corinthians 11:34

[7] 2 Corinthians 12:4

[8] John 12:49-50

[9] Hagin, Kenneth. "Heart Faith Brings Results." *Charisma Magazine*, 2015, www.charismamag.com/anniversary/pages-from-our-past/24035-kenneth-hagin-sr-heart-faith-brings-results.

Chapter 12: The Measure of Faith

[1] PC Study Bible, NT: 2472, *Biblesoft's New Exhaustive Strong's Numbers and Concordance with Expanded Greek-Hebrew Dictionary*. Copyright 1994, 2003, 2006 Biblesoft Inc. and International Bible Translators Inc.

[2] Acts 9:36-42

[3] Acts 14:8-10

[4] John 14:12

[5] Matthew 8:10

[6] Wommack, Andrew. "Faith of God." Andrew Wommack Ministries, 28 Jan. 2020, www.awmi.net/reading/teaching-articles/faith_god/.

[7] 2 Peter 1:3

Chapter 13: Increase our Faith

[1] 2 Peter 1:3

Chapter 14: Activating Faith

[1] Desilva, Dawna, and Teresa Liebscher. *Sozo - Saved, Healed, Delivered*. Sozo Ministry, 2011.

[2] PC Study Bible, NT: 4982, *Thayer's Greek Lexicon*, PC Study Bible formatted Electronic Database. Copyright 2006 by Biblesoft, Inc.

[3] PC Study Bible, NT: 4982, *Biblesoft's New Exhaustive Strong's Numbers and Concordance with Expanded Greek-Hebrew Dictionary*. Copyright 1994, 2003, 2006 Biblesoft Inc. and International Bible Translators Inc.

[4] McIntyre, Joe. E.W. *Kenyon and His Message of Faith: The True Story*. Creation House, 1997. (Page 52)

[5] Ibid. (Page 53)

Chapter 16: Take Captive every Thought

[1] PC Study Bible, NT:225, *Vine's Expository Dictionary of Biblical Words*, Copyright 1985, Thomas Nelson Publishers.

Chapter 17: Healthy Thinking (Part 1)

[1] How Many Times Does Your Heart Beat in a Lifetime?" Wonderopolis, www.wonderopolis.org/wonder/how-many-times-does-your-heart-beat-in-a-lifetime.

[2] Morton, J L., "Color & Vision Matters." Color & Vision Matters, www.colormatters.com/color-and-vision/color-and-vision-matters.

[3] Morrison, Jessica. "Human Nose Can Detect 1 Trillion Odours." *Nature News*, Nature Publishing Group, 20 Mar. 2014, www.nature.com/news/human-nose-can-detect-1-trillion-odours-1.14904#/b1.

[4] "10 Fun Facts about Your Brain." *10 Fun Facts about Your Brain*, Piedmont Healthcare, www.piedmont.org/living-better/10-fun-facts-about-your-brain.

Chapter 18: Healthy Thinking (Part 2)

[1] Leaf, Caroline. *Switch on Your Brain: The Key to Peak Happiness, Thinking, and Health.* BakerBooks, a Division of Baker Publishing Group, 2015.

[2] Luke 6:45

[3] Leaf, Caroline. *Switch on Your Brain: The Key to Peak Happiness, Thinking, and Health.* BakerBooks, a Division of Baker Publishing Group, 2015.

[4] Ibid

[5] Virkler, Mark. *How to Hear Gods Voice: An Interactive Learning Experience.* Destiny Image Publishers, 2005.

Chapter 19: Hearing God

[1] Romans 8:14

[2] Virkler, Mark. *How to Hear Gods Voice: An Interactive Learning Experience.* Destiny Image Publishers, 2005.

Chapter 20: Value and Worth

[1] "Just Tickled." *People.* 47 (1). January 13, 1997. Retrieved 11 June 2014.

[2] Mills, Harry (2000), *Artful Persuasion: How to Command Attention, Change Minds, and Influence People*, – via Questia (subscription required), New York: AMACOM, p. 253, ISBN 0-8144-7063-7.

[3] Forsberg, Chris. "One Expensive Stained Shirt." Boston.com, *The Boston Globe*, 24 June 2008, www.boston.com/sports/celticsblog/2008/06/24/one_expensive_s.

[4] "Report: Bonds' 756th HR Ball, with Asterisk, May Be on Display by Opening Day." ESPN, ESPN Internet Ventures, 6 Mar. 2008, www.espn.com/mlb/news/story?id=3279476&cid=1139733341&ei=F3HQR43vGJyMoAPK6fjmDg.

[5] Rea, Naomi. "'I Have Never Seen Such Chaos' Mass Confusion Ensues After the Louvre Moved the Mona Lisa to a Different Gallery." Artnet News, 1 Aug. 2019, news.artnet.com/art-world/louvre-mona-lisa-crowd-1613794.

[6] *"Why Is the Mona Lisa so Expensive and What It Has to Do with Information Storage."*

REFERENCES

ART, 27 June 2019, art.art/blog/mona-lisa-expensive-information-storage/

Chapter 21: Forgiveness

[1] 1 Corinthians 13:5

[2] PC Study Bible, NT: *Adam Clark's Commentary,* Electronic Database. Copyright 1996, 2003, 2005, 2006 by Biblesoft, Inc.

[3] PC Study Bible, *IVP Bible Background Commentary: New Testament* by Craig S. Keener Copyright 1993 by Craig S. Keener. Published by Intervarsity Press.

[4] Hogue, Rodney. *Forgiveness.* Rodney Hogue, 2008.

Chapter 23: Identity (Part 1)

[1] Foster, Jack. *"21 Terrifying Cyber Crime Statistics & Trends (2017-2018)."* VPN Geeks, 30 Oct. 2019, www.vpngeeks.com/21-terrifying-cyber-crime-statistics-in-2018/.

[2] PC Study Bible, *Theological Wordbook of the Old Testament.* Copyright 1980 by Moody Bible Institute of Chicago.

[3] PC Study Bible, NT: 6754, *Vine's Expository Dictionary of Biblical Words,* Copyright 1985, Thomas Nelson Publishers.

[4] PC Study Bible, NT: 1823, *Biblesoft's New Exhaustive Strong's Numbers and Concordance with Expanded Greek-Hebrew Dictionary.* Copyright 1994, 2003, 2006 Biblesoft Inc. and International Bible Translators Inc.

Chapter 24: Identity (Part 2)

[1] Hagin, Kenneth E. In Him. Rhema Bible Church, 1979.

[2] Kenyon, E. W. *Identification: A Romance in Redemption.* Kenyons Gospel Publishing Society, 1998.

Chapter 25: Holy Spirit

[1] PC Study Bible, NT: 1411, *Biblesoft's New Exhaustive Strong's Numbers and Concordance with Expanded Greek-Hebrew Dictionary.* Copyright 1994, 2003, 2006 Biblesoft Inc. and International Bible Translators, Inc.

[2] PC Study Bible, NT: 5547, *Thayer's Greek Lexicon,* PC Study Bible formatted Electronic Database. Copyright 2006 by Biblesoft, Inc.

Chapter 26: Baptism in Holy Spirit

[1] Acts 2:15

[2] Acts 2:39

Chapter 27: How to Receive the Baptism of the Holy Spirit

[1] Matthew 3:11

Chapter 28: Benefits of Praying in Tongues

[1] 1 Corinthians 14:5

[2] 1 Corinthians 14:13

[3] Hyatt, Eddie L. 2000 Years of Charismatic Christianity: a 21st Century Look at Church History from a Pentecostal/Charismatic Perspective. Hyatt International Ministries, 1998. Page 62.

[4] PC Study Bible, NT: 3618, Biblesoft's New Exhaustive Strong's Numbers and Concordance with Expanded Greek-Hebrew Dictionary. Copyright 1994, 2003, 2006 Biblesoft Inc. and International Bible Translators Inc.

Chapter 29: Authority of the Believer

[1] PC Study Bible, NT:6175, *The Online Bible Thayer's Greek Lexicon* and *Brown Driver & Briggs Hebrew Lexicon*, Copyright 1993, Woodside Bible Fellowship, Ontario, Canada. Licensed from the Institute for Creation Research.

Chapter 30: Biblical Basis for Healing

[1] PC Study Bible, NT: 5060, *Biblesoft's New Exhaustive Strong's Numbers and Concordance with Expanded Greek-Hebrew Dictionary*. Copyright 1994, 2003, 2006 Biblesoft Inc. and International Bible Translators Inc.

[2] Prince, Joseph. *Health and Wholeness through the Holy Communion.* 4th ed., Joseph Prince, 2006. Page 35

[3] PC Study Bible, NT: 3068, *Biblesoft's New Exhaustive Strong's Numbers and Concordance with Expanded Greek-Hebrew Dictionary*. Copyright 1994, 2003, 2006 Biblesoft Inc. and International Bible Translators Inc.

[4] PC Study Bible, NT: 2483, *The Online Bible Thayer's Greek Lexicon* and *Brown Driver & Briggs Hebrew Lexicon*, Copyright 1993, Woodside Bible Fellowship, Ontario, Canada. Licensed from the Institute for Creation Research.

[5] PC Study Bible, NT: 3510, *Biblesoft's New Exhaustive Strong's Numbers and Concordance with Expanded Greek-Hebrew Dictionary*. Copyright 1994, 2003, 2006 Biblesoft Inc. and International Bible Translators Inc.

Chapter 32: Deliverance

[1] Clark, Randy. *Empowered, A School of Healing and Impartation Workbook.* 5th ed., Apostolic Network of Global Awakening, 2012. (Pages 97-102)

Chapter 33: The Old Covenant

[1] Valkanet, Rich. "Complete Biblical Timeline." Bible Timeline, Discovery Bible and Biblos.com, 2010, biblehub.com/timeline/.

[2] Loughran, David B. "The Sacrificial System." *Animal Sacrifices - The Sacrificial System ... A Voice In The Wilderness* - Canada, 1996, www.avoiceinthewilderness.org/laws/sacrific2.html.

REFERENCES

³ Ghose, Tia. "Animal Sacrifice Powered Ancient Jerusalem's Economy." LiveScience, Purch, 4 Sept. 2013, www.livescience.com/39307-jerusalem-animal-sacrifice-found.html.

Chapter 35: The Church

¹ PC Study Bible, NT: 1577, *Thayer's Greek Lexicon*, PC Study Bible formatted Electronic Database. Copyright 2006 by Biblesoft, Inc.

² Richards, Larry, 1931. *Expository Dictionary of Bible Words*. Grand Rapids, Mich.: Regency Reference Library, 1985.

Chapter 36: The Sovereignty of God

¹ Ephesians 6:12

² James 4:7

Chapter 37: Under Law or Under Grace?

¹ Hecht, Mendy. "The 613 Commandments (Mitzvot)." *Mitzvahs & Traditions*, AskMoses.com, 27 Oct. 2008, www.chabad.org/library/article_cdo/aid/756399/jewish/The-613-Commandments-Mitzvot.htm.

² PC Study Bible, NT: 2673, *Biblesoft's New Exhaustive Strong's Numbers and Concordance with Expanded Greek-Hebrew Dictionary*. Copyright 1994, 2003, 2006 Biblesoft Inc. and International Bible Translators Inc.

³ "Covenant." Dictionary.com, www.dictionary.com/browse/covenant.

⁴ "Testament." Dictionary.com, www.dictionary.com/browse/testament.

Chapter 38: The Purpose of the Law

¹ Genzlinger, Neil. "The Military That Was Only for Show." *The New York Times*, 20 May 2013, www.nytimes.com/2013/05/21/arts/television/the-ghost-army-on-pbs-about-the-23rd-headquarters.html.

² PC Study Bible, NT: 3807, *Biblesoft's New Exhaustive Strong's Numbers and Concordance with Expanded Greek-Hebrew Dictionary*. Copyright 1994, 2003, 2006 Biblesoft Inc. and International Bible Translators Inc.

³ PC Study Bible, Galatians 3:23, *Jamieson, Fausset, and Brown Commentary*, Electronic Database. Copyright © 1997, 2003, 2005, 2006 by Biblesoft, Inc. All rights reserved.

Chapter 39: The Right Way to use the Law

¹ PC Study Bible, *Barnes' Notes*, Electronic Database Copyright © 1997, 2003, 2005, 2006 by Biblesoft, Inc.

² Bumgardner, Wendy. *"Walking Time for Mile, 5K, 10K, Half-Marathon, Marathon, and More."* Verywell Fit, Verywell Fit, 5 Mar. 2020, www.verywellfit.com/miles-and-kilometers-how-far-is-that-3435412.

Chapter 40: How Jesus Fulfilled the Law

[1] PC Study Bible, NT: 4137, *Biblesoft's New Exhaustive Strong's Numbers and Concordance with Expanded Greek-Hebrew Dictionary*. Copyright 1994, 2003, 2006 Biblesoft Inc. and International Bible Translators Inc.

[2] PC Study Bible, NT: 4137, *Thayer's Greek Lexicon*, Electronic Database. Copyright © 2000, 2003, 2006 by Biblesoft, Inc.

[3] Free, Joseph P., and Howard F. Vos. *Archaeology and Bible History*. Zondervan Publ. House, 1997. Page 241

Chapter 41: No More Consciousness of Sin

[1] PC Study Bible, NT: 3993, *Vine's Expository Dictionary of Biblical Words*, Copyright 1985, Thomas Nelson Publishers.

[2] PC Study Bible, NT: 4862, *Biblesoft's New Exhaustive Strong's Numbers and Concordance with Expanded Greek-Hebrew Dictionary*. Copyright 1994, 2003, 2006 Biblesoft Inc. and International Bible Translators Inc.

[3] PC Study Bible, NT: 4894, *Thayer's Greek Lexicon*, Electronic Database. Copyright © 2000, 2003, 2006 by Biblesoft, Inc.

Chapter 42: Christology

[1] GotQuestions.org. "Home." GotQuestions.org, 13 Sept. 2008, www.gotquestions.org/Christology.html.

[2] Patton, Francis L., et al. *Biblical and Theological Studies*. Solid Ground Christian Books, 2003. (Might be better reference)

[3] PC Study Bible, Philippians 2:6, from *Bible Knowledge Commentary/Old Testament*, Copyright © 1983, 2000 Cook Communications Ministries.

[4] PC Study Bible, NT: 2758, *Biblesoft's New Exhaustive Strong's Numbers and Concordance with Expanded Greek-Hebrew Dictionary*. Copyright 1994, 2003, 2006 Biblesoft Inc. and International Bible Translators Inc.

Chapter 43: The Lord's Supper

[1] PC Study Bible, NT: 2605, *Thayer's Greek Lexicon*, Electronic Database. Copyright © 2000, 2003, 2006 by Biblesoft, Inc.

[2] PC Study Bible, NT: 371. *Vine's Expository Dictionary of Biblical Words*, Copyright © 1985, Thomas Nelson Publishers

[3] Prince, Joseph. *Health and Wholeness through the Holy Communion*. 4th ed., Joseph Prince, 2006. Page 52

[4] PC Study Bible, Wigram, George V. *The Englishmans Greek Concordance*: Numerically Coded to Strongs Exhaustive Concordance. Mott Media, 1982.

[5] PC Study Bible, NT: 1252, *Thayer's Greek Lexicon*, Electronic Database. Copyright © 2000, 2003, 2006 by Biblesoft, Inc.

REFERENCES

⁶ Prince, Joseph. *Health and Wholeness through the Holy Communion*. 4th ed., Joseph Prince, 2006. Page 39

Chapter 44: Paul's Thorn

[1] PC Study Bible, *Adam Clarke's Commentary*, Electronic Database. Copyright © 1996, 2003, 2005, 2006 by Biblesoft, Inc.

[2] PC Study Bible, *Barnes' Notes*, Electronic Database Copyright © 1997, 2003, 2005, 2006 by Biblesoft, Inc.

[3] Ibid

[4] PC Study Bible, *Bible Knowledge Commentary/Old Testament* Copyright © 1983, 2000 Cook Communications Ministries; *Bible Knowledge Commentary/New Testament* Copyright © 1983, 2000 Cook Communications Ministries.

[5] PC Study Bible, NT: 5229. *Vine's Expository Dictionary of Biblical Words*, Copyright © 1985, Thomas Nelson Publishers

[6] Ibid: NT: 2852

[7] PC Study Bible, NT: 769, *Thayer's Greek Lexicon*, Electronic Database. Copyright © 2000, 2003, 2006 by Biblesoft, Inc.

Chapter 45: Blessed or Cursed?

[1] "Curse." Merriam-Webster.com Dictionary, *Merriam-Webster*, https://www.merriam-webster.com/dictionary/merit. Accessed 3 Apr. 2020.

Chapter 46: God Wants You Blessed

[1] Howard L. Dayton, Jr., *Leadership*, Spring, 1981, p. 62.

[2] "Ordinance." Merriam-Webster.com Dictionary, *Merriam-Webster*, https://www.merriam-webster.com/dictionary/ordinance. Accessed 14 Apr. 2020.

Chapter 47: When Prayers seem Unanswered

[1] Odom, Robert. "Jewish Division of Day Into Hours." *Ministry Magazine*, www.ministrymagazine.org/archive/1946/04/jewish-division-of-day-into-hours.

Chapter 48: Self-Centeredness

[1] *A Matter of a Few Degrees* - media.ldscdn.org. http://media.ldscdn.org/pdf/magazines/ensign-may-2008/2008-05-23-a-matter-of-a-few-degrees-eng.pdf

[2] Wommack, Andrew. *Self-Centeredness, Level 2, Lesson 1, The Complete Discipleship Evangelism 48-Lesson Course, Condensed Version and Workbook*. Don Krow, 2004.

Chapter 50: Charismatic Church History

[1] PC Study Bible, Schaff, Philip. *History of the Christian Church* / by Philip Schaff. C. Scribners Sons, 1885.

² 1-300, AD. *"Whatever Happened to the Twelve Apostles?"* Christianity.com, Salem Web Network, 28 Apr. 2010, www.christianity.com/church/church-history/timeline/1-300/whatever-happened-to-the-twelve-apostles-11629558.html.

³ International Bible Society. *"How Were the Books of the Bible Chosen?"* Biblica, 10 Aug. 2017, www.biblica.com/resources/bible-faqs/how-were-the-books-of-the-bible-chosen/.

⁴ The Editors of Encyclopedia Britannica. *"St. Justin Martyr."* Encyclopedia Britannica, Encyclopedia Britannica, Inc., 28 Mar. 2020, www.britannica.com/biography/Saint-Justin-Martyr.

⁵ Hyatt, Eddie L. *2000 Years of Charismatic Christianity: a 21st Century Look at Church History from a Pentecostal/Charismatic Perspective.* Hyatt International Ministries, 1998. Page 76.

⁶ Clark, Randy. *Empowered, A School of Healing and Impartation Workbook.* 5th ed., Apostolic Network of Global Awakening, 2012. (Page 55)

⁷ Ibid. 55

⁸ Hyatt, Eddie L. *2000 Years of Charismatic Christianity: a 21st Century Look at Church History from a Pentecostal/Charismatic Perspective.* Hyatt International Ministries, 1998. Page 17.

⁹ Clark, Randy. *Empowered, A School of Healing and Impartation Workbook.* 5th ed., Apostolic Network of Global Awakening, 2012. (Page 56)

¹⁰ Hyatt, Eddie L. *2000 Years of Charismatic Christianity: a 21st Century Look at Church History from a Pentecostal/Charismatic Perspective.* Hyatt International Ministries, 1998. Page 18.

¹¹ Clark, Randy. *Empowered, A School of Healing and Impartation Workbook.* 5th ed., Apostolic Network of Global Awakening, 2012. (Page 56)

¹² Ibid. 58

¹³ Ibid. 59

¹⁴ Hyatt, Eddie L. *2000 Years of Charismatic Christianity: a 21st Century Look at Church History from a Pentecostal/Charismatic Perspective.* Hyatt International Ministries, 1998. Page 47.

¹⁵ Ibid. 58

¹⁶ Ibid. 62

Chapter 51: 1 John 1:9

¹ Prince, Joseph. *Destined To Reign: The Secret to Effortless Success, Wholeness, and Victorious Living.* Harrison House, Inc., 2007. Page 107.

² PC Study Bible, *Wiersbe's Expository Outlines on the New Testament.* Copyright © 1992 by Chariot Victor Publishing, an imprint of Cook Communication Ministries.

³ Pavao, Paul F., *"Gnostic Beliefs."* Christian History for Everyman, www.christian-history.org/gnostic-beliefs.html.

⁴ PC Study Bible, *Wiersbe's Expository Outlines on the New Testament.* Copyright © 1992

REFERENCES

by Chariot Victor Publishing, an imprint of Cook Communication Ministries.

[5] Pavao, Paul F. *"Gnostic Beliefs." Christian History for Everyman*, www.christian-history.org/gnostic-beliefs.html.

[6] "Docetism." Wikipedia, Wikimedia Foundation, 4 Feb. 2020, en.wikipedia.org/wiki/Docetism#CITEREFSmithWace1877.

[7] PC Study Bible, *Bible Knowledge Commentary/Old Testament*, Copyright © 1983, 2000 Cook Communications Ministries; *Bible Knowledge Commentary/New Testament* Copyright © 1983, 2000 Cook Communications Ministries.

[8] Ibid.

www.ingramcontent.com/pod-product-compliance
Lightning Source LLC
Chambersburg PA
CBHW050852160426
43194CB00011B/2122